Explore new ideas!

Reading/Writing Workshop

Read exciting literature, science and social studies texts!

(tl) JP5/ZOB/WENN.com/Newscom; (rl) Jimmy Holder; (cr) ericfoltz/iStock/360/Getty Images; (b) Nathan Love

Become an expert writer!

Build vocabulary and knowledge to unlock the Wonders of reading!

Use your student login to explore your interactive Reading/Writing Workshop, practice close reading, and more.

Go Digital! www.connected.mcgraw-hill.com

An English Language Arts Program

Program Authors

Diane August

Donald R. Bear

Janice A. Dole

Jana Echevarria

Douglas Fisher

David Francis

Vicki Gibson

Jan Hasbrouck

Margaret Kilgo

Jay McTighe

Scott G. Paris

Timothy Shanahan

Josefina V. Tinajero

Mc
Graw
Hill
Education

Cover and Title Pages: Nathan Love

www.mheonline.com/readingwonders

Copyright © 2017 McGraw-Hill Education

Send all inquiries to:
McGraw-Hill Education
2 Penn Plaza
New York, NY 10121

ISBN: 978-0-02-133031-7
MHID: 0-02-133031-X

Printed in the United States of America

4 5 6 7 8 9 QVS 21 20 19 18 17   C

Unlock the
Wonders
of
Reading

With your *Reading/Writing Workshop* you will:

- Closely read and reread literature and informational text

- Discuss what you have read with your peers

- Become a better writer and researcher

- Look for text evidence as you respond to complex text

Get Ready to Become:

- Lifelong Learners

- Critical Thinkers

- Part of the Community of Learning

READ and REREAD

Exciting Literature

Open your book and fire up your imagination! You'll find folktales, fantasies, other stories, poems, and dramas. They're all there waiting for you to explore and share.

Informational Texts

Build knowledge with many kinds of informational texts, including biographies, narrative nonfiction, and news articles. Sometimes the real world is more exciting than fiction.

Different texts can challenge you in different ways. If you don't understand something, what's the first thing you should do? You should figure out why you don't understand it. After all, you can't find a solution until you know what the problem is!

VOCABULARY

If you come across an unfamiliar word, look for context clues. Some texts contain technical terms. You might want to look these up in a dictionary.

MAKE CONNECTIONS

Sometimes you may need to make inferences about the text. For example, the reasons a character does something are not always stated. In nonfiction, you can connect information to find the essential idea.

ILLUSTRATIONS AND TEXT FEATURES

Are there any illustrations that can give you clues about the plot or how the characters feel? In nonfiction, are there any maps or diagrams that can help you understand information in the text?

TEXT STRUCTURE

How is the text organized? Does the author compare and contrast information? Is there a series of problems presented? Are there steps in a process?

COLLABORATE What do you do when you come across a word that you don't understand?

L👀K
for Text Evidence

When you answer a question about your reading, you often have to look for evidence in the text to support or even find the answer. Here are some tips to help you find what you are looking for.

Long ago, in China, a poor woman and her son, Ping, lived in a tiny hut. The woman earned a living weaving beautiful brocade hangings, which her son sold.

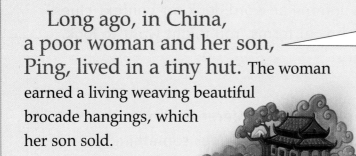

Stated
Here I can locate specific information that tells me where Ping lived.

It took three years to complete the brocade, and it was her finest work. However, soon afterward, a great wind swept into their hut and carried it away! The woman was grief-stricken.

Unstated
This text evidence allows me to make the inference that the brocade was very dear to the woman.

Text Evidence

Evidence is either stated or implied. If it is stated, you can find it directly in the text. If it is implied, that means that it is not directly stated in the text. Here's how to tell if a question will have a stated or an implied answer:

It's Stated — Right There!

The answers to questions that ask you to locate specific facts or events can usually be found stated in a single sentence or paragraph. For example: *What happened to the brocade?*

Other questions require you to combine stated information from more than one place. A question such as *What happens during Ping's search for the brocade?* requires you to look throughout the text.

It's Unstated — Here Is My Evidence

The answers to some questions are not stated. These kinds of questions require you to analyze information, put the answer in your own words, and support it with text evidence.

To answer a question such as *What was the theme of this story?* look for evidence in what the characters do and say and how they interact with one another. In a nonfiction text, look for signal words and phrases.

 Find the stated text evidence that tells what Ping's mother did for a living.

Be an Expert Writer

Remember that good writing represents clear ideas, is well organized, and contains text evidence and details from reliable sources. See how Candice answered a question about a text she read.

Candice's Model

CCSS **Write to Sources**

Write About the Text

 Candice

 Pages 78–81

I answered the question: *In your opinion, do kids spend too much time using electronic devices? Include logical reasons.*

Student Model: *Opinion*

I don't think kids spend too much time using electronic devices. Technology will only become more advanced, and the use of electronic devices helps kids learn.

Some research shows that using computers and playing video games benefits kids. For example, one study showed that kids who utilized lots of

Sentence Structure
I combined two sentences with a conjuction to help the rhythm of my writing.

Logical Order
I supported my opinion with reasons and evidence from the text.

media did more physical activities than kids who didn't. Another study by the National Institute of Health says that some video games can help increase attention. They can give kids structure for learning and help them learn to switch tasks. The use of electronic devices has many good effects for kids.

Grammar
Avoid **sentence fragments.** Correct **run-on sentences.**
Grammar Handbook
See pages 450 and 454.

Strong Conclusion
My final sentence sums up my opinion.

Your Turn
Explain why you agree or disagree with the author's viewpoint in "Plugged In." Use details from the text.
Go Digital!
Write your response online. Use your editing checklist.

86   W.5.1b, L.5.3a See the California Standards section.

W.5.1d See the California Standards section.   87

W6

Write About the Text

When you write about something you have read closely, you should introduce your topic clearly. Cite evidence from the text that supports your opinions. When you do research, make sure you use multiple reliable sources and then provide a list of the sources you have used. Use the question checklist below.

Opinions Are my opinions supported by facts and details? Did I cite text evidence from any texts I have read to support my opinions and conclusions?

Informative Texts Did I develop my topic with facts, details, and quotations? Did I write a conclusion that is connected to the information I presented?

Narrative Texts When you write a narrative, use your imagination to develop real or fictional events. The checklist below will help make stories memorable.

- **Sequence** Did I use a variety of transitional words and phrases to manage the order of events?

- **Dialogue** Did I use dialogue and description to develop experiences? Did I show the responses of characters to different situations?

What is your favorite subject to write about? Tell a partner why.

Unit 1

Eureka! I've Got It!

The Big Idea

(t) Valerie Decampo; (b) James Bernardin

Go Digital! Find all lessons online at www.connected.mcgraw-hill.com.

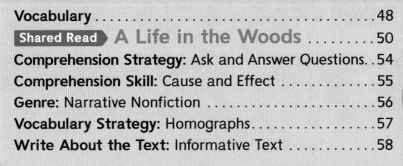

Unit 2

TAKING THE NEXT STEP

The Big Idea

(t) Diane Greenseid; (b) Peter Francis

Go Digital! Find all lessons online at www.connected.mcgraw-hill.com.

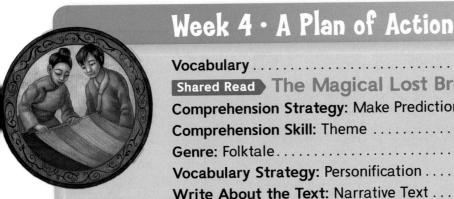

(t) Coal River Folklife Project collection (AFC 1999/008), American Folklife Center, Library of Congress; (b) Peter Zander/Workbook Stock/Getty Images

Unit 3

Getting from Here to There

The Big Idea
What kinds of experiences can lead
to new discoveries? **160**

(t) Westend61/Getty Images; (b) Maryn Roos

Go Digital! Find all lessons online at www.connected.mcgraw-hill.com.

Unit 4

IT'S UP TO YOU

The Big Idea
How do we decide what's important? . .**232**

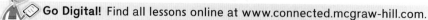 **Go Digital!** Find all lessons online at www.connected.mcgraw-hill.com.

(t) Aurora Photos/Alamy; (b) Robert Kirk/Photodisc/Getty Images

Unit 5

What's Next?

The Big Idea
In what ways can things change? **304**

Go Digital! Find all lessons online at www.connected.mcgraw-hill.com.

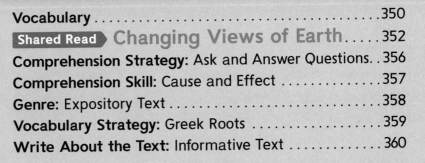

Unit 6

Linked In

The Big Idea

How are we all connected? 376

(t) Sean Qualls; (b) Marcelo Baez

 Go Digital! Find all lessons online at www.connected.mcgraw-hill.com.

Week 3 · Adaptations 406

Week 4 · Making a Difference 420

Week 5 · Out in the World 434

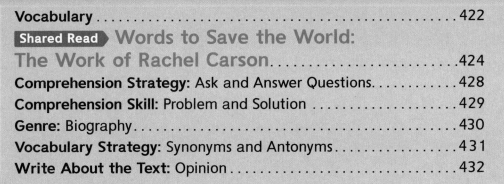

Eureka! I've Got It!

Ideas

A person with wisdom once said,
"An idea must begin in your head.
It may come as you sit
Or while strolling a bit,
Or even while lying in bed!"

An idea is a lot like a seed.
To get started, it's all that you need.
Each time that you think,
Your idea takes a drink,
Until it's grown big, yes, indeed!

You plant your ideas and then grow 'em,
Develop your thoughts and you'll show 'em.
Add a word at a time,
Plus a few words that rhyme,
And you'll end up creating a poem!

—Meish Goldish

THE BIG
Idea

Where can an idea begin?

Essential Question

How do we get the things we need?

Go Digital!

SL.5.1c See the California Standards section.

What Do We Need?

From the time we get up in the morning to the time we go to sleep at night, we need things to help us survive. We meet these needs in a variety of ways.

► Finding water, building shelter, and weaving clothes are some ways we meet our needs.

► This woman is meeting a need by harvesting rice, a food upon which millions of people depend.

Talk About It

Write words you have learned about meeting a need. Then talk about one way that you have found to get the things you need.

Meeting Needs

Vocabulary

Use the picture and the sentences to talk with a
partner about each word.

afford

Jill looked at the price tag to see if she
could **afford** to buy the blouse.

Name something you would like to be
able to afford.

loan

Lin asked her mom for a **loan** of
five dollars.

When have you made a loan to
someone?

profit

Jem and Ana set up a lemonade stand
and made a **profit** of five dollars from
the sales.

When have you made a profit?

prosper

When enough rain falls and the weather
is good, a garden can **prosper**.

What other things help people to
prosper?

risk

Firefighters take a great **risk** when they enter a burning building.

In what other jobs do people take a risk?

savings

Ray sets aside one dollar a week from his allowance and puts it in his **savings**.

What would you like to do with some savings?

scarce

Water can become **scarce** after many hot weeks with no rain.

What is another word for scarce?

wages

Sam and his brother earn **wages** for raking leaves every autumn.

What is a synonym for wages?

Your Turn

COLLABORATE

Pick three words. Write three questions for your partner to answer.

Go Digital! *Use the online visual glossary*

(t to b) Vince Streano/Stone/Getty Images; PhotoLink/Getty Images; Chun Lei/Corbis; Swell Media/Getty Images

L.5.6 See the California Standards section.

A Fresh Idea

Essential Question

How do we get the things we need?

Read about how one girl meets a need in her neighborhood.

One bright Saturday morning, Mali and her mom walked around the neighborhood. That is, her mom walked, but Mali ran, skipped, jumped over puddles, and visited the neighbors' dogs. Mali paused to look at the budding trees on her block. "I can't wait until summer," she said, "especially for Mrs. Fair's great tomatoes at her market stand." She pointed.

Mali's mom stood looking at the empty lot where the market set up every summer weekend. She looked at Mali. "Honey, Mrs. Fair told me last week that she had to close her stand. She's really getting too old to run it anymore."

Mali turned, stared, and put her hands on her hips. "But Mrs. Fair's stand can't close!" she said. "It's the only place in the neighborhood we can buy fresh, delicious tomatoes." Then she added, to show she wasn't being selfish, "Everyone needs fruits and vegetables for a healthy diet."

After they got home, Mali headed out to her backyard swing to think. "If only I could plant a garden," she thought, "but our yard is way too small." Just then, she noticed her neighbor, Mr. Taylor, looking at his daffodils. Mali knew he was thinking about how he had planted those flowers with his wife. This was the first spring since his wife had died, and Mali saw the sadness on his face. Then she had an idea.

Valerie Decampo

Mali cleared her throat, and Mr. Taylor looked up. Mali decided to walk over to the fence. "Hi, Mr. Taylor," she said. He waved, and turned away. "Wait!" Mali cried. Taking a **risk** while she still felt brave, she rushed to gather her thoughts: "Mr. Taylor, Mrs. Fair isn't doing her tomato stand anymore because she's getting old. So I'd like to grow tomatoes. I don't want to get in the way of your flowers, though. I mean, I really like tomatoes."

Suddenly, Mr. Taylor smiled. "Mali, I'm not sure what you're talking about, but you've made me smile. Reasons to smile have been **scarce** lately. What do you want to do?"

As Mr. Taylor listened, an idea came to him. "I still need a place to plant my flowers, but there's room for tomatoes. How about I make you a **loan**? I'll let you use a plot of land in my yard. I'll help you, and when your garden starts to **prosper**, you can repay me with a few tomatoes."

Mali and Mr. Taylor shook hands on this deal. "But first," Mr. Taylor said, "you'll have to make an investment by buying some tomato plants at the nursery."

Mali thought. "Well, I have some **savings** from my allowance, and I was saving to buy a computer game." She paused. "But I'd rather have tomatoes, so let's start right away!"

The next day, Mali bought all the tomato plants she could **afford**. Mr. Taylor taught Mali how to prepare the soil and place the plants. Finally, Mali placed stakes in the ground to help hold the plants up. Mr. Taylor explained, "Once the tomatoes come, the heavy fruit makes the branches bend." Then all they could do was water, pull weeds, and wait.

When the fruit ripened, there were more juicy, red tomatoes than even Mali could have imagined. "There is no way I can eat all these," she realized. On Saturday, Mali and Mr. Taylor carried several crates of ripe tomatoes to the market, and by the day's end they had sold them all. "Not only did I get back the money I invested," said Mali, "but I also made a **profit** of twenty dollars!"

Mr. Taylor said, "Those are also your **wages**! You've earned that money."

Mali beamed and said, "Mr. Taylor, maybe you could sell some of your flowers, and we could run a market stand together!" Mr. Taylor, picturing a garden of zinnias and marigolds, was already looking forward to next summer.

Make Connections

How did Mali and Mr. Taylor each get something they needed? ESSENTIAL QUESTION

How has someone helped you get something you needed? TEXT TO SELF

Valerie Decampo

Reread

When you read a story for the first time, you may find that some details, descriptions, or events are confusing. As you read "A Fresh Idea," you can stop and reread difficult parts of the story to make sure you understand them.

 Find Text Evidence

You may not be sure how Mali got her idea to grow a garden of her own, with Mr. Taylor's help. Reread the fourth paragraph on page 23 of "A Fresh Idea."

> page 23
>
> Just then, she noticed her neighbor, Mr. Taylor, looking at his daffodils. Mali knew he was thinking about how he had planted those flowers with his wife. This was the first spring since his wife had died, and Mali saw the sadness on his face. Then she had an idea.

When I reread, I see that Mr. Taylor knows how to plant gardens. He is also sad because his wife died. Mali got her idea after noticing Mr. Taylor's flowers and his sadness.

 COLLABORATE

Your Turn

Why does Mali decide to sell her tomatoes? Reread page 25. Remember to use the strategy Reread.

Valerie Decampo

Sequence

The sequence is the order in which the **plot events** happen in a story. The sequence of events includes the most important events at the beginning, middle, and end. Sequence also includes when **characters** and **settings** are introduced.

 Find Text Evidence

When I read the paragraphs on page 23 of "A Fresh Idea," I can see the sequence of events that leads to Mali's idea. The beginning of the story introduces Mali, her mom, and their neighborhood. Then we learn about Mali's problem.

Characters
Mali, Mali's mom, Mr. Taylor
Setting
Mali's neighborhood in spring
Beginning
Mali learns that the tomato stand will not be at the summer market anymore. Mali sees her neighbor in his garden and gets an idea. Mr. Taylor lets Mali use his land.

↓

Middle

↓

End

Your Turn

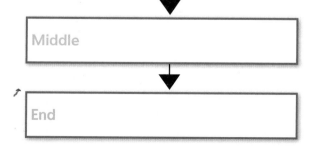

COLLABORATE

Reread "A Fresh Idea." List events in the middle and end of the story in your graphic organizer. Select important details that show the sequence of events.

Go Digital!
Use the interactive graphic organizer

Realistic Fiction

The selection "A Fresh Idea" is realistic fiction.

Realistic fiction:

- Tells about characters, settings, and events that are like people, places, and events in real life
- Includes dialogue and descriptive details
- Often includes illustrations

Find Text Evidence

I can tell that "A Fresh Idea" is realistic fiction. Details about the neighborhood, as well as the illustrations, show me that this story could happen in real life. Also, the characters say and do things that people might say and do in real life.

page 23

One bright Saturday morning, Mali and her mom walked around the neighborhood. That is, her mom walked, but Mali ran, skipped, jumped over puddles, and visited the neighbors' dogs. Mali paused to look at the budding trees on her block. "I can't wait until summer," she said, "especially for Mrs. Fair's great tomatoes at her market stand." She pointed.

Mali's mom stood looking at the empty lot where the market set up every summer weekend. She looked at Mali. "Honey, Mrs. Fair told me last week that she had to close her stand. She's really getting too old to run it anymore."

Mali turned, stared, and put her hands on her hips. "But Mrs. Fair's stand can't close!" she said. "It's the only place in the neighborhood we can buy fresh, delicious tomatoes." Then she added, to show she wasn't being selfish, "Everyone needs fruits and vegetables for a healthy diet."

After they got home, Mali headed out to her backyard swing to think. "If only I could plant a garden," she thought, "but our yard is way too small." Just then, she noticed her neighbor, Mr. Taylor, looking at his daffodils. Mali knew he was thinking about how he had planted these flowers with his wife. This was the first spring since his wife had died, and Mali saw the sadness on his face. Then she had an idea.

23

Use Illustrations Illustrations can give readers visual clues about characters, settings, and events.

COLLABORATE

Your Turn

List three examples of details, dialogue, or illustrations in "A Fresh Idea" that show you this is realistic fiction. Tell your partner why these things make the story realistic.

Context Clues

When you read a sentence and do not know what a word means, you can look at the other words and phrases in the sentence to help you figure out the meaning.

Find Text Evidence

When I read the sentence, Finally, Mali placed stakes in the ground to help hold the plants up, *I'm not sure what "stakes" are. I can use the phrase, "to help hold the plants up" to help me figure out what stakes do.*

Mr. Taylor taught Mali how to prepare the soil and place the plants. Finally, Mali placed stakes in the ground to help hold the plants up. Mr. Taylor explained, "Once the tomatoes come, the heavy fruit makes the branches bend."

Your Turn

COLLABORATE

Use sentence clues to figure out the meanings of the following words from "A Fresh Idea."

plot, *page 24*

nursery, *page 24*

ripened, *page 25*

Valerie Decampo

Pages 22–25

Write About the Text

José

I responded to the prompt: *Write a diary entry from Mali's point of view about her plans for next summer's garden. Use descriptive details.*

Student Model: *Narrative Text*

October 28

This morning Mr. Taylor and I were in our garden. Golden leaves covered the ground. The dead leaves made me feel sad. I was looking forward to spring, but Mr. Taylor insisted that fall is best for gardeners. He said it's a good time to think about what to plant for next year.

Point of View

My diary entry uses the pronoun *I* to show that it is written from Mali's perspective.

Descriptive Details

I included sensory language to tell how the character feels.

Jupiterimages/Creatas/360/Getty Images

I wasn't sure why Mr. Taylor thought

the fall was so great for gardeners

until I looked at his marigolds with all

of their yellow, orange, and red petals.

Some were the exact colors of peppers,

pumpkins, and tomatoes. That inspired

me. I think I now know what Mr. Taylor

and I will be planting

next year!

Grammar

A **sentence** is a group of words that expresses a complete thought.

Grammar Handbook See page 450.

Strong Conclusion

My final sentence completes Mali's thoughts following the day's events.

Your Turn

Write a diary entry from Mr. Taylor's point of view about how he felt when Mali asked him for help. Use descriptive details.

Go Digital!
Write your response online.
Use your editing checklist.

Essential Question

What can lead us to rethink an idea?

Go Digital!

Sean Davey/Australian Picture Library/Corbis

SL.5.1c See the California Standards section.

On Second Thought

Before trying out a new idea, we first learn all we can in order to get the desired result. If we do not accomplish the goal, we work to figure out what caused the problem.

▷ After a wipe-out like this one, this surfer may ask himself, "What went wrong?"

▷ Every wave is different, and each mistake will teach him more about his options for next time!

Talk About It

Write words you have learned about rethinking an idea. Then talk about a time you had to rethink the way you did something.

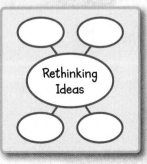

Rethinking Ideas

Vocabulary

Use the picture and the sentences to talk with a partner about each word.

accomplish

With Grandpa's help, I was able to **accomplish** my project more quickly.

What would you like to accomplish today?

anxious

Rita was **anxious** about the research project, so she checked many sources.

Describe a situation that made you feel anxious.

assemble

When all the students **assemble** in the room, we will begin the play.

Where else might a large group assemble?

decipher

The archeologists had to **decipher** the code in the rock drawings in order to understand what they meant.

When is handwriting hard to decipher?

distracted

When my friend **distracted** my attention, her dog swiped my frozen treat.

What things have distracted your attention from studying?

navigate

We used a map to help **navigate** our way around the park.

In what other ways do people navigate?

options

The grocery store offered many different vegetable **options**.

What is a synonym for options?

retrace

Carl was able to **retrace** his footsteps to find his way home.

What is another word or phrase for retrace?

COLLABORATE

Your Turn

Pick three words. Write three questions for your partner to answer.

Go Digital! *Use the online visual glossary*

L.5.6 See the California Standards section.

WHITEWATER ADVENTURE

Essential Question

What can lead us to rethink an idea?

Read about how Nina and her family use trial and error to rethink solutions to a problem.

James Bernardin

I don't know about you, but I never pictured my family on a whitewater rafting vacation in Colorado. We had tried rafting several times before with instructors and guides. All of us liked it! I come from a family of excellent athletes, and I sometimes have to work hard at holding my own. I didn't even mind when my sister, Marta, who is fourteen, kept correcting my technique. Because she's three years older, Marta believes it's her mission in life to make sure I do everything perfectly. "Nina, hold your paddle this way. Nina, plant your feet firmly," she corrects. Honestly, sometimes she's full of herself, although I guess she means well.

That morning, Dad had us **assemble** our equipment, as we had learned. He then took us through his checklist. Only Dad could read his checklist because his handwriting was so hard to **decipher**. "Paddles – check, helmets – check, life jackets – check, buckets – check," until everything was accounted for. Then we boarded our raft for our second solo trip and headed down the beautiful Colorado River.

Mom had mapped out our route—a novice's course with just enough whitewater to make it exciting. It felt great to **navigate** the raft, paddling in rhythm with everyone else. Dad and I sat in the rear, or stern, of the raft. Mom and Marta sat in the front, or the bow. From time to time, waves slapped against the sides of the raft, spraying water in our faces.

Suddenly, I was **distracted** by a bear coming out of the trees, but it turned around and began to **retrace** its steps. All of us must have been distracted by that bear because, in the blink of an eye, we ran into a problem! Our raft came to a complete halt.

"What's wrong?" I asked, hoping I didn't sound nearly as **anxious** as I felt.

"Yikes!" exclaimed Mom. "We're stuck on some rocks!"

"Maybe a river guide will come by and give us a shove," suggested Marta. However, there wasn't a soul in sight. She tried shouting, "HELLO, OUT THERE!" All we heard back was an echo. To make matters worse, storm clouds were gathering. The last thing we needed now was a rainstorm.

"Don't worry, folks, I know what we can do," said Dad. "It's the front of the raft that's stuck, so let's all sit in the stern. Our weight will probably shift the raft off the rocks." Carefully, Mom and Marta moved to the rear. Nothing happened.

James Bernardin

"Let's try swaying from side to side," urged Mom, looking up at the darkening sky. So we swayed and swayed, but the raft didn't move an inch. Dad even tried jumping a couple of times, but that didn't work either. Now it started to drizzle, and although no one wanted to admit it, we were running out of **options**.

"Wait!" I yelled. I thought back to our rafting lessons. "What if we tried to lift the side of the raft away from the rocks?" I asked hesitantly.

"Quick, let's try it!" said Mom. We went to the front of the raft and lifted the side away from the rocks. Then we heard a little popping noise. We held our breath.

"Did we tear the raft?" cried Marta.

"No, we broke the suction between the raft and the rocks!" said Dad, as he pushed off the rocks with his paddle.

"We did it!" yelled Marta. "I mean, you did it, Nina—that was truly brilliant!"

"Good thinking, Nina!" cheered Mom and Dad.

By this time, it was raining steadily, so we paddled really hard to return to land and wait indoors for the rain to stop. And how was I feeling? It's kind of hard to describe. I was on cloud nine! I felt like I could **accomplish** anything I wanted.

Make Connections

Talk about why Nina and her family had to rethink solutions to the problem of being stuck on the rocks. Compare the different ideas they came up with. ESSENTIAL QUESTION

When have you had to rethink an idea in order to solve a problem? TEXT TO SELF

Reread

When you read a story for the first time, you may find that some of the events, descriptions, or details are confusing. As you read "Whitewater Adventure," you can stop and reread difficult parts of the story to check your understanding.

 Find Text Evidence

You may not be sure how Nina feels about her older sister, Marta. Reread the first paragraph of "Whitewater Adventure" on page 37.

page 37

I don't know about you, but I never pictured my family on a whitewater rafting vacation in Colorado. We had tried rafting several times before with instructors and guides. All of us liked it! I come from a family of excellent athletes, and I sometimes have to work hard at holding my own. I didn't even mind when my sister, Marta, who is fourteen, kept correcting my technique. Because she's three years older, Marta believes it's her mission in life to make sure I do everything perfectly. "Nina, hold your paddle this way. Nina, plant your feet firmly," she corrects. Honestly, sometimes she's full of herself, although I guess she means well.

At first, I'm not sure what Nina means by "it's her mission in life to make sure I do everything perfectly." When I reread the paragraph, I can infer that Nina is being sarcastic, because her sister Marta often corrects her.

Your Turn

COLLABORATE

Why is Nina's solution to the problem successful? Reread page 39 to answer the question. As you read other selections, remember to use the strategy Reread.

Problem and Solution

The plot of a story usually involves a problem that the main character or characters in the story need to solve. What the characters want to do or change is called the **problem**. The way the problem is solved is called the **solution**.

 Find Text Evidence

When I read the beginning of "Whitewater Adventure" on page 37, I learn that the characters are Nina, Marta, Mom, and Dad, and that they are whitewater rafting on the Colorado River. When I read what Mom said on page 38, I learn about the problem they encounter.

Character
Nina, Marta, Mom, Dad

Setting
Colorado River; a raft

Problem
The raft gets stuck on some rocks.

↓

Events

↓

Solution

COLLABORATE

Your Turn

Reread the remaining section of "Whitewater Adventure." Complete the rest of your graphic organizer by recording the events that show how the family tries to solve the problem, and then telling their solution.

Go Digital!
Use the interactive graphic organizer

Realistic Fiction

The selection "Whitewater Adventure" is realistic fiction.

Realistic fiction:

- Tells about characters and events that resemble people and events in real life
- May have adventure involving actions to reach a goal
- May create suspense through dialogue and details

Find Text Evidence

I can tell that "Whitewater Adventure" is realistic fiction. Rafting is an adventure that could happen in real life, and it happens in a place that actually exists. The author also creates suspense.

page 38

Suddenly, I was **distracted** by a bear coming out of the trees, but it turned around and began to **retrace** its steps. All of us must have been distracted by that bear because, in the blink of an eye, we ran into a problem! Our raft came to a complete halt.

"What's wrong?" I asked, hoping I didn't sound nearly as **anxious** as I felt.

"Yikes!" exclaimed Mom. "We're stuck on some rocks!"

"Maybe a river guide will come by and give us a shove," suggested Marta. However, there wasn't a soul in sight. She tried shouting, "HELLO, OUT THERE!" All we heard back was an echo. To make matters worse, storm clouds were gathering. The last thing we needed now was a rainstorm.

"Don't worry, folks, I know what we can do," said Dad. "It's the front of the raft that's stuck, so let's all sit in the stern. Our weight will probably shift the raft off the rocks." Carefully, Mom and Marta moved to the rear. Nothing happened.

38

Suspense Suspense is what you feel when you are uncertain and excited about how events in a story will turn out. Unexpected events help create suspense.

COLLABORATE

Your Turn

List three details in "Whitewater Adventure" that show the story is realistic fiction. Then identify ways the author builds suspense.

Idioms

An idiom is an expression that cannot be understood from the meanings of the individual words in it. To figure out the meaning of an **idiom**, you have to use clues in the sentence or the surrounding sentences.

 Find Text Evidence

When I read the end of the first paragraph on page 37, I see an idiom. In the sentences that came before, Marta is always correcting Nina, as if Marta thinks of herself as an expert. The idiom she's full of herself *means she thinks she knows everything.*

> "Nina, hold your paddle this way. Nina, plant your feet firmly," she corrects. Honestly, sometimes she's full of herself, although I guess she means well.

Your Turn

COLLABORATE

Use context clues in the sentence or the surrounding sentences to help you figure out the meanings of the following idioms from "Whitewater Adventure."

holding my own, *page 37*

in the blink of an eye, *page 38*

on cloud nine, *page 39*

James Bernardin

Write About the Text

Pages 36–39

Maddy

I responded to the prompt: *Imagine that the raft sprang a leak while the family was in the river. Write about the event. Use descriptive details.*

Student Model: *Narrative Text*

My family and I were having fun on the river, when suddenly the river was at our ankles. Our raft had sprung a leak! "Quick, Mom! Reach for that big tree limb!" I shouted. "We can use it to tug the raft to shore."

"Good idea, Nina," Mom agreed.

"Let's get it done, team!"

Style and Tone

I used exclamatory sentences to show that my tone is excited.

Dialogue

I used realistic conversation to show how the characters responded to the event.

We all grabbed the limb and pulled our raft toward land. Our ship was sinking quickly, and it took all of our might. After a few minutes, we got the job done. Finally, we climbed onto dry land. Then we pulled the raft onto the river bank with sighs of relief. We were safe!

Sequence

I used transitions, such as *after a few minutes,* to show the order of events.

Grammar

This is an example of a **simple subject** and a **simple predicate**.

Grammar Handbook See page 451.

Your Turn

Imagine Nina's dad lost his paddle on the way back to shore. Write about the event using descriptive details.

Go Digital!
Write your response online.
Use your editing checklist.

Essential Question

How can experiencing nature change the way you think about it?

Go Digital!

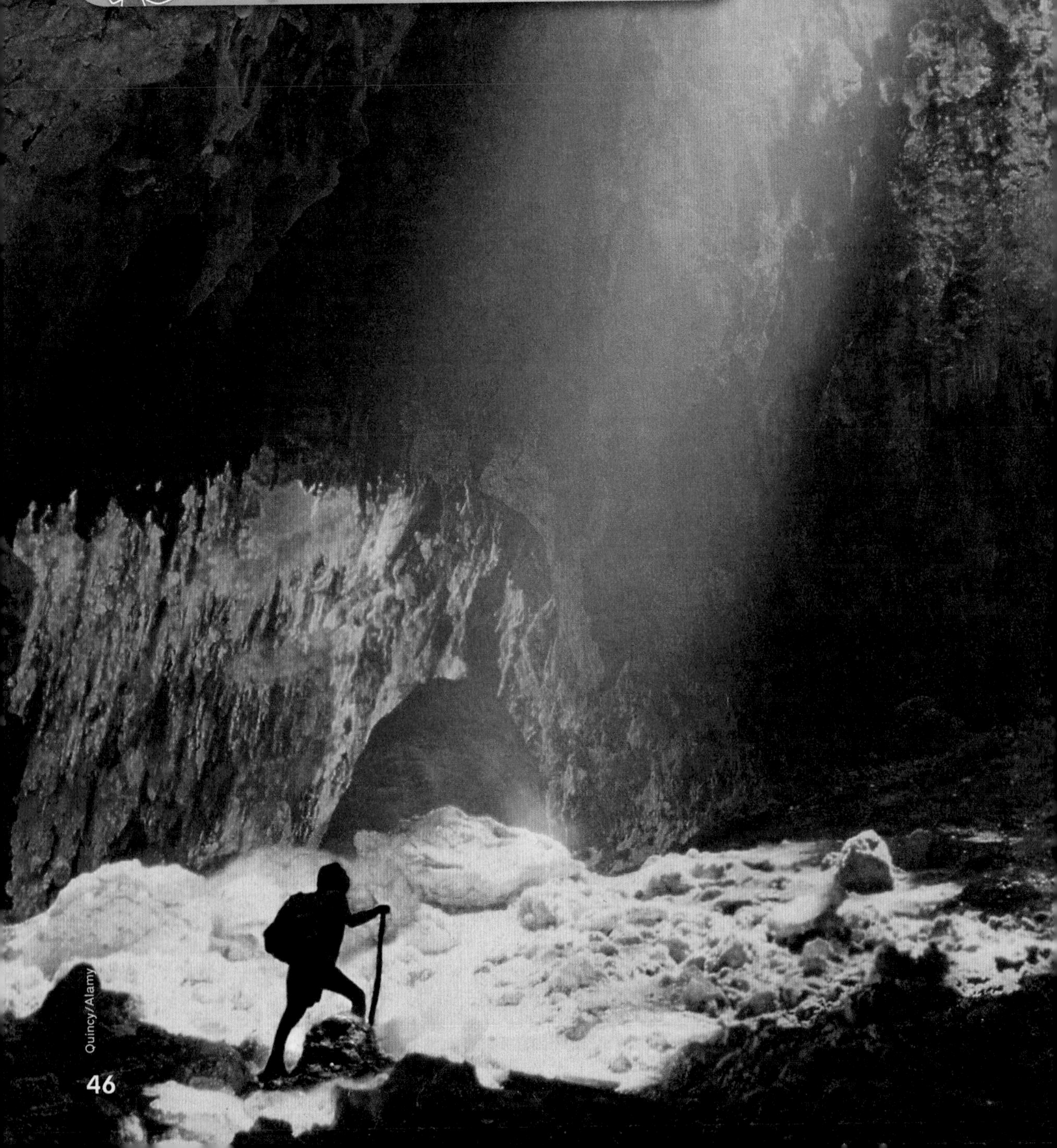

Quincy/Alamy

Close Encounters

What have you discovered in nature that was like nothing you had seen before? You don't have to be a naturalist to have an amazing encounter with the great outdoors.

▶ Many natural wonders are under ground. Caves like this one display formations that may change the way you see rocks!

▶ Above ground, you can find surprises while hiking among the trees. California redwoods, for example, can grow to be over 320 feet tall. That's taller than the Statue of Liberty!

Talk About It

Write words you have learned about ways to experience nature. Then talk about how an experience you had in nature affected you.

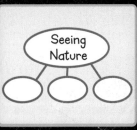

Vocabulary

Use the picture and the sentences to talk with a
partner about each word.

debris

The science class picked up **debris** that
had washed up on the beach.

What is a synonym for debris?

emphasis

When Elena said, "Shhh," she put her
finger to her lips for **emphasis**.

How can you show emphasis when
you talk?

encounter

During a hike, you might have an
encounter with a butterfly.

What is a synonym for encounter?

generations

My grandma has a pie recipe that has
been in my family for many **generations**.

How many generations of a family might
be at a holiday meal?

indicated

The thermometer **indicated** that it was hot outside.

What is a synonym for indicated?

naturalist

The **naturalist** told us about many of the plants and animals she studied.

What is something you might ask a naturalist?

sheer

When we looked up at the **sheer** rock, we knew it would be impossible to climb.

What else might you describe as sheer?

spectacular

The mountaintop provides **spectacular** views.

What else might you describe as spectacular?

COLLABORATE

Your Turn

Pick three words. Write three questions for your partner to answer.

Go Digital! *Use the online visual glossary*

(t to b) FogStock LLC/Photolibrary; Sandro Vannini/Corbis; Johner/Johner Images/Getty Images; David Epperson/Photographer's Choice/Getty Images

L.5.6 See the California Standards section.

A Life in the Woods

Essential Question

How can experiencing nature change the way you think about it?

Read about how Thoreau's stay in the woods changed his view of nature.

Into the Woods

Henry David Thoreau raised his pen to write, but the chatter of guests in the next room filled his ears. He stared at the page. "Concord, 1841" was all that he had written. How would he write a book with such noise in his family's house? Thoreau headed outside, shutting the door with **emphasis**. He would have to find a place of his own.

Thoreau walked out of town. Tall white pines soon replaced the painted houses. He listened to the rustling of the leaves. What if I could stay here, he thought. He could live off the land, close to nature, and begin his book. It would take work, but he could do it.

Years passed, but Thoreau still did not have a place in the woods. One day, his friend Ralph Waldo Emerson had an idea. Emerson was a well-known writer who had bought some land near Walden Pond. Because he and Thoreau shared the same interest in nature, Emerson decided to let Thoreau use part of this land.

In March of 1845, Thoreau began to build a cabin. By July, it was ready. He could live and write in the woods.

(bkgd) Galen Rowell/Mountain Light/Alamy; (inset) Aaron Roeth Photography; (r) FPG /Taxi/Getty Images

Cabin Life

Thoreau's move to the woods **indicated** that he liked to be alone. But Thoreau did not feel that way. "I have a great deal of company in my house," he wrote. Red squirrels woke him by running up and down the **sheer** sides of his cabin. A snowshoe hare lived in the **debris** under his cabin, thumping against the floorboards. A sparrow once perched on his shoulder. Thoreau recorded these experiences in his journal. How easily writing came to him with the beauty of nature around him!

On Walden Pond

Thoreau was a **naturalist**. He noticed the habits of animals. Each **encounter** showed him something new. One afternoon, Thoreau tried to get a close look at a loon, but the bird quickly dove into the pond. He knew loons could travel long distances under water, so he guessed where it would come up. But every time Thoreau paddled to one spot, the loon came up somewhere else and let out a call—a howling laugh. What a silly loon, Thoreau thought. But after a while, Thoreau felt as though the bird was laughing at him because he still could not catch up to it. Thoreau wrote in his journal:

Thoreau published his book *Walden* in 1854.

His white breast, the stillness of the air, and the smoothness of the water were all against him. At length he uttered one of those prolonged howls, as if calling on the god of the loons to aid him, and immediately there came a wind from the east and rippled the surface, and filled the whole air with misty rain, and I was impressed.

The **spectacular** scene made Thoreau wonder at the loon. It no longer seemed a silly animal, but one with some mysterious power. As months went by, Thoreau also became aware of each animal's ability to stay alive. "His power of observation seemed to indicate additional senses," Emerson once remarked. In winter, as he warmed his cabin by fire, he watched in awe as the moles warmed their nest by their own body heat. He understood forest life as never before.

Back to Concord

Like the geese that move to new ponds at the season's end, so too did Thoreau leave Walden. He had done what he had set out to do, and had learned much from the woods around him. He packed his few belongings and his stack of journals and returned to Concord. Now, he would turn his journal entries into a book. **Generations** to come would know life on Walden Pond!

Make Connections

Talk about how Thoreau's experiences at Walden Pond changed his view of nature. ESSENTIAL QUESTION

Think about a time that you saw something in nature close-up. How did it change your idea about it? TEXT TO SELF

Rick & Nora Bowers/Alamy

Ask and Answer Questions

When you read, you can ask yourself questions to check your understanding. Asking questions such as *What just happened?* or *Why did that happen?* can help you look for answers. You can also ask and answer questions about the whole selection.

🔍 Find Text Evidence

After you read the first paragraph of "A Life in the Woods" on page 51, you might ask yourself: *Why did Thoreau have to find a place of his own?* Reread the paragraph to find the answer.

page 51

Into the Woods

Henry David Thoreau raised his pen to write, but the chatter of guests in the next room filled his ears. He stared at the page. "Concord, 1841" was all that he had written. How would he write a book with such noise in his family's house? Thoreau headed outside, shutting the door with **emphasis**. He would have to find a place of his own.

Thoreau walked out of town. Tall white pines soon replaced the painted houses. He listened to the rustling of the leaves. What if I could stay here, he thought. He could live off the land, close to nature, and begin his book. It would take work, but he could do it.

I read that Thoreau wondered how he could write a book with such noise in his family's house. From this I can infer that Thoreau needed to find a place of his own because the noise in his family's house made it impossible for him to write.

COLLABORATE

Your Turn

Reread the next to last sentence in "Back to Concord" on page 53. Ask and answer a question about this sentence.

Cause and Effect

To explain how and why things happen, authors may organize information to show cause and effect. A **cause** is an event or action that makes something happen. An **effect** is what happens as the result of a cause. To identify cause-and-effect relationships, look for signal words and phrases, such as *because, so,* and *as a result.*

 Find Text Evidence

When I read the section "Into the Woods" from "A Life in the Woods" on page 51, I can look for signal words that show cause-and-effect relationships. I see the signal word because *in the sentence, "Because he and Thoreau shared the same interest in nature, Emerson decided to let Thoreau use part of this land."*

Cause	Effect
Emerson and Thoreau shared an interest in nature.	Emerson let Thoreau use his land.

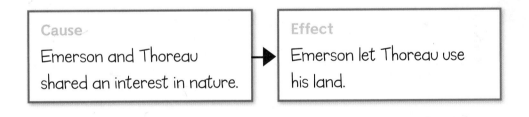

COLLABORATE

Your Turn

Reread "A Life in the Woods." Find cause-and-effect relationships and list them in your graphic organizer.

Go Digital!
Use the interactive graphic organizer

Narrative Nonfiction

The selection "A Life in the Woods" is a narrative nonfiction text.

Narrative nonfiction:

- Gives facts about real people and events
- Tells about events in the sequence that they happened
- May include both primary and secondary sources

🔍 Find Text Evidence

I can tell that "A Life in the Woods" is narrative nonfiction. It gives facts about a real person, Henry David Thoreau, using primary and secondary sources. It also tells about events in Thoreau's life at Walden Pond in the order that they happened.

page 52

Secondary Source A secondary source retells or interprets information from a primary source.

Primary Source A primary source provides first-hand information about a topic. Autobiographies, journals, and letters are examples.

Cabin Life

Thoreau's move to the woods **indicated** that he liked to be alone. But Thoreau did not feel that way. "I have a great deal of company in my house," he wrote. Red squirrels woke him by running up and down the **sheer** sides of his cabin. A snowshoe hare lived in the **debris** under his cabin, thumping against the floorboards. A sparrow once perched on his shoulder. Thoreau recorded these experiences in his journal. How easily writing came to him with the beauty of nature around him!

On Walden Pond

Thoreau was a **naturalist**. He noticed the habits of animals. Each **encounter** showed him something new. One afternoon, Thoreau tried to get a look at a loon, but the bird quickly dove into the pond. He knew loons could travel long distances under water, so he guessed where it would come up. But every time Thoreau paddled to one spot, the loon came up somewhere else and let out a call—a howling laugh. What a silly loon, Thoreau thought. But after a while, Thoreau felt as though the bird was laughing at him because he still could not catch up to it. Thoreau wrote in his journal:

His white breast, the stillness of the air and the smoothness of the water were all against him. At length he uttered one of those prolonged howls, as if calling on the god of the loons to aid him, and immediately there came a wind from the east and rippled the surface, and filled the whole air with misty rain, and I was impressed.

WALDEN.

By HENRY D. THOREAU,

Thoreau published his book *Walden* in 1854.

52

 COLLABORATE

Your Turn

Reread the passage "Cabin Life" on page 52. Find a sentence that must have come from a primary source. How is a primary source unique?

Homographs

Homographs are words that are spelled the same but have different meanings. Two homographs may or may not sound the same. When you see a homograph in a sentence, use sentence clues to find the correct meaning of the word.

 Find Text Evidence

When I read the fourth sentence of "On Walden Pond" on page 52, I see a word that has two meanings: dove. *I can use the phrase* dove into the pond *to help me choose the correct meaning. That also helps me figure out the right way to say the word.*

Thoreau tried to get a close look at a loon, but the bird quickly dove into the pond.

Your Turn

COLLABORATE

Use sentence clues to figure out the meanings of the following homographs in "A Life in the Woods."

felt, *page 52*

wind, *page 52*

moles, *page 53*

Write About the Text

Pages 50–53

Sofia

I answered the question: *Why did the author include an excerpt from Thoreau's journal in "A Life in the Woods"? Include text evidence.*

Student Model: *Informative Text*

Topic Sentence

My first sentence addresses the author's main reason for including the excerpt.

The author included the journal excerpt to help readers connect to Thoreau's experience living in the woods. The author states that Thoreau's house was too noisy for him to write, but he was able to write in the quiet of the woods.

Supporting Details

I included text evidence to support my reasoning.

The excerpt shows Thoreau himself writing about the forest life around him, and this helps the experience seem more real. Thoreau's writing allows readers to almost hear the loon laughing and feel the wind blowing, just as he did.

Grammar

This **compound sentence** joins two ideas by using a comma and the conjunction *and*.

Grammar Handbook *See page 452.*

Strong Words

I used precise language to help create a clear picture in the reader's mind.

Your Turn

What effect did living in the woods have on Thoreau? Use text evidence to support your answer.

Go Digital!
Write your response online.
Use your editing checklist.

Rick & Nora Bowers/Alamy

Essential Question

How does technology lead to creative ideas?

Go Digital!

Strokes of Genius

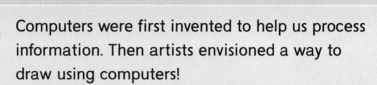

Computers were first invented to help us process information. Then artists envisioned a way to draw using computers!

▶ Using a special "pen" and "pad," I make my artistic ideas come to life on the screen in front of me.

▶ I can also animate my drawings on the computer. It makes me wonder what the next breakthrough in making art will be!

Talk About It

Write words you have learned about inventions. Then talk about an invention you like, and what it allows you to do.

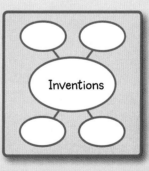

Inventions

Vocabulary

Use the picture and the sentences to talk with a
partner about each word.

breakthrough

Sam had been trying to think of a project
idea when he finally had a **breakthrough**.

What kind of breakthrough would you
like to see?

captivated

Josh was **captivated** by the action
movie in 3-D.

What is something that has
captivated you?

claimed

After her flight landed, Marika happily
claimed her suitcase.

What is something you claimed
that was yours?

devices

Many people use electronic **devices**
every day to tell time, read, and
communicate.

What devices do you use?

enthusiastically

Fans cheered **enthusiastically** when their team won.

What events make you react enthusiastically?

envisioned

As Sara stared at the map, she **envisioned** traveling all over the world.

Tell about something you have envisioned.

passionate

Cal is **passionate** about protecting all animals from harm.

Describe a person who is passionate about something.

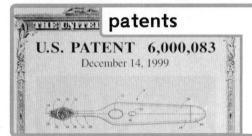

patents

U.S. PATENT 6,000,083
December 14, 1999

Inventors who have **patents** for their inventions can make money from them.

What inventions do you think have patents?

Your Turn

COLLABORATE

Pick three words. Write three questions for your partner to answer.

Go Digital! *Use the online visual glossary*

(t to b) Chris Whitehead/Cultura/Corbis; Fuse/Getty Images; Ed Bock/Getty Images; Mark Duncan/AP Images

Fantasy
Becomes Fact

Essential Question

How does technology lead to creative ideas?

Read about how a science fiction writer's ideas led to new technology.

Inventing the Future

Have you ever imagined ways of traveling into space? Or have you used a tool and wished it did something more? One person who thought just this way was the science fiction writer Arthur C. Clarke. Arthur is most famous for writing novels and stories about science and the future. But you may not know that real inventions came about as a result of things he first imagined!

In his writings, Arthur envisioned technologies that did not yet exist, but might. This was no accident. Arthur studied and used scientific knowledge all during his lifetime. Arthur wrote about advanced computers and spaceships. Years later, these technologies were developed.

Science at an Early Age

Even as a child, Arthur was passionate about science. Born in England in 1917 in a small town by the sea, Arthur spent his school years enthusiastically reading his favorite science fiction magazine. He was fascinated by astronomy and built a telescope when he was just 13. He also started writing his own science fiction stories. He even published them in a school magazine. Arthur loved imagining the future.

Arthur's own future became uncertain as a teenager, when his father died. Since his mother could not afford to send him to college, Arthur moved to London at the age of 19 and got an office job. In his free time, he worked at the subjects he loved. He also continued to write science fiction. His love of science and its possibilities would soon be useful.

Arthur C. Clarke's interest in science and space exploration lasted all his life. He sometimes constructed his own tools for his research.

(l) David Rajecky www.davidrajecky.cz; (r) SSPL via Getty Images

In 1939 Arthur joined the Royal Air Force to help fight the Second World War. It was there that Arthur began to invent. Arthur became an expert in the radar systems used to guide planes and detect enemies. This technology gave Arthur ideas. He imagined an amazing breakthrough in communication systems. He proposed a wireless system using space stations. This system required rockets to carry satellites into space. Then the satellites would help transmit signals around the Earth. Since satellites and space stations did not exist, this idea was a demonstration of Arthur's imagination. He had learned much about space.

As with any inventor, Arthur built on technologies that already existed to create his system. For example, rockets had been invented but could not yet travel into space. In 1957, Russia used a rocket to launch *Sputnik 1*, which became the first manmade object to orbit Earth. In the 1960s, a satellite communications system was created. It was just like the one Arthur had envisioned years before. Years later, the same kind of satellite was used to make cell phone communication possible. Although Arthur claimed the communications system as his own idea, he did not apply for patents. As a result, he never made money from his idea.

Satellites like this one began with the launch of *Sputnik 1,* which weighed less than 200 pounds and was only about 23 inches in diameter.

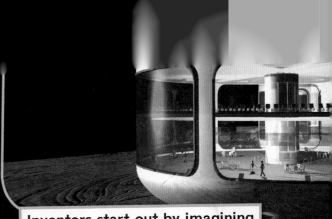

In 1968, Arthur published one of his best-known novels, *2001: A Space Odyssey*. In the novel, Arthur imagined a computer that controlled almost everything. Arthur's computer idea, HAL, could actually think for itself. Today, computers cannot think for themselves. However, they do control many of the devices in our homes, cars, planes, and spacecraft. HAL could recognize human voices as well as speak back. This technology did not exist when the book was written, but it is common today. Arthur's novel also predicted advances such as space stations and rocket-powered missions to far-off

Inventors start out by imagining what the future will look like.

planets. He even predicted people reading news on electronic screens!

Arthur C. Clarke's science fiction books have captivated readers around the world. Many of the technologies he wrote about seemed like fantasy at the time, but they turned into fact. His creative ideas may have inspired others to invent the very technologies he imagined.

Make Connections

Talk about how existing technology helped Arthur C. Clarke imagine other inventions. ESSENTIAL QUESTION

What are some ways you would like to improve a machine or other object that you use in your everyday life? TEXT TO SELF

Ask and Answer Questions

To help their understanding, readers ask themselves questions before, during, and after they read. You might ask: *What is the main idea of this section?* and *Do I need to reread this text?*

Find Text Evidence

As you read the section "Predicting the Future" in "Fantasy Becomes Fact" on page 66, you may not understand how Arthur built on technologies that already existed. You may ask: *What technologies existed at that time?*

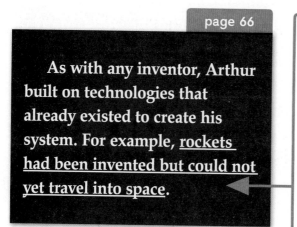

page 66

As with any inventor, Arthur built on technologies that already existed to create his system. For example, <u>rockets had been invented but could not yet travel into space.</u>

As I read the next few sentences in the paragraph, I get the answer to my question. Rockets existed, but they had not yet gone into space. Arthur's idea was that rockets could take satellites into space to help with a wireless communication system.

COLLABORATE

Your Turn

Ask yourself a question about the inventions Arthur imagined in *2001: A Space Odyssey.* Then reread "Can Science Fiction Come True?" to answer it.

Sequence

Sequence, or time order, is one way an author organizes and presents information. Understanding the sequence of events helps readers identify and remember key events. Signal words and phrases such as *years later, as a child,* or *in 1968* are clues that help you understand the sequence.

Find Text Evidence

As I read "Fantasy Becomes Fact," I can look for events that show how Arthur C. Clarke became an important inventor and writer. In the section "Science at an Early Age" on page 65, I see that Arthur built a telescope. I also see a signal phrase that tells me when this happened: "he was just 13."

Even as a child, Arthur was passionate about science.

⬇

Arthur spent his school years reading science fiction.

⬇

At 13, he built a telescope and began writing science fiction.

Your Turn

Reread the remaining sections of "Fantasy Becomes Fact." Look for words and phrases that signal a sequence of events. List the events in your graphic organizer.

Go Digital!
Use the interactive graphic organizer

RI.5.3 See the California Standards section.

Biography

A biography is the true story of a person's life written by another person. A biography may be about someone who lived in the past or someone who is alive today. The author of a biography writes in the third person, using pronouns such as *he* or *she*. A biography may include illustrations.

Find Text Evidence

I can tell that "Fantasy Becomes Fact" is a biography because it tells me facts about a real person, Arthur C. Clarke. The author tells who Arthur C. Clarke was, when and where he lived, and why he is important. The illustrations and photos give me more information.

page 66

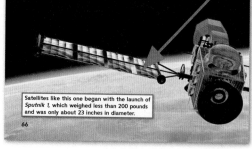

Predicting the Future

In 1939 Arthur joined the Royal Air Force to help fight the Second World War. It was there that Arthur began to invent. Arthur became an expert in the radar systems used to guide planes and detect enemies. This technology gave Arthur ideas. He imagined an amazing breakthrough in communication systems. He proposed a wireless system using space stations. This system required rockets to carry satellites into space. Then the satellites would help transmit signals around the Earth. Since satellites and space stations did not exist, this idea was a demonstration of Arthur's imagination. He had learned much about space.

As with any inventor, Arthur built on technologies that already existed to create his system. For example, rockets had been invented but could not yet travel into space. In 1957, Russia used a rocket to launch *Sputnik 1*, which became the first manmade object to orbit Earth. In the 1960s, a satellite communications system was created. It was just like the one Arthur had envisioned years before. Years later, the same kind of satellite was used to make cell phone communication possible. Although Arthur claimed the communications system as his own idea, he did not apply for patents. As a result, he never made money from his idea.

Satellites like this one began with the launch of *Sputnik 1*, which weighed less than 200 pounds and was only about 23 inches in diameter.

66

Use Illustrations and Photographs Illustrations and photographs give readers an idea of what the people, places, and things discussed in a text looked like.

COLLABORATE

Your Turn

List five facts you learned about Arthur C. Clarke. What do the illustrations and photos tell you?

Greek Roots

A root is the basic part of a word that gives the word its meaning. Many words in English have roots that come from ancient Greek. Knowing Greek roots can help you figure out the meaning of some unfamiliar words.

 Find Text Evidence

In "Science at an Early Age" on page 65, I can use what I know about Greek roots to figure out the meaning of telescope. *I know that* tele *means "at a distance" and* scop *means "see." The sentence talks about Arthur's interest in astronomy, so a telescope is a tool that helps people see things that are far away.*

> He was fascinated by astronomy and built a telescope when he was just 13.

Your Turn

COLLABORATE

Use what you know about Greek roots to figure out the meanings of the following words found in "Fantasy Becomes Fact."

biography, *page 64, "Genre" label*
astronomy, *page 65*
phone, *page 66*

Nikreates/Alamy

Write About the Text

Pages 64–67

Evan

I answered the question: *What was the author's purpose in writing "Fantasy Becomes Fact"? Include text evidence.*

Student Model: *Informative Text*

The author wrote "Fantasy Becomes Fact" to show that big dreams can actually become reality. He wants to inspire people to learn more about the things that interest them.

The author stated that Arthur C. Clarke had always loved science. He built a telescope when he was only thirteen. Then he started writing science fiction stories as he got older.

Precise Language
I used the word *inspire* to show the level of the author's enthusiasm.

Sequence
I used signal words to show the order of events.

As a young adult, Arthur fought in World War II, but this didn't stop his imagination. The radar he used during the war gave him ideas for satellites and space stations before they even existed. After the war, he wrote a novel that predicted what computers would become capable of doing. Arthur C. Clarke proved that it is worthwhile to have big dreams!

Grammar

Combine sentences by joining two shorter sentences with a conjunction.

Grammar Handbook See page 453.

Reasons and Evidence

I included facts about Arthur C. Clarke's life to support my points.

Your Turn

How did the author help us to understand Clarke's idea for a wireless system? Include text evidence.

Go Digital!
Write your response online.
Use your editing checklist.

W.5.2b, L.5.la, L.5.3a See the California Standards section.

73

Essential Question

What are the positive and negative effects of new technology?

Go Digital!

SL.5.lc See the California Standards section.

It's a Wired World

From our homes to our businesses, our highways to our hospitals, new technology is everywhere! With careful analysis, we can understand its effects.

► This plastic hand is no toy. It is a bionic hand built to replace a missing human hand. The digits are even powered to move individually!

► Every new technology can have effects beyond what even the creators dreamed of.

Talk About It

COLLABORATE

Write words you have learned about the effects of new technology. Then talk about a new technology you know about and what effects it has.

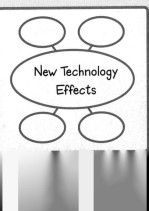

New Technology Effects

Vocabulary

Use the picture and the sentences to talk with a partner about each word.

access

In order to **access** the locked room, Brad had to punch in a special number code.

How do you access information on a computer?

advance

Many citizens have marched on Washington to **advance** people's rights.

What would you do to advance a cause you believed in?

analysis

A magnifying glass helped Karina make a careful **analysis** of the seashell.

How do you do an analysis of information for a report?

cite

When doing research, it is important to identify and **cite** sources of information.

What sources might you cite when writing a report about a country?

counterpoint

The positive review from one critic was in **counterpoint** to another's bad review.

What opinion have you had in counterpoint to that of a friend?

data

The students gathered **data** for their experiment by measuring a bubble's size.

What data would you need to write a weather report?

drawbacks

Limited room for passengers and little trunk space are **drawbacks** of a small car.

What are some drawbacks to going on a hike without the right equipment?

reasoning

James used his **reasoning** skills before deciding on his next chess move.

What other situations require good reasoning?

COLLABORATE

Your Turn

Pick three words. Write three questions for your partner to answer.

Go Digital! **Use the online visual glossary**

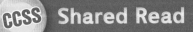
Essential Question

What are the positive and negative effects of new technology?

Read two different viewpoints about how technology affects kids.

JGI Jamie Grill/Blend Images/Getty Images

Are Electronic Devices Good for Us?

Plugged In

Kids need to spend time using electronic devices.

Do you love to surf the Internet, listen to music, IM, and talk on a cell phone? You are not alone. A recent study has some surprising news: Kids in the United States between the ages of 8 and 19 spend seven and a half hours a day on electronic devices. These include computers, smart phones, and video games. Some adults try to **advance** the idea that these devices waste kids' time. However, some research surveys say this idea is inaccurate. In fact, the **data** show that technology can benefit kids.

Critics say that kids stare at computers and TVs all day and do not get enough exercise. The facts stand in **counterpoint** to this belief. One study compared kids who use media a lot to those who do not. The "heavy" media users actually spent more time in physical activity than "light" media users.

One study by the National Institutes of Health says that action video games may help increase kids' visual attention. In addition, using interactive media can give kids good structure for learning. It can also help them learn to switch tasks effectively. Kids also need to use the Web to **access** information. Many argue that learning to use the Web responsibly sharpens kids' **reasoning** abilities.

Today's world is wired, and not just for fun. The jobs of the future depend on kids who plug in!

A Source of News for Teens

For the latest news, teens used to rely on newspapers, television, and magazines. See how many teens now get their news online.

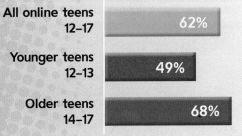

All online teens 12–17	62%
Younger teens 12–13	49%
Older teens 14–17	68%

Tuned Out

Electronic media is harming kids.

Are kids tuning out by tuning in to electronic devices? An alarming report states that young people spend an hour more per day on computers, smart phones, television, and other electronic media than they did 5 years ago. Nearly 7 out of 10 kids have cell phones. Just 5 years ago, 4 out of 10 had them. Are these devices harmless or hurtful to the well-being of young people? A close **analysis** of several studies shows that there are plenty of disadvantages to these devices.

The Internet is supposed to be a great tool for learning. Do kids who love computers do better in the classroom? To **cite** one report, access to electronic devices does not automatically bring high marks in school. See the graphs below.

Many young people use more than one electronic device at a time.

The Effect of Media Use on Grades

These pie graphs show how the use of media affects grades.

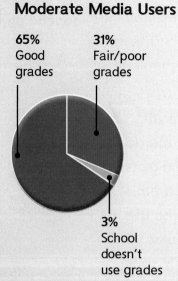

Heavy Media Users

51% Good grades   47% Fair/poor grades

Moderate Media Users

65% Good grades   31% Fair/poor grades

3% School doesn't use grades

Light Media Users

60% Good grades   23% Fair/poor grades

10% School doesn't use grades

The effects of using electronic devices on kids will continue to be studied. These devices seem to be here to stay.

Some argue that the devices get kids involved and help them make friends. Claims like these are incorrect. A study done by the Pew Research Center discusses teenagers' use of online social networks. Teens do this to keep in touch with friends they already have, not to make new ones. In addition, trying to meet people online can be dangerous.

There are other serious **drawbacks** to new technology. One issue is multitasking, or trying to do many tasks at the same time. Is it possible to do more than one task at a time well? Some studies say kids' thinking improves when they do several tasks at once. Still, experts point out that much more research needs to be done on this.

New electronic devices hit stores every year. Kids should know that there is more to life than what they see on a screen.

Make Connections

Talk about the positive and negative effects of electronic devices on kids. ESSENTIAL QUESTION

What is your opinion of electronic devices? Compare your opinion to the views discussed in the two articles. TEXT TO SELF

(l) Andrew Bret Wallis/Photographer's Choice RF/Getty Images; (r) Thomas Barwick/Iconica/Getty Images

Reread

Rereading a text—including opening and closing paragraphs—can help clarify points an author makes. Rereading can also help you check your understanding of how ideas are presented and supported by an author.

Find Text Evidence

When I reread the end of the opening paragraphs of "Plugged In" on page 79 and "Tuned Out" on page 80, I can better understand what the different authors will be writing about.

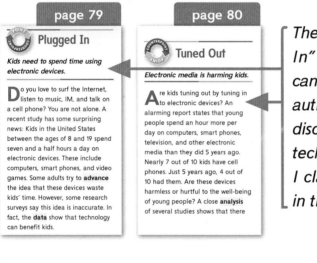

page 79	page 80
Plugged In	**Tuned Out**
Kids need to spend time using electronic devices.	*Electronic media is harming kids.*

Do you love to surf the Internet, listen to music, IM, and talk on a cell phone? You are not alone. A recent study has some surprising news: Kids in the United States between the ages of 8 and 19 spend seven and a half hours a day on electronic devices. These include computers, smart phones, and video games. Some adults try to **advance** the idea that these devices waste kids' time. However, some research surveys say this idea is inaccurate. In fact, the **data** show that technology can benefit kids.

Are kids tuning out by tuning in to electronic devices? An alarming report states that young people spend an hour more per day on computers, smart phones, television, and other electronic media than they did 5 years ago. Nearly 7 out of 10 kids have cell phones. Just 5 years ago, 4 out of 10 had them. Are these devices harmless or hurtful to the well-being of young people? A close **analysis** of several studies shows that there

The author of "Plugged In" says that technology can benefit kids. The author of "Tuned Out" discusses disadvantages of technology. By rereading, I clarify the different ideas in the articles.

Your Turn

Reread the conclusions of "Plugged In" on page 79 and "Tuned Out" on page 81. How are the conclusions similar or different? As you read, use the strategy Reread.

Author's Point of View

When arguing for or against an idea in a text, authors give reasons and evidence to support their points, and include both facts and opinions. Facts are statements that can be proven. Opinions are personal feelings and cannot be proven. Facts, opinions, and word choice help show readers a point of view.

Find Text Evidence

For "Plugged In" on page 79, the author's position is stated in this sentence: Kids need to spend time using electronic devices. *The author supports this point with evidence about exercise and learning. Finally, the author argues that technology creates the jobs of the future. From these details I can identify the point of view.*

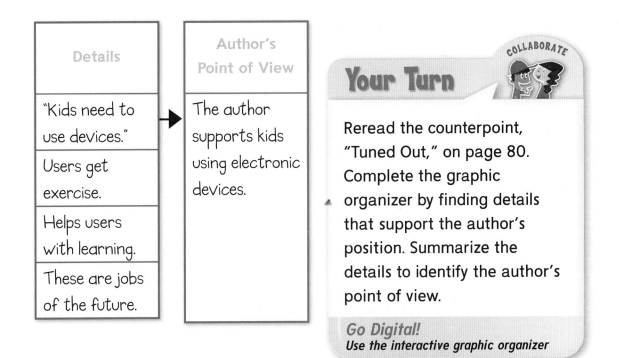

Details	Author's Point of View
"Kids need to use devices."	The author supports kids using electronic devices.
Users get exercise.	
Helps users with learning.	
These are jobs of the future.	

Your Turn COLLABORATE

Reread the counterpoint, "Tuned Out," on page 80. Complete the graphic organizer by finding details that support the author's position. Summarize the details to identify the author's point of view.

Go Digital!
Use the interactive graphic organizer

Persuasive Article

The selections "Plugged In" and "Tuned Out" are persuasive articles.

Persuasive articles:

- Persuade a reader to be for or against an idea
- Include reasons and evidence that support opinions
- Include text features, such as headings and graphs

Find Text Evidence

I can tell that "Plugged In" on page 79 is a persuasive article. The opening paragraph clearly states an argument. The second paragraph cites a study that supports the argument. Headings help focus each section, and a graph adds more support.

page 79

Are Electronic Devices Good for Us?

Plugged In

Kids need to spend time using electronic devices.

Do you love to surf the Internet, listen to music, IM, and talk on a cell phone? You are not alone. A recent study has some surprising news: Kids in the United States between the ages of 8 and 19 spend seven and a half hours a day on electronic devices. These include computers, smart phones, and video games. Some adults try to **advance** the idea that these devices waste kids' time. However, some research surveys say this idea is inaccurate. In fact, the **data** show that technology can benefit kids.

Critics say that kids stare at computers and TVs all day and do not get enough exercise. The facts stand in **counterpoint** to this belief. One study compared kids who use media a lot to those who do not. The "heavy" media users actually spent

more time in physical activity than "light" media users.

One study by the National Institutes of Health says that action video games may help increase kids' visual attention. In addition, using interactive media can give kids good structure for learning. It can also help them learn to switch tasks effectively. Kids also need to use the Web to **access** information. Many argue that learning to use the Web responsibly sharpens kids' **reasoning** abilities.

Today's world is wired, and not just for fun. The jobs of the future depend on kids who plug in!

A Source of News for Teens

For the latest news, teens used to rely on newspapers, television, and magazines. See how many teens now get their news online.

All online teens 12–17	62%
Younger teens 12–13	49%
Older teens 14–17	68%

79

Headings A heading tells what a section of text is mainly about.

Graphs A graph is a diagram that compares two or more quantities of something. Bars or sections of different sizes show differences in amount. Labels identify the graph's main parts.

Your Turn

COLLABORATE

List three parts of the bar graph on page 79 of "Plugged In."

Greek and Latin Prefixes

Prefixes are word parts added to the beginning of a word that change the word's meaning. Prefixes that come from ancient Greek and Latin, such as *dis-*, *in-*, *tele-*, and *multi-*, are common in many English words. Knowing Greek and Latin prefixes can help you figure out the meaning of unfamiliar words.

 ## Find Text Evidence

On page 80 of "Tuned Out," I can use my knowledge of Greek and Latin prefixes to figure out the meaning of disadvantages. *The prefix* dis- *means "opposite," so if* advantages *means "qualities that help," then* disadvantages *must mean "harmful qualities."*

> page 80
>
> Are these devices harmless or hurtful to the well-being of young people? A close analysis of several studies shows that there are plenty of disadvantages to these devices.

Your Turn

COLLABORATE

Use the Greek and Latin prefixes below to define these words from "Plugged In" and "Tuned Out."

Latin prefix: *in-* = not	**inaccurate,** *page 79*
Greek prefix: *tele-* = distant	**television,** *page 80*
Latin prefix: *multi-* =many	**multitasking,** *page 81*

Write About the Text

Pages 78–81

Candice

I answered the question: *In your opinion, do kids spend too much time using electronic devices? Include logical reasons.*

Student Model: *Opinion*

I don't think kids spend too much time using electronic devices. Technology will only become more advanced, and the use of electronic devices helps kids learn.

Some research shows that using computers and playing video games benefits kids. For example, one study showed that kids who utilized lots of

Sentence Structure
I combined two sentences with a conjunction to help the rhythm of my writing.

Logical Order
I supported my opinion with reasons and evidence from the text.

media did more physical activities than kids who didn't. Another study by the National Institute of Health says that some video games can help increase attention. They can give kids structure for learning and help them learn to switch tasks. The use of electronic devices has many good effects for kids.

Grammar

Avoid **sentence fragments.** Correct **run-on sentences**.

Grammar Handbook See pages 450 and 454.

Strong Conclusion
My final sentence sums up my opinion.

Your Turn

Explain why you agree or disagree with the author's viewpoint in "Plugged In." Use details from the text.

Go Digital!
Write your response online.
Use your editing checklist.

Andrew Bret Wallis/Photographer's Choice RF/Getty Images

TAKING THE NEXT STEP

The Crow and the Pitcher

A fable by Aesop

A crow, whose throat was parched and dry with thirst, saw a pitcher in the distance. In great joy he flew to it, but found that it held only a little water, and even that was too near the bottom to be reached, for all his stooping and straining. Next he tried to overturn the pitcher, thinking that he would at least be able to catch some of the water as it trickled out. But this he was not strong enough to do. At last he collected as many stones as he could carry and dropped them one by one with his beak into the pitcher, until he brought the water within his reach and thus saved his life.

Necessity is the mother of invention.

THE BIG IDEA

What does it take to put a plan into action?

?

Essential Question

What do good problem solvers do?

Go Digital!

Francis G. Mayer/Corbis

SL.5.lc See the California Standards section.

A Stitch in Time

In May of 1776, a committee led by General George Washington had an idea for what would be the first American flag. They asked seamstress Betsy Ross for help.

▷ General Washington explained his proposal for the flag, which included a six-pointed star.

▷ Betsy Ross showed him how to make a five-pointed star with a simple fold and one snip! With little debate, Washington changed the design!

Talk About It

Write words you have learned about solving a problem. Then talk about how this committee solved a problem.

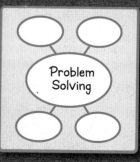

Problem Solving

Vocabulary

Use the picture and sentences to talk with a partner about each word.

committees

I am on one of the **committees** to plan our class trip.

What committees could help plan a school talent show?

convention

Ms. Blake attends a **convention** of music teachers every year.

What kind of convention would you like to attend?

debate

The council members will **debate** the benefits and costs of a new park before they vote on it.

What is a synonym for debate?

proposal

The mayor shared a **proposal**, or plan, to build a new community center.

Do you have a proposal that would improve your community?

representatives

Our government **representatives** help make laws to benefit our country.

What qualities should good representatives have?

resolve

To try to **resolve** the argument over food choices, Mrs. Marks asked Jeremy to discuss the importance of nutrition.

What steps help you resolve a problem?

situation

The icy roads caused a dangerous driving **situation**.

What kinds of weather can cause serious situations?

union

The United States is a **union** of 50 states that joined together.

What two states in the country are not physically connected to the rest of the union?

Your Turn
COLLABORATE

Pick three words. Write three questions for your partner to answer.

Go Digital! *Use the online visual glossary*

Creating a Nation

Essential Question

What do good problem solvers do?

Read about how American colonists tried to solve their problems with Great Britain.

Taxes and Protests

In 1765, King George III of Great Britain needed money to rule his empire. How could he raise it? With taxes! Parliament, the law-making branch of the British government, passed a new tax called the Stamp Act. Every piece of paper sold in the American colonies had to carry a special stamp. Want to buy a newspaper? Stamp! Pay the tax.

To most colonists, the Stamp Act was unfair. The British had the right to choose **representatives** to speak for them in Parliament. The colonists had no such right. How could Parliament tax them if they had no voice in government?

The colonists held protests against the Stamp Act. Consequently, it was repealed, or canceled. But more taxes followed. Women protested a tax on cloth imported from Britain. How? They wove their own cloth at home.

Boston Tea Party: Some colonists disguised themselves as Native Americans.

Before long, the **situation** grew worse. In 1770, British soldiers fired into a disorderly crowd in Boston. Five colonists died. This tragedy is known as the Boston Massacre.

By 1773, most taxes had been repealed, or canceled, except the one on tea. One night, colonists held a protest called the Boston Tea Party. Dressed in disguise, they slipped onto three British ships in Boston Harbor and then they tossed the ships' cargo—tea—overboard.

Revolution Begins

An angry King George punished the colonies by ordering the port of Boston closed and town meetings banned. Colonists called these harsh actions the "Intolerable Acts." However, they could not agree on how to **resolve** the problems with Great Britain. Patriots wanted to fight for independence. Loyalists wanted peace with the king. Many colonists were undecided.

Finally, colonists called for representatives from each colony to attend a **convention**. This important meeting, the First Continental Congress, took place in 1774 in Philadelphia. After discussion, the delegates decided to send a peace **proposal** to the king. Congress ended, but the trouble continued. In April 1775, there were rumors that the British were marching to Lexington and Concord, villages near Boston, to capture weapons that the patriots had hidden there.

The colonial militias were ready. Militias were groups of volunteers willing to fight. British troops attacked. The militias fired back. Surprisingly, the British retreated, or went back.

Now that war had begun, the patriots called for a Second Continental Congress in May. Delegates made George Washington commander of the new Continental Army. Congress also sent another peace proposal to King George.

As war continued, Congress formed **committees** to do important tasks. Five delegates were chosen to write a declaration of independence. This committee gave the job to one of its members—Thomas Jefferson.

(bkgd) Oleksiy Maksymenko/Alamy

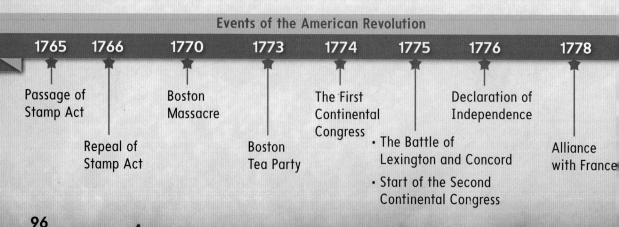

Events of the American Revolution

1765	1766	1770	1773	1774	1775	1776	1778
Passage of Stamp Act		Boston Massacre		The First Continental Congress		Declaration of Independence	
	Repeal of Stamp Act		Boston Tea Party		• The Battle of Lexington and Concord		Alliance with France
					• Start of the Second Continental Congress		

Independence Declared

Jefferson knew he had to convince many colonists of the need for independence. As a result, he combined a variety of ideas to make his case. Individuals, he explained, had certain rights. These included life, liberty, and the pursuit of happiness. Governments were created to protect those rights. Instead, King George had taken away colonists' rights and freedoms. Therefore, the colonies had to separate from Britain.

Congress went on to **debate** Jefferson's points. As a result, his strong words against slavery were deleted. There were other compromises, too. But on July 4, 1776, Congress approved the Declaration of Independence. A nation was born. Washington's army fought on. Finally, in 1778, France joined the fight on America's side. This was a turning point. In 1781, British troops surrendered in the war's last major battle. That year, Congress approved the Articles of Confederation. This document outlined a government for the former colonies. The United States was created as a confederation, or a **union**, of separate states. The Articles gave the states, rather than a central government, the power to make most decisions.

In 1783, King George finally recognized the nation's independence. By then, though, the United States government clearly wasn't working very well. The states often didn't agree with one another.

The revolution had ended. The work of shaping a government had just started. It would continue with a Constitutional Convention in 1787.

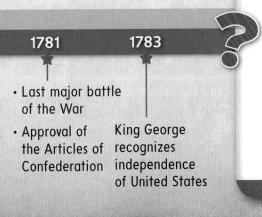

1781
- Last major battle of the War
- Approval of the Articles of Confederation

1783
King George recognizes independence of United States

Make Connections

Talk about some of the ways American colonists tried to solve their problems with Great Britain. **ESSENTIAL QUESTION**

Think of a time you tried to solve a problem. How does your experience compare to the colonists'? **TEXT TO SELF**

Reread

When you find that you are puzzled or confused by something you read, you may have to go back and reread an earlier part of the selection. Rereading can help you check your understanding of facts and explanations in "Creating a Nation."

 Find Text Evidence

When you read the second paragraph of the section "Taxes and Protests" on page 95, you may be confused about why the colonists had a problem with the Stamp Act.

> **page 95**
>
> To most colonists, the Stamp Act was unfair. The British had the right to choose **representatives** to speak for them in Parliament. The colonists had no such right. How could Parliament tax them if they had no voice in government?

When I reread How could Parliament tax them if they had no voice in government?, *I see that the tax seemed unfair because the colonies had no say in making the law.*

Your Turn

"Revolution Begins" on page 96 discusses how King George punished the colonists. Why did he punish them? Reread to find the answer.

Problem and Solution

When an author uses a problem and solution text structure, the author presents a **problem** and then tells the **solution**, or the steps taken to solve the problem. Signal words and phrases, such as *consequently, as a result, therefore,* and *so,* can help you identify the solution.

Find Text Evidence

When I read "Independence Declared" on page 97, I realize that Thomas Jefferson's problem was to convince undecided colonists of the need for independence. The signal words as a result tell me that I will read Jefferson's solution: He combined a variety of ideas to make his case for independence.

Problem	Solution
Some colonists didn't want independence.	Jefferson combined ideas to convince them.

Your Turn

COLLABORATE

Reread "Creating a Nation." Find other problems faced by the colonists and list them in your graphic organizer. Then identify how the colonists solved the problems.

Go Digital!
Use the interactive graphic organizer

Expository Text

The selection "Creating a Nation" is expository text.

Expository text:
- gives facts, examples, and explanations about a topic
- may include text features such as headings, charts, diagrams, or time lines that organize information

🔍 Find Text Evidence

I can tell that "Creating a Nation" is expository text. It gives facts about events that led up to and followed the American Revolution. It provides examples of the colonists' problems with Great Britain. I also see headings and a time line to organize information.

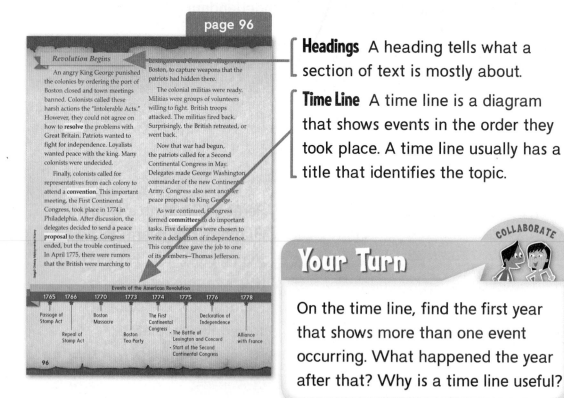

Headings A heading tells what a section of text is mostly about.

Time Line A time line is a diagram that shows events in the order they took place. A time line usually has a title that identifies the topic.

page 96

Revolution Begins

An angry King George punished the colonies by ordering the port of Boston closed and town meetings banned. Colonists called these harsh actions the "Intolerable Acts." However, they could not agree on how to **resolve** the problems with Great Britain. Patriots wanted to fight for independence. Loyalists wanted peace with the king. Many colonists were undecided.

Finally, colonists called for representatives from each colony to attend a **convention**. This important meeting, the First Continental Congress, took place in 1774 in Philadelphia. After discussion, the delegates decided to send a peace **proposal** to the king. Congress ended, but the trouble continued. In April 1775, there were rumors that the British were marching to

Lexington and Concord, villages near Boston, to capture weapons that the patriots had hidden there.

The colonial militias were ready. Militias were groups of volunteers willing to fight. British troops attacked. The militias fired back. Surprisingly, the British retreated, or went back.

Now that war had begun, the patriots called for a Second Continental Congress in May. Delegates made George Washington commander of the new Continental Army. Congress also sent another peace proposal to King George.

As war continued, Congress formed **committees** to do important tasks. Five delegates were chosen to write a declaration of independence. This committee gave the job to one of its members—Thomas Jefferson.

Events of the American Revolution

1765	1766	1770	1773	1774	1775	1776	1778
Passage of Stamp Act		Boston Massacre		The First Continental Congress		Declaration of Independence	
	Repeal of Stamp Act		Boston Tea Party		• The Battle of Lexington and Concord		Alliance with France
					• Start of the Second Continental Congress		

96

Your Turn

COLLABORATE

On the time line, find the first year that shows more than one event occurring. What happened the year after that? Why is a time line useful?

Context Clues

Writers may define or restate the meaning of a difficult word by using commas and the clue word *or.* They may also place a definition in parentheses following the word. At other times, the writer will define the word in a nearby sentence.

Find Text Evidence

When I read the sentence "By 1773 most taxes had been repealed, or canceled, except the one on tea," *I'm not sure what* repealed *means. But I see from the comma and the words* or canceled *that* repealed *means "canceled."*

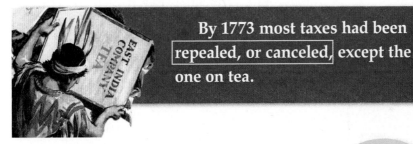

By 1773 most taxes had been repealed, or canceled, except the one on tea.

Your Turn

COLLABORATE

Use context clues to figure out the meaning of the following words in "Creating a Nation." Remember to look in the same sentence or nearby sentences for a definition or restatement of each word's meaning.

Parliament, *page 95*
militias, *page 96*
retreated, *page 96*
Confederation, *page 97*

Write About the Text

Pages 94–97

Oscar

I answered the question: *How does the sequence of events help the reader understand why the colonies declared independence from Great Britain? Use text evidence.*

Student Model: *Informative Text*

The sequence of events shows how the unfair treatment of the colonists continued over several years. These events caused them to declare independence. The colonists initially became upset with Great Britain because they were being taxed but had no voice in the government. This led to protests. During one protest, British soldiers killed five colonists.

Main Idea
My topic sentence clearly states the most important point of my paragraph.

Sequence
I linked the events with words such as *initially*.

Hola Images/Getty Images

The problems didn't end there. King George III punished the colonists further with the Intolerable Acts. Then, in 1775, British troops marched near Boston. The colonists had had enough. War broke out. In 1776, Congress approved the Declaration of Independence. A new nation was born.

Grammar

This is an example of a **proper noun** because it names a particular person.

Grammar Handbook See page 455.

Problem and Solution

I explained how the colonists resolved their issues with Great Britain.

Your Turn

What is the author's point of view about Great Britain's actions toward the colonists? Use text evidence.

Go Digital!
Write your response online.
Use your editing checklist.

English School/Bridgeman Art Library/Getty Images

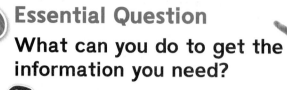

Essential Question

What can you do to get the information you need?

Go Digital!

SL.5.1c See the California Standards section.

Hello Lovely/Corbis

Search High and Low

The world is full of things to explore! Now, how do you begin looking for the answers to your questions?

▶ Reading a book or surfing the Web might be a way to start. Your search may take you to the bottom of the ocean, on a trip up a mountain, or deep into a forest.

▶ Searches reveal answers, and just as often they lead to more questions. No matter what your expectations, you're sure to learn something new!

Talk About It COLLABORATE

Write words you have learned about seeking information. Then talk about one thing you would like to know, and how you might find out about it.

Seeking Information

Vocabulary

Use the picture and the sentences to talk with a
partner about each word.

circumstances

There are many **circumstances** that can
make roads impossible to drive on.

Under what circumstances might schools
be closed?

consideration

My mom gives careful **consideration** to
the fresh fruits she buys.

What is a synonym for consideration?

consults

A driver **consults** a map to find which
road to travel on.

Explain why someone consults a
dictionary.

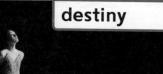

destiny

Lena loves ballet so much, I think her
destiny is to become a dancer.

What might the destiny of a
hard-working student be?

expectations

Jamie's present lived up to her **expectations**.

Tell about something that lived up to your expectations.

presence

The visitors were thrilled to be in the **presence** of the Queen of England.

When have you been in the presence of someone well-known?

reveal

The actor opened the curtain to **reveal** what was behind it.

Why don't magicians reveal their secrets?

unsure

The chess player was **unsure** of what move to make next.

What is an antonym for unsure?

Your Turn

COLLABORATE

Pick three words. Write three questions for your partner to answer.

Go Digital! **Use the online visual glossary**

A Modern Cinderella

Essential Question

What can you do to get the information you need?

Read how a dancing Prince tries to get information about a mystery girl.

Once upon a time—the time being the other night—the Prince was as joyous as a gamer with the new highest score. He had just danced with an amazing young woman at the Royal Palace. It was during the taping of his weekly TV show, *Dancing with the Prince*. He had only agreed to do the show to help his mother, the Queen, raise money for charity. But when the prince twirled this lovely dancer in the presence of the audience and judges, he felt as if he were floating on a cloud.

However, circumstances changed as soon as the music stopped at midnight. As the applause began, the young woman's cell phone rang, and she rushed from the palace. All she left behind was a purple sneaker.

The Prince fell into a dungeon of despair. "I must find her again," he cried, "and in time for tomorrow night's final show!" How should he search? He clutched the purple sneaker in his hand.

Seeing the Prince's tears, the Queen advised, "He who consults the right sources will surely succeed." The Prince's mind raced like a galloping horse on his favorite game, "Horse Chaser." After much consideration, he made a plan. First, he interviewed everyone who had attended the show, but no one could help. Next, the Prince searched the Internet. He entered the phrase "great dancer with purple shoe," but he found no one. Then the Prince put up posters of the purple sneaker all over the kingdom's social network. Yet no one recognized the shoe or knew its owner.

The Prince held the purple sneaker in one hand and his computer compass in the other. "I will continue my quest," he cried, "even if I must personally travel the entire kingdom." With that, the Prince powered up his royal electric skateboard and set out!

At the first house, a woman came out to greet the Prince. He held out the sneaker and announced, "This shoe will tell me if you are my destiny." The excited woman struggled to jam her large foot into the shoe, but the sneaker was much too small.

At the next house, another woman eagerly tried on the sneaker. The shoe flopped and fell off. At every home the Prince visited, the purple sneaker seemed as big as a boat or as small as a seed. Every foot failed to meet his expectations.

As the day wore on, the Prince grew sadder. His discouraged heart was a cell phone in need of recharging. Finally, there was only one house left to visit. When the Prince arrived, three sisters stood in front, offering their feet. (They'd been following the newsfeed.) The shoe fit none of them.

"Does anyone else live here?" a weary Prince asked the sisters. From inside the house came a chime. The sisters' eyes became narrow slits. A young woman stepped outside and handed a phone to the oldest sister.

The Prince quickly held out the sneaker and requested, "Please try this on."

She did, and it fit her foot perfectly!

"You're my missing dancer!" the Prince cried." Will you be my dance partner forever?"

The young woman smiled and replied, "Thanks, but not right now. I'll dance tomorrow, but I have a lot of plans. First I want to travel."

The Prince begged, "Please, say yes! After all, this is a fairy tale, where anything can happen."

"Sorry, Prince," the woman said. "You'll just have to wait."

"That's cool," the Prince sighed, "but at least reveal your name."

"It's Cinderella," the woman replied. She scribbled on a piece of paper. "Here's my number. Let's stay in touch. TTYLP."

The Prince looked puzzled and was unsure of how to reply.

"It means Talk To You Later, Prince," Cinderella explained.

"TTYLC," the Prince replied as he waved to Cinderella and rode away.

And they texted happily ever after.

Make Connections

Talk about how the Prince got the information he needed. What things did he do? **ESSENTIAL QUESTION**

When have you had to search for something or someone? How did you search? **TEXT TO SELF**

Make Predictions

Predicting future events in the plot helps keep readers involved in a story. As you read, use evidence from the story to confirm your predictions. If a prediction is not correct, you can revise it.

Find Text Evidence

After I read the opening of "A Modern Cinderella" on page 109, I made predictions about further events in the story.

page 109

The Prince fell into a dungeon of despair. "I must find her again," he cried, "and in time for tomorrow night's final show!" How should he search? He clutched the purple sneaker in his hand.

Seeing the Prince's tears, the Queen advised, "He who consults the right sources will surely succeed." The Prince's mind raced like a galloping horse on his favorite game, "Horse Chaser." After much consideration, he made a plan. First, he interviewed everyone who had attended the show, but no one could help. Next, the Prince searched the Internet. He entered the phrase "great dancer with purple shoe," but he found no one. Then the Prince put up posters of the purple sneaker all over the kingdom's social network. Yet no one recognized the shoe or knew its owner.

Because the Prince says I must find her again, I predicted that the Prince would not give up his search until he found the dancer. When I continued reading, I confirmed my prediction.

COLLABORATE

Your Turn

What predictions did you make while reading this story? Tell what evidence you used to confirm or revise them.

Compare and Contrast

The events that occur in the beginning, middle, and end of the story may be similar to or different from one another. You compare and contrast events to help you remember what happened and in what order events occurred.

 Find Text Evidence

As "A Modern Cinderella" begins, the first event is the Prince meeting an unknown woman. Next, the young woman disappears. I can compare events before and after midnight and see that they are very different for the Prince.

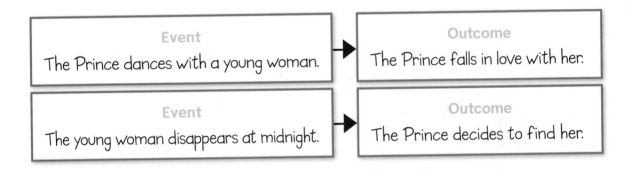

Event		Outcome
The Prince dances with a young woman.	➤	The Prince falls in love with her.
The young woman disappears at midnight.	➤	The Prince decides to find her.

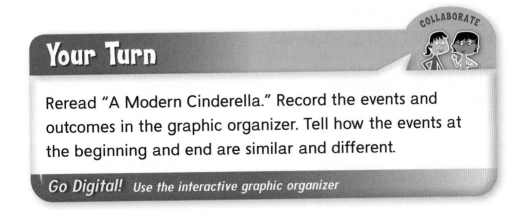

Your Turn

Reread "A Modern Cinderella." Record the events and outcomes in the graphic organizer. Tell how the events at the beginning and end are similar and different.

Go Digital! *Use the interactive graphic organizer*

Fairy Tale

The selection "A Modern Cinderella" is a fairy tale.
        A **fairy tale** may include:
        • a made-up setting, such as "once upon a time"
        • a prince or princess and magical characters
        • illustrations

Find Text Evidence

*I can tell that "A Modern Cinderella" is a fairy tale. The first
sentence begins with "Once upon a time," which is the way
many fairy tales start. One of the main characters is a prince
who has a made-up TV show. The name Cinderella in the title
and the illustrations also suggest that the selection is a fairy tale.*

page 110

The Prince held the purple sneaker
in one hand and his computer compass
in the other. "I will continue my quest,"
he cried, "even if I must personally travel the
entire kingdom." With that, the Prince powered
up his royal electric skateboard and set out!

At the first house, a woman came out to
greet the Prince. He held out the sneaker
and announced, "This shoe will tell me if
you are my destiny." The excited woman
struggled to jam her large foot into the
shoe, but the sneaker was much too small.

At the next house, another woman eagerly tried on the
sneaker. The shoe flopped and fell off. At every home the
Prince visited, the purple sneaker seemed as big as a boat or as
small as a seed. Every foot failed to meet his expectations.

As the day wore on, the Prince grew sadder. His discouraged
heart was a cell phone in need of recharging. Finally, there was
only one house left to visit. When the Prince arrived, three
sisters stood in front, offering their feet. (They'd been following
the newsfeed.) The shoe fit none of them.

"Does anyone else live here?" a weary Prince asked the
sisters. From inside the house came a chime. The sisters' eyes
became narrow slits. A young woman stepped outside
and handed a phone to the oldest sister.

110

Use Illustrations Illustrations
give readers visual clues about
characters, settings, and events.
For example, the style of the
illustrations tells you if a story is
meant to be serious or humorous.

COLLABORATE

Your Turn

What details in "A Modern
Cinderella" show the story is a fairy
tale? How has it been updated?

Simile and Metaphor

Writers compare one thing to another to create a picture in the reader's mind. A simile compares two things using the word *like* or *as*. A metaphor compares two things without using *like* or *as*.

Simile: The sun shone like a giant flashlight in the sky.

Metaphor: The sun was a giant flashlight in the sky.

 Find Text Evidence

On page 109 of "A Modern Cinderella," I see a simile. The Prince's mind is compared to the speed of a galloping horse to show how quickly it is working.

> The Prince's mind raced like a galloping horse on his favorite game, "Horse Chaser."

Your Turn

COLLABORATE

Identify the simile or metaphor in sentences from "A Modern Cinderella." Tell what is being compared. What does the simile or metaphor tell you about the Prince?

The Prince was as joyous as a gamer with the new high score. *page 109*

The Prince fell into a dungeon of despair. *page 109*

His discouraged heart was a cell phone in need of recharging. *page 110*

Peter Francis

Pages 108–111

Write About the Text

Kara

I responded to the prompt: *Write a dialogue between Cinderella and the mysterious caller after Cinderella left the dance. Use details from the story.*

Student Model: *Narrative Text*

"Ms. Wish! Where are you?"

Cinderella called out. She was out of

breath, having run from the palace

after missing her friend's call.

"I'm over here," Ms. Wish called out

from a park bench. "Holy cow! You're

missing one of your sneakers!"

"I know," Cinderella said, surprised

that she could lose a sneaker she'd

been wearing. "I should go find it. I just

Strong Opening
My first sentence introduces a new character whom readers will want to learn more about.

Style and Tone
I used slang in the dialogue to give my writing an informal voice and playful attitude.

Jodi Matthews/iStock/360/Getty Images

bought them yesterday, and I've been

wanting a purple pair for months."

"Don't bother," Ms. Wish said, as

she smiled mysteriously and pulled a

pair of silver sneakers from her bag.

"Put these on and let's get you home.

My plan for you might work better

this way." In two flashes of light,

they were gone.

Develop Characters

I included details about how Cinderella thinks and feels to make her seem more real.

Grammar

Most **plural nouns** are formed by adding -s or -es.

Grammar Handbook See page 456.

Your Turn

Add an event to the story. What did the Prince do and say in the beginning of his show, *Dancing with the Prince?*

Go Digital!
Write your response online.
Use your editing checklist.

Essential Question

How do we investigate questions about nature?

Go Digital!

Nature in Focus

When we move in to study a creature in nature close up, what is it we hope to see?

▶ Sometimes we have a theory about what an insect, such as this grasshopper, looks like. Did you imagine such an intricate design?

▶ What's the best way to study nature? To make a careful observation, you may need more than just the naked eye!

Talk About It

Write words you have learned about investigating nature. Then talk about one way you have studied something in nature.

Investigating Nature

Vocabulary

Use the picture and the sentences to talk with a
partner about each word.

behaviors

We rewarded our dog with a treat for
all its good **behaviors**.

What kinds of behaviors are encouraged
at school?

disappearance

A detective investigated the
disappearance of the painting.

What explains the disappearance of
snow in spring?

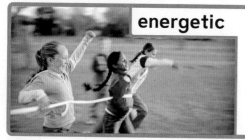

energetic

Rina is so **energetic**, she ran three races
and was not even tired.

What is another word or phrase for
energetic?

flurry

The wind blew a **flurry** of blossoms off
the cherry trees.

What might cause a flurry of birds in
the sky?

migrate

Some birds **migrate** to warmer places each winter.

What kinds of animals migrate to or from your area when seasons change?

observation

Binoculars helped Carlos's **observation** of the ships at sea.

What other tools help with observation?

theory

Nan had a **theory** about how the pillow got shredded.

What theory might explain why your pet is not hungry for dinner?

transformed

Large, colorful clothes and face paint **transformed** Nora into a clown.

How is an empty stage transformed for a show?

Your Turn

COLLABORATE

Pick three words. Write three questions for your partner to answer.

Go Digital!   *Use the online visual glossary*

Growing in Place

The Story of
E. Lucy Braun

iris

? Essential Question

How do we investigate questions about nature?

Read about how Lucy Braun's classification of plants continues to help scientists today.

Taking Root

How could two different things have the same name? Emma Lucy Braun might have wondered that as a child. Born in Cincinnati, Ohio, in 1889, Emma shared her first name with her mother. To avoid confusion, she used her middle name, Lucy. Naming things correctly became the basis for her life's work on plants.

Even as a child, Lucy was interested in plants. She often joined her older sister Annette and their parents on **energetic** walks through the nearby woods. Lucy enjoyed all the plants and wildflowers. Some seemed to shout at her with their wild colors. Others hid behind rocks and logs.

Lucy asked her mother how to tell all the plants apart. Lucy's mother taught her to develop her powers of **observation**. She pointed out the number and shape of leaves on a stem. Lucy kept a record of their observations. She also learned to draw what she saw. Then she could compare and contrast all sorts of plants.

Lucy and her mother gathered specimens for their herbarium, a collection of dried plants. They preserved leaves and flowers between sheets of paper. Lucy became more and more interested in botany, the study of plants. In high school, she started collecting and drying plants for her own herbarium. She continued adding plants all her life.

pink redstem filagrees

Branching Out

Lucy and Annette attended the University of Cincinnati. Annette wanted to become an entomologist and study insects. Lucy took classes in geology, or the study of rocks and minerals. Her work with geologists **transformed** how she looked at the natural world. She continued her studies in botany, as well.

Lucy also became interested in ecology. Ecology looks at how living things interact with their environments. Fellow ecologists helped her test an important **theory**. Lucy believed that plant life in some areas had been able to **migrate** over time. She mapped this movement back to when glaciers covered those regions with ice!

Lucy Braun's Snakeroot: This plant grows in Kentucky and Tennessee.

iris

robin's egg

nest

In Full Bloom

In 1917, Lucy began to teach botany at the University of Cincinnati. She and Annette lived in a house near the woods. Even at home the sisters continued their scientific **behaviors**. Lucy tended both indoor and outdoor gardens. Annette studied the moths that fluttered in a **flurry** of wings around lights outside. The sisters named part of their house "the science wing."

Lucy collected plants from all around the country. She photographed many of them, too. Color photography was still new at the time. Because of that, people enjoyed her lectures and slide shows a great deal.

By making sketches, scientists learn to see details in natural objects.

(bkgd) RoseAnn Hayes; (inset) J.S. Peterson/USDA

The Fruits of Her Labor

Later in her life, Lucy wrote many field guides. Field guides are books that identify plants found in a particular area. In 1950, she published her most important guide. It describes the plants in the forests of the eastern United States. Ecologists still use it to study changes in the forests over time.

Today, Lucy has a few plants named after her. One of them, Lucy Braun's snakeroot, is currently threatened. Lucy's work in conservation, the protection of nature, may help scientists prevent its **disappearance**.

Lucy Braun lived to be 81 years old. In her years as a botanist, Lucy collected nearly 12,000 plants! Today her herbarium is part of the Smithsonian Institution in Washington, D.C. Visitors can study the plants she collected all her life.

Plant Identification

Become a budding botanist! Follow these steps to identify plants in your area.

Materials: a magnifying glass and a reliable field guide

1. Identify the state or region and habitat where the plant grows.
2. Identify whether the leaf is evergreen or broad leaf.
3. Draw or photograph the leaf to record its shape and other details.
4. Observe the arrangement of leaves on the stem. See if they are opposite each other or not.
5. Narrow the list of possible plants in the field guide. Then find an exact match.

Make Connections

Talk about how the advice of Lucy's mother was helpful to Lucy's study of nature. ESSENTIAL QUESTION

Tell about a collection that you have or might like to start. How could you organize your collection? TEXT TO SELF

Reread

When you read informational text, such as a biography, you may find that some details confuse you. Rereading can help you check your understanding of facts and other information.

Find Text Evidence

You may not understand why the author mentions that new color photography played a role in Lucy's lectures. Reread that passage on page 124 of "Growing in Place."

page 124

In Full Bloom

In 1917, Lucy began to teach botany at the University of Cincinnati. She and Annette lived in a house near the woods. Even at home the sisters continued their scientific **behaviors**. Lucy tended both indoor and outdoor gardens. Annette studied the moths that fluttered in a **flurry** of wings around lights outside. The sisters named part of their house "the science wing."

Lucy collected plants from all around the country. She photographed many of them, too. Color photography was still new at the time. Because of that, people enjoyed her lectures and slide shows a great deal.

When I reread, I see the phrase <u>Because of that</u>. *"That" refers to the newness of color photography. This means audiences enjoyed Lucy's presentations because they featured color photographs, which many people had never seen.*

Your Turn

Why did Lucy and her sister create a "science wing" in their home? Reread "In Full Bloom" on page 124 to find the answer. As you read, use the strategy Reread.

Sequence

The author of a biography often presents information in **sequence**, or in the order the events happened in the person's life. Signal words and phrases, such as *in 1917*, *later*, and *today*, are clues to help you understand the sequence of events.

Find Text Evidence

As I read "Growing in Place," I look for events that show how Lucy Braun became an important scientist. In "Taking Root" on page 123, the phrase Even as a child *tells me when Lucy became interested in plants. The phrase* In high school *tells me when Lucy started her herbarium. These events affected her future life.*

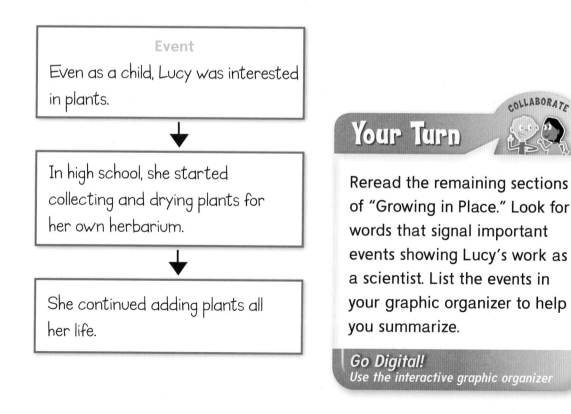

Event

Even as a child, Lucy was interested in plants.

↓

In high school, she started collecting and drying plants for her own herbarium.

↓

She continued adding plants all her life.

Your Turn

COLLABORATE

Reread the remaining sections of "Growing in Place." Look for words that signal important events showing Lucy's work as a scientist. List the events in your graphic organizer to help you summarize.

Go Digital!
Use the interactive graphic organizer

Biography

The selection "Growing in Place" is a biography.

A **biography:**

- Tells the true story of another person's life
- Is told in the third person, using pronouns such as *he* and *she*
- May include photographs and illustrations

Find Text Evidence

I can tell that "Growing in Place" is a biography because it provides facts about a real person, Lucy Braun. As I read and look at illustrations, I learn more about why she is an important scientist.

page 124

Branching Out

Lucy and Annette attended the University of Cincinnati. Annette wanted to become an entomologist and study insects. Lucy took in geology, or the study of rocks and minerals. Her work with geologists **transformed** how she looked at the natural world. She continued her studies in botany, as well.

Lucy also became interested in ecology. Ecology looks at how living things interact with their environments. Fellow ecologists helped her test an important **theory**. Lucy believed that plant life in some areas had been able to **migrate** over time. She mapped this movement back to when glaciers covered those regions with ice!

Lucy Braun's Snakeroot: This plant grows in Kentucky and Tennessee.

In Full Bloom

In 1917, Lucy began to teach botany at the University of Cincinnati. She and Annette lived in a house near the woods. Even at home the sisters continued their scientific **behaviors**. Lucy tended indoor and outdoor gardens. Annette studied the moths that fluttered in a **flurry** of wings around lights outside. The sisters named part of their house "the science wing."

Lucy collected plants from all around the country. She photographed many of them, too. Color photography was still new at the time. Because of that, people enjoyed her lectures and slide shows a great deal.

iris

robin's egg

nest

By making sketches, scientists learn to see details in natural objects.

124

Use Illustrations and Photographs

Illustrations and photographs show readers what the people and things discussed in the text look like. **Labels** identify the images, and **captions** may add information.

Your Turn

COLLABORATE

List three facts that show how Lucy Braun became an important scientist. What information did you learn from the illustrations?

Greek and Latin Suffixes

A **suffix** is added to the end of a word to change its meaning. Many words in English have suffixes that come from ancient Greek and Latin. You can use the suffix as a clue to the meaning of the word.

 Find Text Evidence

I can use what I know about the suffix -ist to figure out the meaning of the word botanist *on page 125 of "Growing in Place." The Greek suffix -ist means "one who specializes in." The sentence talks about Lucy's collection of plants, so I can figure out that a* botanist *is "someone who specializes in the study of plants."*

> In her years as a botanist, Lucy collected nearly 12,000 plants!

Your Turn

Use what you know about Greek suffixes to figure out the meanings of the following words found in "Growing in Place."

entomologist, *page 124*

ecologists, *page 124*

geologists, *page 124*

RoseAnn Hayes

Pages 122–125

Write About the Text

Darius

I answered the question: *How does the Plant Identification sidebar support the information in the text? Use text evidence.*

Student Model: *Informative Text*

Strong Opening
My topic sentence summarizes how the sidebar supports the text.

The sidebar supports the information in the text by explaining how to identify plants. It says to identify where a plant grows and tell if its leaf is an evergreen or a broad leaf. This process is based on what Lucy Braun did.

Fuse/Getty Images

Lucy looked at the shapes of leaves as she walked in the woods. She drew the plants she saw, which the sidebar says to do. It also tells readers to use a field guide to find a plant's exact match. Lucy wrote many of those field guides. They are still used today!

Grammar

Leaf becomes a **plural noun** by changing the *-f* to *-v* and adding *-es*.

Grammar Handbook See page 456.

Supporting Details
I included text evidence to show how the sidebar is related to Lucy's work.

Strong Conclusion
I used an exclamatory sentence to show the impact that Lucy's field guides still have.

Your Turn

What influences in Lucy's life led to her becoming a scientist?

Go Digital!
Write your response online.
Use your editing checklist.

Essential Question

When has a plan helped you accomplish a task?

Go Digital!

SL.5.1c See the California Standards section.

Carving Out a Plan

Whenever I have a project to do, a plan gives me guidance and helps me complete all my tasks.

▷ I wanted to make a sand sculpture of a swan. First I studied swans, then I made drawings, and finally I decided how large to make the sculpture.

▷ An outcome like this is no accident. With good planning, the right tools, and real effort, beautiful things can happen!

Talk About It

Write words you have learned about using a plan to do something. Then talk about how a plan has helped you complete a task.

Making a Plan

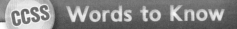
Vocabulary

Use the picture and the sentences to talk with a
partner about each word.

assuring

One job of a coach is **assuring** athletes
that practicing will make them better.

What might a coach say when assuring a
team?

detected

By the way he sniffed, I knew my dog
detected another animal.

What have you detected by looking?

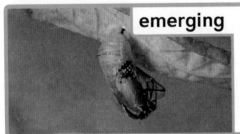

emerging

I watched as the colorful butterfly was
emerging from its chrysalis.

What word or phrase has the same
meaning as emerging?

gratitude

Lena and I gave flowers to our aunt to
show our **gratitude** for her help.

What are other ways people show their
gratitude?

guidance

With my Uncle Rico's **guidance**, I learned how to play guitar.

Whose guidance has helped you learn a new skill?

outcome

The team was pleased with the winning **outcome** of the game.

When has the outcome of a game surprised you?

previous

The **previous** month, July, was summer vacation.

What was the name of your previous teacher?

pursuit

On the nature documentary, I watched a lion in **pursuit** of a zebra.

What might a house cat be in pursuit of?

Your Turn

COLLABORATE

Pick three words. Write three questions for your partner to answer.

Go Digital! *Use the online visual glossary*

(t to b) Terry Vine/Blend Images/Getty Images, moodboard/Corbis, Image Source/Getty Images, S. Purdy Matthews/Stone/Getty Images

The Magical Lost Brocade

?

Essential Question

When has a plan helped you accomplish a task?

Read about how Ping follows a plan to find
a lost brocade.

Long ago, in China, a poor woman and her son, Ping, lived in a tiny hut. The woman earned a living weaving beautiful brocade hangings, which her son sold. She wished she could give Ping a better home, but alas, that was impossible. So she decided to weave a brocade of a magnificent house with gardens. At least they could look at something lovely. It took three years to complete the brocade, and it was her finest work. However, soon afterward, a great wind swept into their hut and carried it away! The woman was grief-stricken. So Ping went off in **pursuit** of the brocade, **assuring** his mother he would bring it home.

Ping walked for three days and came to a stone house. A bearded man sat outside. "I'm searching for my mother's brocade," Ping said.

"A brocade flew by three days ago," said the man. "Now it's in a palace far away. I'll explain how you can get there and lend you my horse." Ping thanked the man and bowed deeply to express his **gratitude**.

"First, you must ride through Fire Valley," said the man. "You must cross over it regardless of the scorching heat, without uttering a word. If you utter even a single sound, you'll burn!" He continued, "After you've crossed Fire Valley, you'll arrive at Ice Ocean. You must ride through the icy waters without shivering. If you shiver even once, the **outcome** will be terrible! The sea will swallow you up!" The old man paused before concluding, "When you emerge from the sea, you'll be facing the Mountain of the Sun. The mountain is as steep as a straight line up to the sky! The palace sits on top of the mountain, and the brocade is in the palace."

"It sounds like an extremely difficult journey," said Ping, "but I'll do my very best." He mounted the horse and traveled for three days, reaching the Fire Valley. As he crossed the valley, angry flames leaped out at him. The intense heat brought tears to Ping's eyes, but he said nothing.

When he reached the other side of the valley, he saw the Ice Ocean. With Ping's gentle **guidance,** the horse entered the frigid waters. The sea touched Ping with icy fingers, but he didn't shiver once. So horse and rider crossed the sea, **emerging** safely on the other side.

Next, Ping approached the Mountain of the Sun. He rode up the steep mountain, grasping the reins for dear life! Finally, he reached the top and dismounted at the palace door.

A lovely princess welcomed him. "I'm Princess Ling," she said. "I thought your mother's brocade was beautiful and wanted to copy it. So I sent a great wind to your home. I've now copied the brocade, so please take it home. Have a safe journey."

Shawna Tenney

"Thank you," said Ping, who stared at the beautiful princess. She was a perfect rose. He wondered if he could see her again and **detected** a knowing smile on her face as they said good-bye.

Ping mounted his horse, placing the brocade under his jacket. First, he rode down the steep Mountain of the Sun. Next, he rode back across Ice Ocean, without shivering once. Then he rode across Fire Valley, without making a sound. Finally, he arrived at the home of the bearded man, who sat outside just as he had the **previous** time. Ping thanked him, returned his horse, and began the long walk home.

Ping arrived home three days later. "Here is your brocade, Mother!" he announced as she cried tears of joy. Together, they unrolled it, and before their eyes, the brocade came to life! Suddenly their hut became a magnificent house with gardens. But that wasn't all—standing before them was Princess Ling! Ping and the princess got married, and a year later, Ping's mother became a loving grandmother. They all lived happily together in their beautiful home and gardens!

Make Connections

Talk about how having a plan helped Ping accomplish his task. How did following the plan lead to his finding the lost brocade? ESSENTIAL QUESTION

When have you followed a plan in order to accomplish a task? Briefly describe the steps of the plan. TEXT TO SELF

Make Predictions

As you read a story, you can show your understanding by predicting what might happen next in the plot. Use evidence from the story to see if your predictions are correct. If they are not correct, you can revise them.

Find Text Evidence

After you read about the tasks Ping must do in order to find the brocade on page 137, you may want to predict whether or not he will succeed before you continue reading.

page 138

"It sounds like an extremely difficult journey," said Ping, "but I'll do my very best." He mounted the horse and traveled for three days, reaching the Fire Valley. As he crossed the valley, angry flames leaped out at him. The intense heat brought tears to Ping's eyes, but he said nothing.

When he reached the other side of the valley, he saw the Ice Ocean. With Ping's gentle **guidance,** the horse entered the frigid waters. The sea touched Ping with icy fingers, but he didn't shiver once. So horse and rider crossed the sea, **emerging** safely on the other side.

On page 138 Ping tells the old man, "_It sounds like an extremely difficult journey, but I'll do my very best._" I predicted Ping would succeed. As I continued reading, I saw my prediction was right.

COLLABORATE

Your Turn

Tell one prediction you made after Ping left the Mountain of the Sun. What evidence did you use? Was your prediction correct? If not, tell how you revised it.

Theme

The theme of a story is the big idea or message about life that the author wants to share. Usually, the theme is not stated directly. To identify the theme, think about what characters do and say and what happens to the characters.

 Find Text Evidence

When I read the end of the first paragraph of "The Magical Lost Brocade" on page 137, Ping makes a promise to his mother and sets off to keep it. I can use what Ping says and does to find the theme of the story.

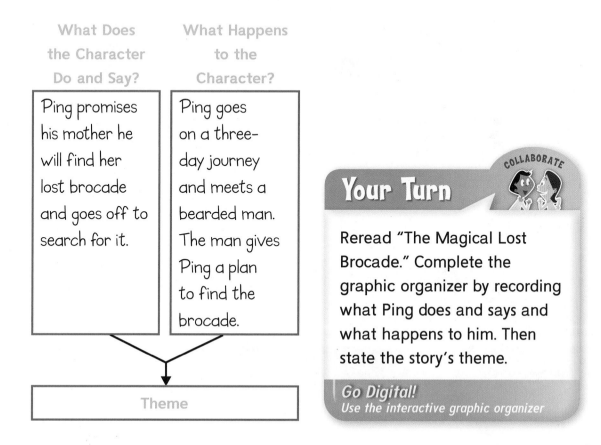

What Does the Character Do and Say?	What Happens to the Character?
Ping promises his mother he will find her lost brocade and goes off to search for it.	Ping goes on a three-day journey and meets a bearded man. The man gives Ping a plan to find the brocade.

Theme

COLLABORATE

Your Turn

Reread "The Magical Lost Brocade." Complete the graphic organizer by recording what Ping does and says and what happens to him. Then state the story's theme.

Go Digital!
Use the interactive graphic organizer

Folktale

The selection "The Magical Lost Brocade" is a folktale.

A **folktale:**

- Describes a hero or heroine's quest or set of tasks he or she must accomplish
- Includes the repetition of actions or words
- Often includes foreshadowing and imagery

Find Text Evidence

I can tell that "The Magical Lost Brocade" is a folktale. It describes Ping's quest to find his mother's brocade, actions are repeated, and events to come are foreshadowed. The tale also contains imagery.

page 137

Long ago, in China, a poor woman and her son, Ping, lived in a tiny hut. The woman earned a living weaving beautiful brocade hangings, which her son sold. She wished she could give Ping a better home, but alas, that was impossible. So she decided to weave a brocade of a magnificent house with gardens. At least they could look at something lovely. It took three years to complete the brocade, and it was her finest work. However, soon afterward, a great wind swept into their hut and carried it away! The woman was grief-stricken. So Ping went off in **pursuit** of the brocade, **assuring** his mother he would bring it home.

Ping walked for three days and came to a stone house. A bearded man sat outside. "I'm searching for my mother's brocade," Ping said.

"A brocade flew by three days ago," said the man. "Now it's in a palace far away. I'll explain how you can get there and lend you my horse." Ping thanked the man and bowed deeply to express his **gratitude**.

"First, you must ride through Fire Valley," said the man. "You must cross over it regardless of the scorching heat without uttering a word. If you utter even a single sound, you'll burn!" He continued, "After you've crossed Fire Valley, you'll arrive at Ice Ocean. You must ride through the icy waters without shivering. If you shiver even once, the **outcome** will be terrible! The sea will swallow you up!" The old man paused before concluding, "When you emerge from the sea, you'll be facing the Mountain of the Sun. The mountain is as steep as a straight line up to the sky! The palace sits on top of the mountain, and the brocade is in the palace."

137

Foreshadowing Foreshadowing gives readers clues about the outcome of events in a story.

Imagery Imagery is words and phrases that help create pictures in a reader's mind.

Your Turn

List two details that show "The Magical Lost Brocade" is a folktale. Then find examples of foreshadowing and imagery.

Personification

Writers sometimes use words in unusual ways to help you better picture an animal, a thing, or an event. Personification gives human qualities to an animal or object.

 Find Text Evidence

When I read the sentence on page 137 of "The Magical Lost Brocade," <u>However, soon afterward, a great wind swept into their hut and carried it away!</u> *I know the writer is using personification. The words* swept *and* carried away *give the wind the movement of a person.*

> However, soon afterward, a great wind swept into their hut and carried it away!

Your Turn

COLLABORATE

Tell which words in the following sentences from "The Magical Lost Brocade" are examples of personification. Explain how each example helps you picture an event.

The sea will swallow you up! *page 137*

As he crossed the valley, angry flames leaped out at him, *page 138*

The sea touched Ping with icy fingers, but he didn't shiver once, *page 138*

Shawna Tenney

Write About the Text

Pages 136–139

Callie

I responded to the prompt: *Add an event to the story. Describe how Princess Ling gets to Ping's house at the end of the story.*

Student Model: *Narrative Text*

Princess Ling called another great wind to take her to Ping's house. She commanded the wind to carry her as fast as a shooting star.

First, there was the problem of the Angry Jungle, where trees and vines suddenly seemed to come to life. As the Princess rode by, they tried to snatch her from the sky.

Grammar

Possessive nouns show who or what owns or has something.

Grammar Handbook See page 457.

Figurative Language

I used a simile to describe the speed that Princess Ling traveled.

Develop Plot

I included conflict in the story to keep readers interested.

Jose Pelaez/Image Source

Then she wrestled with the Desert of Fire, where the rising heat nearly pushed her into orbit.

Her great speed allowed for one stop. She used it to thank the bearded man. Before long, she was at Ping's side, and they lived happily ever after.

Sequence
I used time-order words to help readers understand the sequence of events.

Your Turn

Add another event to the story. Describe a new obstacle that Ping must overcome before he crosses the Ice Ocean.

Go Digital!
Write your response online.
Use your editing checklist.

Essential Question

What motivates you to accomplish a goal?

Go Digital!

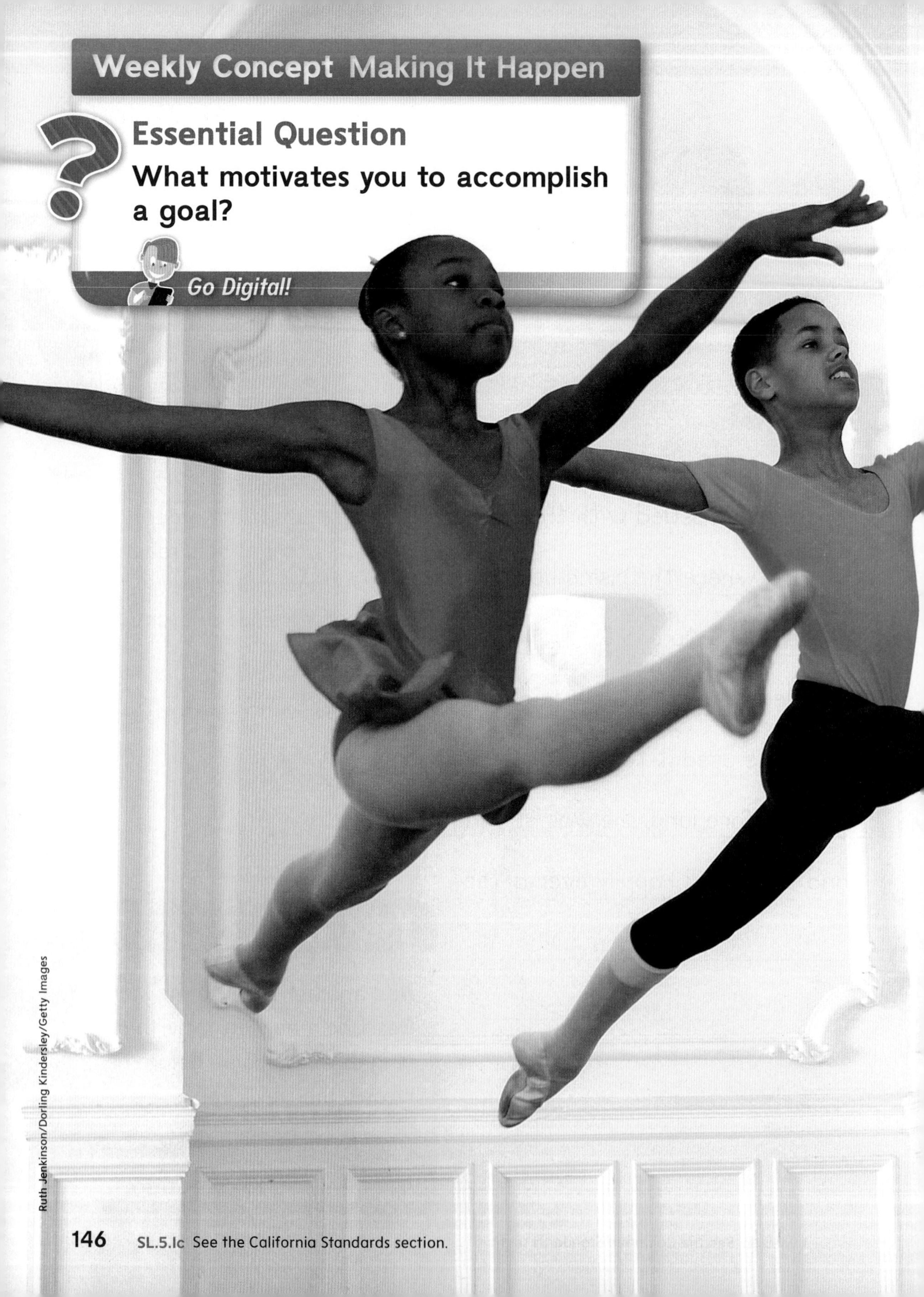

Ruth Jenkinson/Dorling Kindersley/Getty Images

By Leaps and Bounds

When you set a goal for yourself, what does it take to achieve it? How will you know you have accomplished your goal?

▶ These ambitious dancers will have to study, rehearse, and practice for hours each day if they want to be great.

▶ Working hard for success gives them satisfaction and a sense of a job well done.

Talk About It

Write words you have learned about accomplishing a goal. Then talk about a goal you have had, and what motivated you to accomplish it.

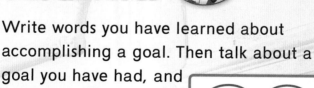

Accomplishing a Goal

147

Vocabulary

Use the picture and the sentences to talk with a
partner about each word.

ambitious

Paulo is an **ambitious** bike rider and
always looks for challenges.

Who do you know that you would
describe as ambitious?

memorized

Pat **memorized** the poem and recited it
perfectly for the class.

What is the name of a poem or song
that you memorized?

satisfaction

Participating in sports, such as
basketball, gave Jason great **satisfaction**.

What activity gives you great
satisfaction?

shuddered

Jill **shuddered** as she bit into the tart,
juicy lemon.

What is a synonym for shuddered?

Poetry Terms

narrative

I like to read **narrative** poems because they tell a story.

Do you prefer narrative poems that tell about fictional or real events?

repetition

The **repetition** of words, phrases, or lines is used for emphasis.

When is the repetition of a word or phrase useful for emphasizing something?

free verse

Some poets enjoy the freedom of writing **free verse** poems that do not have rhyming patterns.

What would be a good topic for a free verse poem?

rhyme

A poem with **rhyme** contains words that end with the same vowel sound.

Can you think of three words that rhyme with funny?

Your Turn

Pick three words and write a question about each for your partner to answer.

Go Digital! **Use the online visual glossary**

A Simple Plan

Each morning when Jack rises,
He schemes a simple plot:
"I think I'll change the world," says he,
"A little, not a lot."
For neighbors he might mow a lawn
Before they know he's done it,
Or lead a soccer match at school,
And not care which team won it.
Some kids would laugh,
but Jack would smile
And look for more to do.
He'd walk your dog or tell a joke,
Or play a song for you.
Jack's brother John just didn't see
What Jack was all about.
John shuddered at Jack's crazy ways,
But Jack had not one doubt.

Essential Question

What motivates you to accomplish
a goal?

Read how two poets describe
unusual goals and why they matter.

(l) Peter Zander/Workbook Stock/Getty Images; (r) Fancy/Alamy

"Who wants to do another's chores?"
John asked. "What does it mean,
'I'll change the world?' You're wasting time.
What changes have you seen?"
"Little brother," Jack explained,
"I used to think like you.
I thought, 'Why bother?' and 'Who cares?'
I see you do that, too.
I'd see some grass not mowed, or else
Kids not getting along,
And in the park no games to play—
I'd wonder what was wrong.
And then I had to ask myself,
What was I waiting for?
The change can start with me, you see,
That key is in my door.
I've memorized a thousand names,
And everyone knows me.
What do *you* do?" John had to think.
And he began to see.
Now each morning when Jack rises,
He hears his brother plan:
"I think I'll change the world," says John,
"If I can't, then who can?"

— Peter Collier

151

RESCUE

From the time we heard of the spill—
a *spill,* as if
someone tipped syrup
onto a tablecloth, as if
salt was shaken to the floor—
my coastal neighbors sailed out, flew
to find the sodden sea birds, bogged down
in waves of oil, a coating
so heavy no wing could lift.
From my own canoe I glimpse a head
once downy, but not drowned—
my heart holds hope!

Reach, lift, and up—
it beats, this bird's heart!
I hold the sickened seagull, know:
Just as one spill can spell disaster,
One boat can bring back life.

— Elena Ruiz

Make Connections

Talk about what motivated the speakers
in each poem to meet a goal. ESSENTIAL
QUESTION

Compare the speakers' feelings in the
poems to the feelings you have when you
try to accomplish a goal. TEXT TO SELF

Narrative and Free Verse

Narrative poetry: • Tells a story. • Has characters and dialogue.
• Can rhyme.
Free verse: • Shares ideas and feelings with no set rhyming
pattern or rhythm. • Has no set line length.

Find Text Evidence

*I can tell that "A Simple Plan" is a narrative poem because it tells
a story and has dialogue between characters. I see that "Rescue" is
free verse because there is no set line length or rhyming patterns.*

page 151

"Who wants to do another's chores?"
John asked. "What does it mean,
'I'll change the world?' You're wasting time.
What changes have you seen?"
"Little brother," Jack explained,
"I used to think like you.
I thought, 'Why bother?' and 'Who cares?'
I see you do that, too.
I'd see some grass not mowed, or else
Kids not getting along,
And in the park no games to play—
I'd wonder what was wrong.
And then I had to ask myself,
What was I waiting for?
The change can start with me, you see,
That key is in my door.
I've memorized a thousand names,
And everyone knows me.
What do *you* do?" John had to think.
And he began to see.
Now each morning when Jack rises,
He hears his brother plan:
"I think I'll change the world," says John,
"If I can't, then who can?"

— Peter Collier

151

"A Simple Plan" is a narrative
poem because it tells a story, has
characters, and includes dialogue.
Like some narrative poems, this
one also rhymes.

COLLABORATE

Your Turn

Reread the poems "A Simple Plan"
and "Rescue." How does the choice
to rhyme or not to rhyme affect the
poems?

Theme

The **theme** is the big idea or message that the poet wishes to communicate. Thinking about the speaker, word choices, and key details that the poet uses can help you figure out the theme of the poem.

 ## Find Text Evidence

Both poems are about accomplishing goals, but each poem has a specific theme. I'll reread "A Simple Plan," think about who is speaking, and look for key details to figure out the poem's theme.

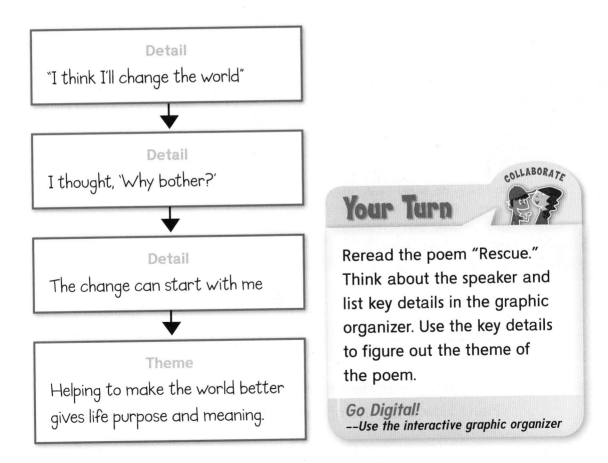

Detail

"I think I'll change the world"

↓

Detail

I thought, 'Why bother?'

↓

Detail

The change can start with me

↓

Theme

Helping to make the world better gives life purpose and meaning.

Your Turn

COLLABORATE

Reread the poem "Rescue." Think about the speaker and list key details in the graphic organizer. Use the key details to figure out the theme of the poem.

Go Digital!
--Use the interactive graphic organizer

Repetition and Rhyme

Poets may use **repetition**, or the repeated use of words, sounds, or phrases, for effect. Repeating a word, phrase, or sentence style helps emphasize the meaning. **Rhyme** is the repetition of the same vowel sound.

Find Text Evidence

Reread the poem "Rescue" on pages 152 and 153. Look for phrases and words that are repeated and the effect they create.

page 152

From the time we heard of the spill—
a *spill*, as if
someone tipped syrup
onto a tablecloth, as if
salt was shaken to the floor—
my coastal neighbors sailed out, flew
to find the sodden sea birds, bogged down
in waves of oil, a coating
so heavy no wing could lift.
From my own canoe I glimpse a head
once downy, but not drowned—
my heart holds hope!

The word "spill" is repeated to emphasize the event. The words "as if" are repeated to emphasize that the spill to come in the poem is worse than spilling syrup or salt.

COLLABORATE

Your Turn

Find examples of rhyme and repetition in "A Simple Plan." How is the use of repetition different in "Rescue"?

BlueMoon Stock/Alamy

Homographs

Homographs are words that are spelled the same but have different meanings and may or may not have the same pronunciation. You can use context clues to help figure out which homograph is correct.

Find Text Evidence

In "A Simple Plan," I see the word park. *I know that* park *can be a verb meaning to place or leave something, and it can also be a noun meaning land set apart for recreation. The phrase "games to play" is a clue that* park *has the second meaning.*

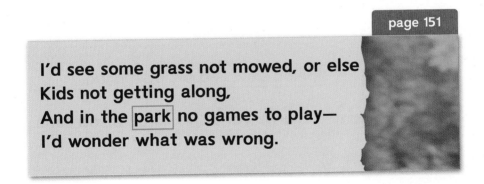

page 151

I'd see some grass not mowed, or else
Kids not getting along,
And in the park no games to play—
I'd wonder what was wrong.

COLLABORATE

Your Turn

Reread the homographs *down* and *spell* in the poem "Rescue." Identify clues that help you figure out the meaning.

Peter Zander/Workbook Stock/Getty Images

Write About the Text

Pages 150–153

Pete

I responded to the prompt: *Write a narrative poem about achieving a goal. Use precise language.*

Student Model: *Narrative Text*

The Race I Ran

I wanted to run a race—

the course stretched three miles long.

Being slow is a bit of a drag.

I didn't want this to be a sad song.

All the runners lined up on our marks.

We got set, then the judge shouted GO!

Figurative Language
I wrote a metaphor to describe running a race with the chance that it might not go so well.

Grammar

A **prepositional phrase** begins with a preposition and ends with a noun or a pronoun.

Grammar Handbook See page 457.

McGraw-Hill Education

A flurry of faces ran by me,

but I wasn't the last one, I know.

Some kids had run up alongside me;

They said that they just ran for fun.

We decided to just do our best,

and in my mind I had already won.

Precise Language
I used specific details to give readers a clear understanding of what I saw at the beginning of the race.

Theme
My message explains that there is more to sports than just winning.

Your Turn

Write a narrative poem about what it feels like to achieve a goal. Use precise language.

Go Digital!
Write your response online.
Use your editing checklist.

W.5.3a, W.5.3b See the California Standards section.

Getting from Here to There

THE BIG IDEA

What kinds of experiences can lead to new discoveries?

Beyond Borders

To tell the truth, as the plane hovered
over the city lights, I felt afraid—the tight
borders, endless sand, and empty expanses.
The different rules. But then I arrived,

and found myself a guest at a table groaning
with meat, bread, dates, tea and more. Laughter
sweetening the night, we shared stories, exchanged
histories. Gentleness entered the room.

Under a new moon's light, I held out my hand
to say good-bye, then walked out into the desert sky's
open arms. A hundred thousand grains of sand
rose with the wind, and resettled—soft and new.

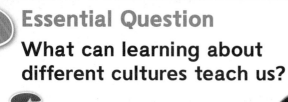

Weekly Concept Cultural Exchange

Essential Question

What can learning about different cultures teach us?

Go Digital!

SL.5.Ic See the California Standards section.

MOVING TO A NEW BEAT

Wherever I travel in the world, I enjoy meeting new people, trying different foods, and learning about the customs of each new place.

▶ One of my favorite things to share with others is African dance. People always become joyful when they move together to music.

▶ When I gain an appreciation of the music and dances of other cultures, I feel joyful, too!

Talk About It

Write words you have learned about cultural exchanges. Then talk about one thing you have learned from another culture.

Cultural Exchange

Vocabulary

Use the picture and the sentences to talk with a
partner about each word.

appreciation

Gram showed her **appreciation** for my
help by giving me a hug.

How do you show appreciation for
someone's help?

blurted

By mistake, I **blurted** out the secret
about the surprise.

How would you feel after you blurted
out a secret?

complimenting

Complimenting me when I do well
makes me feel great.

If you were complimenting a friend,
what would you say?

congratulate

After Niki lost the game, she went over
to **congratulate** the winner.

What might you congratulate
someone for?

contradicted

The witness **contradicted** what he had said earlier, and the lawyer pointed it out.

When have you contradicted something you said previously?

critical

A **critical** person often finds fault with what others do and points it out.

When have you been critical of yourself?

cultural

Languages, foods, and celebrations are examples of **cultural** differences.

Give two examples of cultural activities.

misunderstanding

Mira wore the wrong clothes as a result of a **misunderstanding**.

How would you handle a misunderstanding with a friend?

Your Turn

COLLABORATE

Pick three words. Write three questions for your partner to answer.

Go Digital! *Use the online visual glossary*

(t to b) Stockbyte/Getty Images; Myrleen Pearson/Alamy; Thinkstock/JupiterImages/Alamy; David Sutherland/Photographer's Choice/Getty Images

Shared Read · Genre • Realistic Fiction

A Reluctant TRAVELER

PASSPORT
United States of America

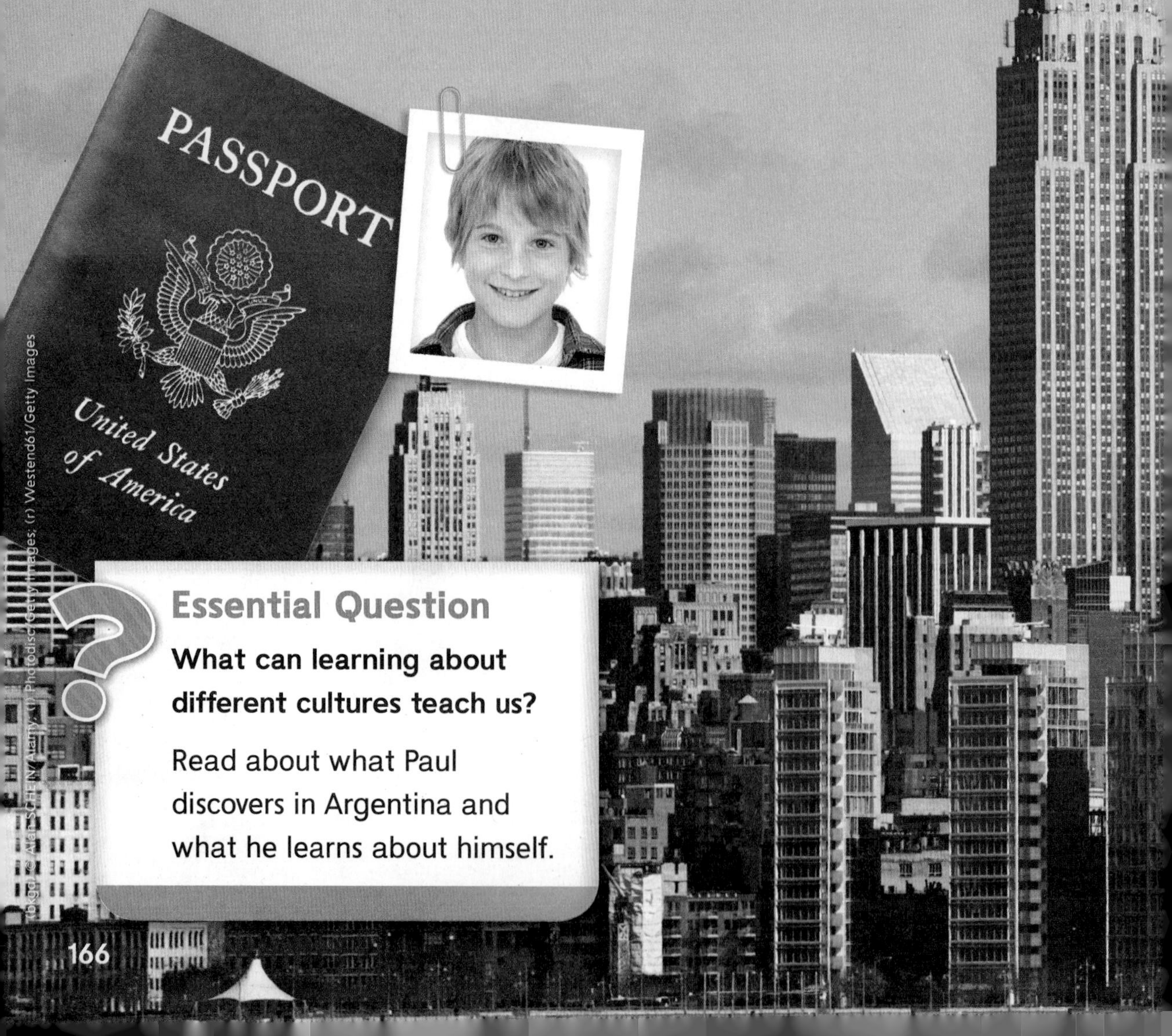

Essential Question

What can learning about different cultures teach us?

Read about what Paul discovers in Argentina and what he learns about himself.

"I think packing winter clothes in August is weird," Paul said, looking from his bedroom window onto West 90th Street. This wasn't going to be a fun vacation. He was sure of it.

His mom **contradicted**, "It's not weird, honey. Argentina's in the Southern hemisphere, and we're in the Northern hemisphere, so the seasons are opposite." To Paul, this was just another reason to want to stay in New York City. Paul wanted to spend the rest of his summer break hanging out with his friends, and not with Aunt Lila and Uncle Art in a faraway country.

Paul's parents, Mr. and Mrs. Gorski, were teachers, and this was a chance they couldn't pass up. Their apartment had been covered with travel guides full of **cultural** information ever since Mrs. Gorski's sister and her husband had relocated to Argentina six months ago. The Gorskis had big plans. Paul, on the other hand, wanted to sleep late and play soccer with his friends. They lived in a city already. Why were they going to Buenos Aires?

As their plane took off, Paul's dad said, "Look down there! That's the island of Manhattan. See? You can even see Central Park!" Paul never realized how completely surrounded by water New York was. Many hours later, as the plane was landing in Buenos Aires, Paul noticed similar outlines of a city on the water, and bright lights, just like home.

New York City

Buenos Aires

"We have so much to show you!" Aunt Lila gushed when they met at the airport. They had a late dinner at a restaurant, just as they often did back home. But the smells coming from its kitchen were new. Uncle Art ordered in Spanish for everyone: *Empanadas* (small meat pies), followed by *parrillada* (grilled meat), *chimichurri* (spicy sauce), and *ensalada mixta* (lettuce, tomatoes, and onions).

Paul made a face. "Don't be **critical**, Paul," his mom said. "Just take a taste." Though some of the foods were new, the spices and flavors were familiar to Paul.

"Mom, I had something like this at César's house," Paul said, after biting into an empanada. "This is really good." As he was **complimenting** the food, Paul felt his bleak mood improving.

Their first full day in Buenos Aires brought a rush of new sights, sounds, and languages. Paul noticed that like New York, Buenos Aires had people from all over the world. His Aunt Lila remarked, "We speak Spanish, but I really need to be multilingual!"

On a plaza, Paul saw a group of people dancing to music he'd never heard. Paul had seen break-dancing on the street, but never dancing like this. "That's the tango," Uncle Art said. "It's the dance Argentina is famous for! Being a soccer player, Paul, I know you have an **appreciation** for people who move well."

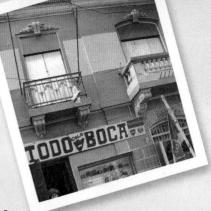

"You know, that *is* pretty cool," Paul admitted.

Around noon, they piled back into the car and drove to the most unusual neighborhood Paul had seen yet. All the buildings were painted or decorated in yellow and blue. "Soccer season has started here," his Aunt Lila said.

"Huh?" Paul asked, wondering if there had been a **misunderstanding**. "Isn't it too cold for soccer?" he asked.

"It's nearly spring. And," his aunt added, "Boca and River are playing at La Bombonera, the famous stadium, this afternoon." She held out her hand, which held five tickets to see these big teams play. Paul couldn't believe it.

"We're in the neighborhood of La Bombonera," Uncle Art said. "When Boca beats their rival, River, the people decorate their neighborhood in Boca colors!"

"Maybe I could paint my room in soccer team colors!" Paul **blurted**.

His mom smiled. "I **congratulate** you, Paul! You've turned out to be a really great traveler." Paul smiled, too.

Make Connections

Talk about what Paul and his family learned about the culture of Argentina. What did Paul learn about himself? ESSENTIAL QUESTION

What has learning about a different culture taught you? TEXT TO SELF

169

Summarize

When you summarize a story, you tell the important events and details in your own words. This helps you remember what you have read. You can summarize a story after you've finished it, or summarize parts of a story while you are reading it.

Find Text Evidence

You can check your understanding of the opening of "A Reluctant Traveler" on page 167 by summarizing the important events and details.

> **page 167**
>
> "I think packing winter clothes in August is weird," Paul said, looking from his bedroom window onto West 90th Street. This wasn't going to be a fun vacation. He was sure of it.
>
> His mom **contradicted**, "It's not weird, honey. Argentina's in the Southern hemisphere, and we're in the Northern hemisphere, so the seasons are opposite." To Paul, this was just another reason to want to stay in New York City. Paul wanted to spend the rest of his summer break hanging out with his friends, and not with Aunt Lila and Uncle Art in a faraway country.
>
> Paul's parents, Mr. and Mrs. Gorski, were teachers, and this was a chance they couldn't pass up. Their apartment had been covered with travel guides full of **cultural** information ever since Mrs. Gorski's sister and her husband had relocated to Argentina six months ago. The Gorskis had big plans. Paul, on the other hand, wanted to sleep late and play soccer with his friends. They lived in a city already. Why were they going to Buenos Aires?

As the story begins, Paul and his mom, who live in New York City, are packing to go on a family vacation in Buenos Aires. They'll stay with Paul's aunt and uncle, but Paul is not sure he wants to make the trip.

Your Turn

COLLABORATE

What are Paul's main experiences on his first night in Buenos Aires? Summarize the events and their effect on Paul. As you read, use the strategy Summarize.

Theme

The **theme** of a story is the overall idea or message about life that the author wants the reader to know. The theme is not stated, but you can find it by thinking about what characters say and do, and what happens to them.

 Find Text Evidence

When I read what Paul says in the first paragraph on page 167 of "A Reluctant Traveler," I see that Paul is not looking forward to his summer vacation. In the next paragraph, I see that his parents are taking him to Argentina to visit his aunt and uncle.

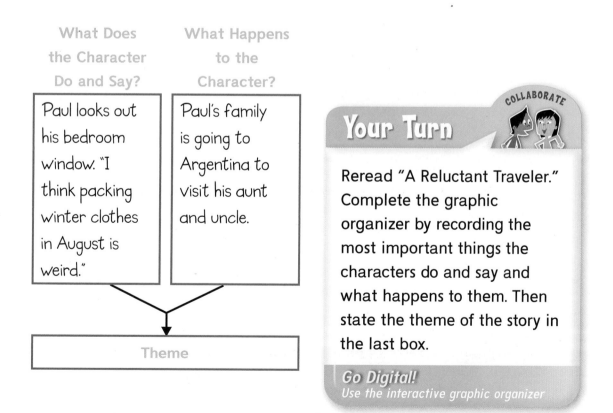

What Does the Character Do and Say?	What Happens to the Character?
Paul looks out his bedroom window. "I think packing winter clothes in August is weird."	Paul's family is going to Argentina to visit his aunt and uncle.

Theme

Your Turn

COLLABORATE

Reread "A Reluctant Traveler." Complete the graphic organizer by recording the most important things the characters do and say and what happens to them. Then state the theme of the story in the last box.

Go Digital!
Use the interactive graphic organizer

Realistic Fiction

The selection "A Reluctant Traveler" is realistic fiction.

Realistic fiction:

- Tells about characters and events that resemble people and events in real life
- Happens in a setting that is real or seems real
- Includes dialogue and descriptive details

🔍 Find Text Evidence

I can tell that "A Reluctant Traveler" is realistic fiction. Paul and his parents travel from New York City to Buenos Aires, which are both real places. Visiting relatives and sightseeing are details that could happen in real life, and the dialogue shows what real people might say.

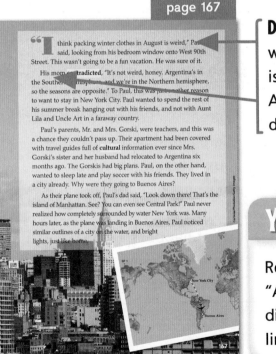

page 167

"I think packing winter clothes in August is weird," Paul said, looking from his bedroom window onto West 90th Street. This wasn't going to be a fun vacation. He was sure of it.

His mom contradicted, "It's not weird, honey. Argentina's in the Southern hemisphere, and we're in the Northern hemisphere, so the seasons are opposite." To Paul, this was just another reason to want to stay in New York City. Paul wanted to spend the rest of his summer break hanging out with his friends, and not with Aunt Lila and Uncle Art in a faraway country.

Paul's parents, Mr. and Mrs. Gorski, were teachers, and this was a chance they couldn't pass up. Their apartment had been covered with travel guides full of **cultural** information ever since Mrs. Gorski's sister and her husband had relocated to Argentina six months ago. The Gorskis had big plans. Paul, on the other hand, wanted to sleep late and play soccer with his friends. They lived in a city already. Why were they going to Buenos Aires?

As their plane took off, Paul's dad said, "Look down there! That's the island of Manhattan. See? You can even see Central Park!" Paul never realized how completely surrounded by water New York was. Many hours later, as the plane was landing in Buenos Aires, Paul noticed similar outlines of a city on the water, and bright lights, just like home.

New York City

Buenos Aires

167

Dialogue Dialogue is the exact words the characters say. Dialogue is shown using quotation marks. A new paragraph indicates a different speaker.

COLLABORATE

Your Turn

Read aloud a line of dialogue in "A Reluctant Traveler." How is the dialogue realistic? What does the line reveal about the character?

Context Clues

When you don't know the meaning of a word, you can look for **cause and effect relationships** between words as clues to the word's meaning. Cause and effect clues may be in the same sentence as the unknown word, or in a nearby sentence.

 Find Text Evidence

To understand what hemisphere *means, I can look at a cause and effect relationship.* Hemisphere *has to do with a location on the earth. Since seasons in the Northern and Southern hemispheres are opposite,* hemisphere *must refer to areas divided by the equator.*

"Argentina's in the Southern hemisphere, and we're in the Northern hemisphere, so the seasons are opposite."

Your Turn

COLLABORATE

Use cause and effect relationships between words as clues to the meanings of the following words from "A Reluctant Traveler."

relocated, *page 167*

bleak, *page 168*

multilingual, *page 168*

Write About the Text

Pages 166–169

Chen

I responded to the prompt: *Write a dialogue between Paul and his mother about the similarities between New York and Buenos Aires.*

Student Model: *Narrative Text*

"Mom," Paul said, as they returned from shopping, "I'm noticing similarities between New York and Buenos Aires."

"What have you noticed?" Mom asked, smiling.

"Well," Paul said, "both cities are located on the water and are lit up by lights at night."

"Nice work, detective," Mom joked.

"What else?"

Supporting Details
I used details from the text to describe the cities.

Formal and Informal Voice
I wrote in an informal tone to make the conversation more realistic.

Yobro10/iStock/360/Getty Images

174 W.5.3b, W.5.3d See the California Standards section.

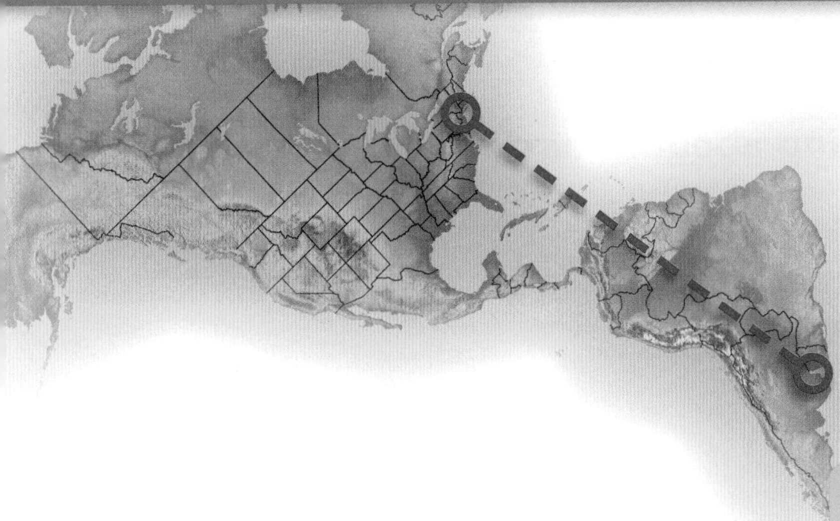

"People in both cities eat dinner late," he said, "and they cook with some of the same spices. Also, they both have people from all over the world."

"Wow! So Buenos Aires is not so bad after all?" Mom said as she winked.

"Yep. I gotta admit that it's pretty cool," Paul agreed.

Cartesia/Photodisc/Getty Images

Grammar

The **action verb** *eat* tells the action of the subject, *people.*

Grammar Handbook
See page 458.

Develop Character

I added an interjection to show how Mom feels about Paul's observations.

Your Turn

Imagine you are Paul. Write a dialogue between Paul and a close friend about the trip.

Go Digital!
Write your response online.
Use your editing checklist.

Essential Question

How can learning about nature be useful?

Go Digital!

(bkgd) Mathieu Belanger/XO2032/Reuters/Corbis; (tr) Kerry Sherck/Aurora/Getty Images; (c) F1 Online/SuperStock; (br) Ryan Donnell/Aurora/Getty Images; (inset) Burke Triolo Productions/Artville/Getty Images

A Fruitful Experience

Human beings depend on nature. Over many years, we have had to figure out what is safe for us to eat, and how to grow the foods we need.

▶ Cranberries, pictured here, grow wild on shrubs and vines, but resourceful people have learned to cultivate them.

▶ These men are standing in a cranberry bog. Flooding the cranberry beds each autumn makes the fruit easier to harvest.

Talk About It COLLABORATE

Write words you might use to describe how learning about nature is useful. Then talk about a time when learning about nature helped you.

Learning from Nature

Vocabulary

Use the picture and the sentences to talk with a
partner about each word.

civilization

I am excited to look at the unique artifacts
that an ancient **civilization** left behind.

What past civilization interests you
most?

complex

The **complex** jigsaw puzzle was a
challenge to finish.

What is an antonym for complex?

cultivate

It takes time and work to **cultivate** a
beautiful garden.

How do you cultivate a friendship?

devise

My mom helped our family **devise** a
plan for eating healthfully.

What healthful plan would you like
to devise?

fashioned

I watched as the potter **fashioned** a vase out of clay.

What other items can be fashioned from clay?

resourceful

Birds are **resourceful** when finding materials to build nests.

What qualities does a resourceful person have?

shortage

The river was drying up from a **shortage** of rainwater.

Why is a shortage of water dangerous?

tormentors

Flies and mosquitoes can be **tormentors** to people in summer.

How can cats be tormentors to birds?

COLLABORATE

Your Turn

Pick three words. Write three questions for your partner to answer.

Go Digital! **Use the online visual glossary**

L.5.6 See the California Standards section.

Survivaland

Essential Question

How can learning about nature be useful?

Read how four friends use their knowledge of nature to survive.

"I'm going to win *Survivaland*!" Raul declared as he started the computer game. His immobile character suddenly sprang into action on screen. He raced across the desert island pursued by a sandstorm.

"Not today," Latrice warned while moving her character on the screen. "I'll be the last player standing on the island!"

Juanita stomped her feet. "No way," she insisted, "I always **devise** a winning game plan."

Jackson frowned. "*Survivaland* is too **complex**," he complained. "You have to know all about nature to win, but in real life, knowing about nature is just not that important."

"You are *so* wrong!" Juanita cried.

A loud *crackle* sounded, and the entire room went dark. When the lights returned seconds later, the four players were very confused. Instead of controlling their characters on the computer screen, they were on the island themselves!

"I can't believe it—we're inside the game!" Raul exclaimed. "And this sandstorm is blinding me! What should we do?" Suddenly, a large sign in the sky flashed a message: RUN WEST TO ESCAPE THE STORM.

"Which way is west?" Jackson called.

"I know," Latrice exclaimed, pointing. "The sun is rising over there, and since the sun ascends in the east and sets in the west, west must be in the opposite direction."

Maryn Roos

181

The four players ran until the sandstorm was safely behind them. "Whew, that was close!" Raul gasped with a **shortage** of breath.

Suddenly Juanita shouted, "No time to relax—there's new trouble overhead!" The group looked up and saw a gigantic butterfly hovering above them. Juanita feared the monster insect might fly down and land on her head.

Just then, Raul spotted onions growing nearby. He quickly pulled one up and smashed it with a stick. He pulled it apart, **fashioned** four onion pieces, and said, "Rub this all over yourselves. NOW!"

The giant butterfly floated down and rested its feet on Juanita, just as she had feared. She shrieked in fright, and the gigantic insect flew away. "I think my screaming scared it off," Juanita sighed.

"No, actually, the onion did," Raul explained. "Because butterflies taste with their feet, I knew that the onion's bitterness would drive the insect away."

Jackson looked perplexed. "Huh? Butterflies taste with their feet?" he exclaimed, confused.

"Yes," Raul replied, "don't you remember learning that last year in science class?"

"I guess I was daydreaming that day," Jackson admitted, adding, "Raul, you're a **resourceful** friend!"

Then, without warning, an enormous crow flew down and announced, "I'm hungry!" When the huge bird walked close to Jackson, Juanita tore off the silver bracelet and ring she was wearing and threw them as far as she could. The crow raced after the jewelry, and the friends ran the other way.

Even after the bird was out of sight, they kept running, and Jackson called to Juanita, "Why did you throw away your jewelry?"

Juanita explained, "I read in a nature book that crows are attracted to shiny objects, so I knew the giant bird would go after the jewelry instead of me!"

"You see?" Raul said, looking at Jackson. "Knowing about nature has saved us again from our **tormentors**."

Finally, the four friends stopped running—but not by choice. They accidentally tripped over a tree log and landed in gooey mud that covered their faces, making it impossible for them to see. They heard another loud crackle. When the four wiped the mud away and opened their eyes, they were back in Raul's game room, in front of the computer screen! All the mud was gone, and the electric blue sky had become four white walls.

"We're off the island!" Latrice cried. "We survived *Survivaland,* and all of us returned to a normal **civilization**!"

"So who won the game?" Raul wondered.

Jackson declared, "I think we all did—but I feel like the biggest winner, because I've managed to **cultivate** a new appreciation for nature."

"Agreed!" the friends cried, as they wondered what game they might like to play next.

Make Connections

Talk about how the four friends used their knowledge of nature to get out of dangerous situations. ESSENTIAL QUESTION

How might you use information about nature to stay safe and healthy? TEXT TO SELF

Maryn Roos

Summarize

When you summarize a story, you can decide which details are most important and retell them in your own words. Ask yourself, *Does this detail help me understand what is happening?* Summarizing helps you remember what you read.

 Find Text Evidence

You can summarize the first few paragraphs of "Survivaland" on page 181 to make sure you understand what has happened to the friends as they start the game.

> **page 181**
>
> "I'm going to win *Survivaland*!" Raul declared as he started the computer game. His immobile character suddenly sprang into action on screen. He raced across the desert island pursued by a sandstorm.
>
> "Not today," Latrice warned while moving her character on the screen. "I'll be the last player standing on the island!"
>
> Juanita stomped her feet. "No way," she insisted, "I always **devise** a winning game plan."
>
> Jackson frowned. "*Survivaland* is too **complex**," he complained. "You have to know all about nature to win, but in real life, knowing about nature is just not that important."
>
> "You are *so* wrong!" Juanita cried.
>
> A loud *crackle* sounded, and the entire room went dark. When the lights returned seconds later, the four players were very confused. Instead of controlling their characters on the computer screen, they were on the island themselves!

Four friends are playing a computer game that tests who can best survive on a desert island. The text on page 181 says, "they were on the island themselves." These important details help me understand what the story is about before I continue reading.

 COLLABORATE

Your Turn

What are the most important details about the outcome of "Survivaland"? Use the strategy Summarize as you read.

Theme

The **theme** of a story is the message about life that the author thinks is important. The theme is usually not stated in the story. To identify the theme, think about what the characters do and say and what happens to them. Then decide what lesson they learn as a result of their words and actions.

Find Text Evidence

On page 181 of "Survivaland," a message appears in the sky, telling the friends to run west to escape the sandstorm. Latrice says, "Since the sun ascends in the east and sets in the west, west must be in the opposite direction." Her knowledge allows the other characters to run to safety and escape the sandstorm.

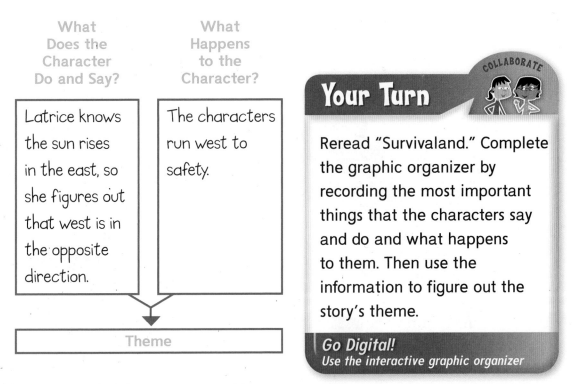

What Does the Character Do and Say?	What Happens to the Character?
Latrice knows the sun rises in the east, so she figures out that west is in the opposite direction.	The characters run west to safety.

Theme

Your Turn COLLABORATE

Reread "Survivaland." Complete the graphic organizer by recording the most important things that the characters say and do and what happens to them. Then use the information to figure out the story's theme.

Go Digital!
Use the interactive graphic organizer

Fantasy

The selection "Survivaland" is a fantasy.

A **fantasy:**

- Has a made-up setting
- Includes characters and events not possible in real life
- May include sensory language and personification

Find Text Evidence

I can tell that "Survivaland" is a fantasy. In the story, the characters meet a giant butterfly and a giant crow, which couldn't exist in real life. Personification occurs when the crow speaks. Sensory language is used to describe the experiences.

page 182

The four players ran until the sandstorm was safely behind them. "Whew, that was close!" Raul gasped with a **shortage** of breath.

Suddenly Juanita shouted, "No time to relax—there's new trouble overhead!" The group looked up and saw a gigantic butterfly hovering above them. Juanita feared the monster insect might fly down and land on her head.

Just then, Raul spotted onions growing nearby. He quickly pulled one up and smashed it with a stick. He pulled it apart, **fashioned** four onion pieces, and said, "Rub this all over yourselves. NOW!"

The giant butterfly floated down and rested its feet on Juanita, just as she had feared. She shrieked in fright, and the gigantic insect flew away. "I think my screaming scared it off," Juanita sighed.

"No, actually, the onion did," Raul explained. "Because butterflies taste with their feet, I knew that the onion's bitterness would drive the insect away."

Jackson looked perplexed. "Huh? Butterflies taste with their feet?" he exclaimed, confused.

"Yes," Raul replied, "don't you remember learning that last year in science class?"

"I guess I was daydreaming that day," Jackson admitted, adding, "Raul, you're a **resourceful** friend!"

Then, without warning, an enormous crow flew down and announced, "I'm hungry!" When the huge bird walked close to Jackson, Juanita tore off the silver bracelet and ring she was wearing and threw them as far as she could. The crow raced after the jewelry, and the friends ran the other way.

182

Sensory Language Language that is sensory involves the five senses: touch, sight, taste, sound, smell.
Personification Personification gives human qualities to animals or objects.

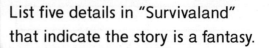

Your Turn

List five details in "Survivaland" that indicate the story is a fantasy.

Context Clues

When you come across an unfamiliar or multiple meaning word in a sentence, you can look for **comparisons** in the text as clues to the word's meaning.

 Find Text Evidence

When I read the first paragraph on page 181 of "Survivaland," I can use the comparisons <u>suddenly sprang into action</u> *and* <u>raced across</u> *to figure out the meaning of* immobile. *It must mean the opposite, "not moving."*

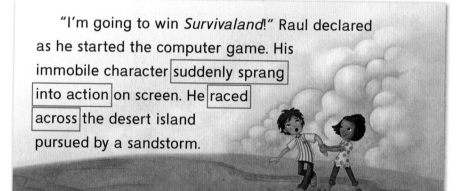

"I'm going to win *Survivaland*!" Raul declared as he started the computer game. His immobile character suddenly sprang into action on screen. He raced across the desert island pursued by a sandstorm.

Your Turn COLLABORATE

Use comparisons to figure out the meaning of each of the following words in "Survivaland."

ascends, *page 181*
hovering, *page 182*
perplexed, *page 182*

Maryn Roos

CCSS Write to Sources

Write About the Text

Miguel

I answered the question: *In your opinion, what is the most important lesson Jackson learned? Provide reasons for your response.*

Student Model: *Opinion*

In my opinion, the most important

lesson Jackson learned was about

the power of nature. He changed

his feelings after each of his friends

shared a key detail about nature that

saved them from danger.

First, Latrice mentioned how to

use the sun's position to figure out

Connotation and Denotation

I chose the word *key* because it has a positive meaning and shows that knowing about nature is a good thing.

Supporting Details

I included text evidence from the story to support my reasoning.

which direction was west. Next, Raul
remembered that butterflies taste
through their feet and do not like
bitterness. Last, Juanita recalled that
crows like shiny objects. All of these
facts helped save the children. Jackson
learned a lesson he is not likely to
forget.

Grammar

Past-tense verbs
tell about an action
that has already
happened.

*Grammar
Handbook
See page 458.*

Strong Conclusion
My final sentence
restates the importance
of the lesson that
Jackson learned.

Your Turn

In your opinion, which friend
was most helpful in surviving
Survivaland? Provide reasons
for your response.

Go Digital!
Write your response online.
Use your editing checklist.

Maryn Roos

Essential Question

Where can you find patterns in nature?

Go Digital!

Niall Benvie/Photolibrary

SL.5.1c See the California Standards section.

Seeing a PATTERN

Though each thing in nature is unique, the repetition of shapes, colors, lines, and behaviors shows us that nature works in patterns.

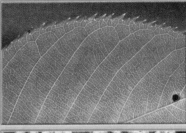

▶ A geographic formation such as this salt marsh is often created over time. Wind and water, for example, create patterns like cut-outs in the landscape.

▶ These pictures of a leaf, coral, and a honeycomb suggest that things on Earth have a pattern.

Talk About It

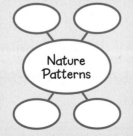

COLLABORATE

Write words you have learned about patterns in nature. Then talk about one pattern in nature you have seen.

Nature Patterns

(t) David Mark/Alamy; (c) Ian Cartwright/Getty Images; (b) Frank May/dpa/Corbis

Vocabulary

Use the picture and sentences to talk with a partner about each word.

contact

When I turned on the gas stove, the flame made **contact** with the metal pot.

What happens when your hand comes into contact with something hot?

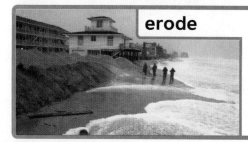

erode

When storms **erode** the beach, they carry sand away from the shore.

Why does the beach get smaller when storms erode it?

formation

The marching band played in **formation** during halftime.

Does formation mean that you make something or destroy it?

moisture

I knew it had rained when I saw drops of **moisture** on the leaves.

What is an antonym for moisture?

particles

Tiny **particles** of sand floated in the light shining across the dunes.

What is a synonym for particles?

repetition

I do each exercise in a **repetition** of ten, and hope to increase it to twenty.

What is a skill you have learned better through repetition?

structure

My little sister built a **structure** with blocks.

Did you ever build a structure, such as a castle or fort?

visible

The boy's face was **visible** through the apartment window.

What is visible from your window?

Your Turn

COLLABORATE

Pick three words. Write three questions for your partner to answer.

Go Digital! *Use the online visual glossary*

Patterns of Change

Essential Question

Where can you find patterns in nature?

Read about patterns you can find in rocks and rock formations.

194

Rock Solid

"Solid as a rock" is a saying often used to describe something that's reliable, that doesn't change. But, in fact, rocks do change. The effects of water, wind, and temperature over long periods of time slowly transform one type of rock into another type of rock. These same forces also shape awe-inspiring landscapes and sketch designs on rock. Nature's patterns are **visible** in some rocks as small as pebbles and in wonders as vast as the Grand Canyon.

The photograph across these pages shows one example of nature's art. This **structure** of rock, known as the Wave **formation**, is made of sandstone. It is sand turned to rock over a long period of time.

Igneous Rocks

Igneous rocks are one type of rock. They are formed from hot, liquid rock called magma. Magma exists far below the Earth's surface, but it sometimes escapes to the surface through cracks, such as the mouths of volcanoes. Then, we call it lava.

This molten rock, or lava, is composed of minerals. As the minerals slowly cool, they form crystals. Eventually, the once fiery liquid hardens into a solid substance.

There are many kinds of igneous rock. Their textures and colors come from their crystallized minerals. You may be familiar with granite, which feels rough and comes in many colors. Another variety of igneous rock is obsidian, which is smooth and often black.

Granite

Obsidian

Sedimentary Rocks

Igneous rocks do not stay the same forever. Water and wind **erode** them, carrying away **particles** of broken rock and depositing them elsewhere. These particles may be left on a beach or riverbank, in a desert or the sea.

Gradually, the particles collect in layers. The **contact** between the particles and the weight of the layers squeeze out any pockets of **moisture** or air. Pressed together, the particles form a new material called sedimentary rock. It is formed from many different sorts of sediment. It can include rocks and sand, as well as biological matter, such as plants, bones, and shells.

Just as there are different kinds of igneous rock, there are different kinds of sedimentary rock. Sandstone is formed from sand. Limestone is composed of bones and shells.

Limestone

Marble

Rock Formations

Over time, a layer can be created entirely of one kind of sedimentary rock. Geologists who study rocks call a layer made of the same material and at about the same time a *stratum*. Another stratum of a different kind can be deposited on top of the first one. The plural for stratum is strata.

Sandstone

Many strata of different kinds of rock can accumulate. Each one will press down on those that came before it. Scientists learn a lot by studying the chronology of layers. The oldest layer will be at the bottom, the youngest at the top.

These layers of sedimentary rock can create dazzling patterns. Each layer will have its own texture and colors. Moreover, water and wind will continue to do their work.

The Rock Cycle

Still, rocks continue to change. There is a third type of rock below the earth's surface, called metamorphic rock. These rocks are pressed down upon by the layers of rock above them. At the same time, they are heated by the magma beneath them. Eventually, the heat will cause some metamorphic rock to melt and become magma.

As the magma slowly cools, it will turn back into igneous rock. The **repetition** of this process is called the rock cycle. The rock cycle is a pattern—a pattern of change that repeats and continues. It transforms liquid rock into a solid substance. It builds cliffs from sand and bones. And it returns rock to liquid form.

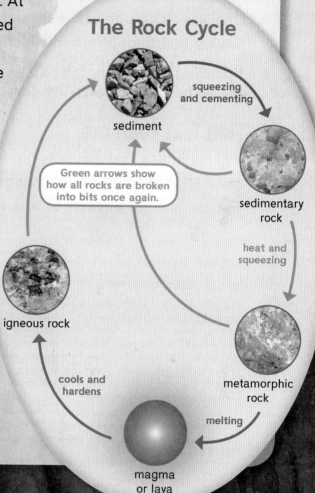

The Rock Cycle

sediment

squeezing and cementing

Green arrows show how all rocks are broken into bits once again.

sedimentary rock

heat and squeezing

igneous rock

metamorphic rock

cools and hardens

melting

magma or lava

Make Connections

Talk about the patterns you can find in sedimentary rocks. Where do you see these patterns? ESSENTIAL QUESTION

Compare the patterns of change in rocks with other patterns you have seen. TEXT TO SELF

Ask and Answer Questions

One way to be sure you understand a science text is to ask and answer questions about the information. You can ask a question such as, *Why does this happen?* Then look for information in the text to help you answer the question.

 ## Find Text Evidence

You might ask *How do rocks change?* when you read the first paragraph of "Patterns of Change" on page 195. As you read, you can look for answers to your question.

---

page 195

Rock Solid

"Solid as a rock" is a saying often used to describe something that's reliable, that doesn't change. But, in fact, rocks do change. The effects of water, wind, and temperature over long periods of time slowly transform one type of rock into another type of rock. These same forces also shape awe-inspiring landscapes and sketch designs on rock. Nature's patterns are **visible** in some rocks as small as pebbles and in wonders as vast as the Grand Canyon.

The photograph across these pages shows one example of nature's art. This **structure** of rock, known as the Wave **formation**, is made of sandstone. It is sand turned to rock over a long period of time.

The text explains that water, wind, and temperature over long periods of time can change one type of rock into another type. They can also shape landscapes and sketch designs on rock.

COLLABORATE

Your Turn

Ask and answer a question about the information in the section "Igneous Rocks" on page 195. As you read, use the strategy Ask and Answer Questions.

Main Idea and Key Details

Most texts have an overall **main idea.** This is what the writer most wants you to know about a topic. To find the **main idea,** identify **key details.** Then decide what all the key details have in common.

 Find Text Evidence

After I read "Sedimentary Rocks" on page 196, I see that the key details are about how different particles form sedimentary rocks. From these details, I can find the main idea.

Main Idea
Particles such as sand or bones and shells form different sedimentary rocks.

Detail
Wind and water carry away rock particles.

Detail
Particles collect in layers and are pressed together.

Detail
Sedimentary rocks are made from the pressed particles.

Your Turn

COLLABORATE

Reread "Rock Formations" on page 196. Use key details to find the main idea of this section.

Go Digital!
Use the interactive graphic organizer

Expository Text

The selection "Patterns of Change" is expository text.

Expository text:

- Explains a topic with reasons and evidence
- Supports reasons and evidence with facts, examples, and concrete details
- May include text features, such as diagrams or time lines

🔍 Find Text Evidence

I can tell "Patterns of Change" is expository text. It provides evidence and gives reasons why patterns occur, supporting these with facts and concrete details. A diagram illustrates information.

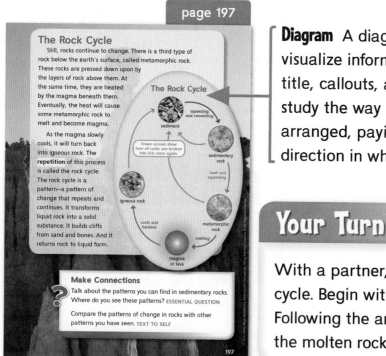

page 197

The Rock Cycle

Still, rocks continue to change. There is a third type of rock below the earth's surface, called metamorphic rock. These rocks are pressed down upon by the layers of rock above them. At the same time, they are heated by the magma beneath them. Eventually, the heat will cause some metamorphic rock to melt and become magma.

As the magma slowly cools, it will turn back into igneous rock. The **repetition** of this process is called the rock cycle. The rock cycle is a pattern—a pattern of change that repeats and continues. It transforms liquid rock into a solid substance. It builds cliffs from sand and bones. And it returns rock to liquid form.

The Rock Cycle

sediment

squeezing and cementing

Green arrows show how all rocks are broken into bits once again.

sedimentary rock

heat and squeezing

igneous rock

cools and hardens

metamorphic rock

melting

magma or lava

Make Connections

Talk about the patterns you can find in sedimentary rocks. Where do you see these patterns? ESSENTIAL QUESTION

Compare the patterns of change in rocks with other patterns you have seen. TEXT TO SELF

197

Diagram A diagram helps readers visualize information. Read the title, callouts, and labels. Then study the way information is arranged, paying attention to the direction in which arrows point.

Your Turn

COLLABORATE

With a partner, describe the rock cycle. Begin with magma or lava. Following the arrows, explain how the molten rock changes.

Greek Roots

If you know the meaning of a word's root, you can use it as a clue to figure out the meaning of an unfamiliar word. Some roots from ancient Greek are *geo*, which means "earth"; *logy*, which means "study"; *chrono*, which means "time"; *bio*, which means "life"; and *morph*, which means "form."

Find Text Evidence

I'm not sure what geologists *means on page 196 of "Patterns of Change." I know that* geo *means "earth" and* logy *means "study." The context clue* who study rocks *also helps me figure out that* geologists *means "someone who studies the earth."*

> Over time, a layer can be created entirely of one kind of sedimentary rock. Geologists who study rocks call a layer made of the same material and at about the same time a *stratum*.

Your Turn

COLLABORATE

Use what you know about Greek roots, along with other context clues, to figure out the meaning of the following words.

biological, *page 196*
chronology, *page 196*
metamorphic, *page 197*

Andrew J. Martinez/Photo Researchers

Patterns of Change

Pages 194–197

Write About the Text

Samantha

I answered the question: *How does the flow chart of the rock cycle help us to better understand the text?*

Student Model: *Informative Text*

> The flow chart helps us better understand the text by using visuals to explain the rock cycle. The arrows show the process of how rocks go through different stages, and how those stages are continuously repeated.
>
> The process begins with broken bits of rock. As these bits get squeezed,

Strong Opening
I wrote a topic sentence that clearly states the main idea of my response.

Grammar

A **helping verb** helps the **main verb** show an action or make a statement.

Grammar Handbook
See page 460.

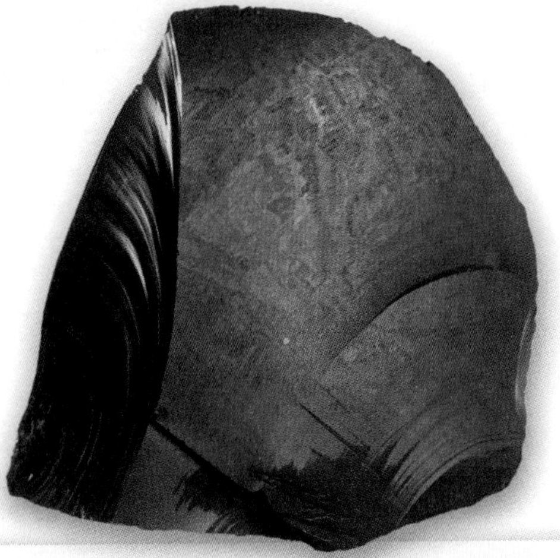

they cement into sedimentary rock. This rock is then heated into metamorphic rock. Next, the rock gets melted by magma. Then the magma cools and forms igneous rock. The process repeats itself. In conclusion, the diagram helps the reader make sense of a challenging text.

Relevant Evidence
I included facts and details from the text that clearly support my response.

Transitions
I used a transition to link my final thought to the rest of my writing.

Your Turn

How does the author help us to understand what *stratum* means?

Go Digital!
Write your response online. Use your editing checklist.

W.5.2b, W5.2e See the California Standards section.

Essential Question

What benefits come from people working as a group?

Go Digital!

SL.5.1c See the California Standards section.

The Art of WORKING TOGETHER

Playing sports, building houses, or performing in a show are just some of the reasons people come together to work in teams.

▶ A group of artists decided to collaborate on an art project for their community.

▶ Many people dedicated their time and talents to planning and painting this mural, and it inspired the whole neighborhood!

Talk About It

Write words you have learned about working as a team. Then talk about a time you were part of a successful team.

Teamwork

Vocabulary

Use the picture and the sentences to talk with a partner about each word.

artificial

Mike's **artificial** leg did not prevent him from playing most sports.

When might you need something to be artificial rather than real?

collaborate

Many students will **collaborate** to create our school's new banner.

What other projects might require you to collaborate with others?

dedicated

Tina **dedicated** herself to learning the song for the choir concert.

When have you dedicated all your efforts to learning something?

flexible

The dancer's body was so **flexible** that he could twist into almost any position.

Why is it important for athletes to be flexible?

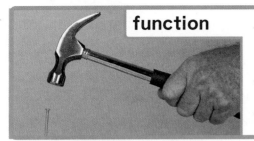

function

The main **function** of a hammer is pounding nails.

What is the main function of another common tool?

mimic

Some insects can **mimic** a tree branch or twig to hide themselves.

What other animals can mimic something?

obstacle

The fallen tree created an **obstacle** in the road, and cars could not get through.

What sort of obstacle have you encountered trying to get somewhere?

techniques

Maria uses a variety of bowing **techniques** when playing her violin.

What are some techniques you use to help you study?

COLLABORATE

Your Turn

Choose three words. Write three questions for your partner to answer.

Go Digital! *Use the online visual glossary*

(t to b) Dynamic Graphics Group/IT Stock Free/Alamy, © Tom Uhlman/Alamy, Marcos Welsch/DesignPics, Image Source/Punchstock

L.5.6 See the California Standards section.

Gulf Spill Superheroes

Essential Question

What benefits come from people working as a group?

Read about how a variety of people worked together after the Deepwater Horizon oil spill in the Gulf of Mexico.

Fans of comic books know that sometimes it takes a team of superheroes to save the day. Each one uses his or her special powers to fight an enemy or solve a problem. On April 20, 2010, the Deepwater Horizon drilling platform exploded in the Gulf of Mexico. Massive fires raged above the waters. Down below, gallons and gallons of oil spewed from a broken pipeline. Such a huge disaster would require the skills and abilities of many heroes working together.

Fire boats at work at the off shore oil rig Deepwater Horizon.

Responders in the Water

Immediately after the explosion, firefighters worked with the U.S. Coast Guard to battle the blaze. Boats and aircraft transported survivors from the platform to safety before the rig sank.

Meanwhile, scientists raced to understand what was happening underwater. Each type of scientist had a specific **function**. Oceanographers mapped out the ocean floor and charted water currents in the area. Biologists looked for ways to protect animals in the region from the spreading oil.

What was most important, engineers discussed **techniques** to fix the broken well. The leak was more than a mile below the Gulf's surface. That was too deep for human divers to work effectively. For that reason, experts relied on robots with **artificial** arms and special tools to stop the spill. Many of their first efforts failed.

After nearly three months, workers finally plugged up the damaged well. It would take many more months to clean up the mess left behind.

◀ Workers move absorbent material to capture some spilled crude oil at Fourchon Beach, Louisiana.

Watchers from the Sky

From the water, it was hard to see where the oil was spreading. Responders had to **collaborate** with other agencies, such as the NASA space program. Satellites in the sky sent information to scientists on the ground. Meteorologists tracked storms that might pose an **obstacle** to the response teams. Photographs helped team leaders decide how to assign their workers.

Pilots and their crews flew over the Gulf region in helicopters and planes. Some studied how the oil slick moved from place to place. Others directed the placement of floating barriers to protect sensitive areas. Some crews transferred needed supplies back and forth between land and sea.

Heroes on Land

As the oil approached land, new responders leapt into action. Veterinarians **dedicated** their efforts to helping out marine animals, such as pelicans and turtles. They would capture and treat affected animals before returning them to the wild. Naturalists and ecologists cleaned up the animals' habitats. Quite often, these groups' efforts overlapped and they helped one another. Volunteers also helped out on many tasks.

Local fishermen also needed help. They relied on crabs, shrimp, and other seafood for their livelihood. Government officials monitored fishing areas to decide which were safe. Bankers and insurance companies also reached out to the fishermen. They helped find ways to make up for the lost income from seafood sales.

Biologists catch an oil-soaked brown pelican to clean and return to the wild.

In Florida, experts worked together in a "think tank." They needed to trap floating globs of oil before they ruined area beaches. They created the SWORD, or Shallow-water Weathered Oil Recovery Device. The SWORD was a catamaran with mesh bags hung between its two pontoons. The small craft would **mimic** a pool skimmer and scoop up oil as it moved. Because of its size and speed, the SWORD could be quite **flexible** responding to spills.

Workers place absorbent materials to catch oil in Orange Beach, Alabama.

As we have seen, the Deepwater Horizon accident required heroic efforts of all kinds. In some cases, workers' jobs were quite distinct. In others, their goals and efforts were similar. The success of such a huge mission depended on how well these heroes worked together. The lessons learned will be quite valuable if and when another disaster happens.

Make Connections

How did people from other locations work together with those responders at the site of the Gulf oil spill?
ESSENTIAL QUESTION

How have others helped you achieve a goal? Explain how you all worked together to meet the challenge.
TEXT TO SELF

Ask and Answer Questions

When you read an article for the first time, you may find some details confusing. As you read "Gulf Spill Superheroes," you can stop, ask yourself questions, and then look for answers.

Find Text Evidence

When you read "Watchers from the Sky" on page 210, you may get confused about how pilots and their crews helped. Ask, *Why would pilots and their crews be in charge of where to place floating barriers?* Then reread to find the answer.

page 210

Watchers from the Sky

From the water, it was hard to see where the oil was spreading. Responders had to **collaborate** with other agencies, such as the NASA space program. Satellites in the sky sent information to scientists on the ground. Meteorologists tracked storms that might pose an **obstacle** to the response teams. Photographs helped team leaders decide how to assign their workers.

Pilots and their crews flew over the Gulf region in helicopters and planes. Some studied how the oil slick moved from place to place. Others directed the placement of floating barriers to protect sensitive areas. Some crews transferred needed supplies back and forth between land and sea.

I reread the beginning of the section: From the water, it was hard to see where the oil was spreading. *People placing the floating barriers needed pilots above to see the oil, so pilots were in charge.*

Your Turn

COLLABORATE

Why did engineers decide to use robots to fix the broken well? Reread page 209 to find the answer. Remember to use the strategy Ask and Answer Questions.

Main Idea and Key Details

The **main idea** of an article is what it is mostly about. Each section and paragraph in an article also has a main idea. To find the main idea, identify **key details** and figure out what they have in common.

 Find Text Evidence

When I read the section "Heroes on Land" on page 210, I see that all the details are about the efforts of people on land working to help others. From this I can find the main idea.

Main Idea

As the oil spill reached land, other responders went to work.

Detail

Veterinarians and naturalists helped animals affected by the oil.

Detail

Business leaders helped fishermen who could not fish in some areas.

Detail

Members of a "think tank" created the SWORD to protect local beaches.

Your Turn COLLABORATE

Reread "Watchers from the Sky" on page 210. Use the graphic organizer to tell how responders in that section helped to deal with the Deepwater Horizon disaster.

Go Digital!
Use the interactive graphic organizer

Expository Text

The selection "Gulf Spill Superheroes" is an expository text.

Expository text:
- Gives factual information about a topic
- May offer the author's conclusions supported by evidence
- May include photographs, captions, and headings

Find Text Evidence

I can tell that "Gulf Spill Superheroes" is expository text about the Gulf Spill responders. Headings organize the text by type of responder. Photos and captions provide additional information.

page 210

Watchers from the Sky

From the water, it was hard to see where the oil was spreading. Responders had to **collaborate** with other agencies, such as the NASA space program. Satellites in the sky sent information to scientists on the ground. Meteorologists tracked storms that might pose an **obstacle** to the response teams. Photographs helped team leaders decide how to assign their workers.

Pilots and their crews flew over the Gulf region in helicopters and planes. Some studied how the oil slick moved from place to place. Others directed the placement of floating barriers to protect sensitive areas. Some crews transferred needed supplies back and forth between land and sea.

Heroes on Land

As the oil approached land, new responders leapt into action. Veterinarians **dedicated** their efforts to helping out marine animals, such as pelicans and turtles. They would capture and treat affected animals before returning them to the wild. Naturalists and ecologists cleaned up the animals' habitats. Quite often, these groups' efforts overlapped and they helped one another. Volunteers also helped out on many tasks.

Local fishermen also needed help. They relied on crabs, shrimp, and other seafood for their livelihood. Government officials monitored fishing areas to decide which were safe. Bankers and insurance companies also reached out to the fishermen. They helped find ways to make up for the lost income from seafood sales.

210

Biologists catch an oil-soaked brown pelican to clean and return to the wild.

Use Photographs and Captions

Photographs help to illustrate the information in the text. Captions provide additional information.

COLLABORATE

Your Turn

List three examples of information that the author of "Gulf Spill Superheroes" includes that show you that this is expository text. Why is this kind of information included?

Latin Roots

Many English words have roots that come from ancient Greek and Latin. A root can be a clue to the meaning of an unfamiliar word. Some roots from ancient Latin are *sensus,* which means "perceive" or "feel"; *habitare,* which means "to live" or "to dwell"; and *port,* which means "carry." The prefix *trans-,* which means "across," also comes from ancient Latin.

 ## Find Text Evidence

I'm not sure what marine *means. I know that the Latin root* mare *means "the ocean or sea." Other context clues talk about how the oil spill affected life in the Gulf of Mexico, so I can figure out that* marine *means "of or relating to the sea."*

Veterinarians dedicated their efforts to helping out marine animals, such as pelicans and turtles.

Your Turn

Use your knowledge of Latin roots to figure out the meanings of the following words from "Gulf Spill Superheroes":

transported, *page 209*
sensitive, *page 210*
habitats, *page 210*

Write About the Text

Pages 208–211

Yolanda

I answered the question: *What do you believe was the biggest obstacle after the oil pipeline broke in the Gulf? Explain your response.*

Student Model: *Opinion*

I believe the biggest obstacle after the pipeline broke was the danger the oil created for animals and their habitats. Biologists had to find ways to protect the animals, and it was hard to tell which way the oil was spreading. Not all animals could be protected.

Animals, such as pelicans and

Focus on a Topic

I only included details from the text that support and explain my opinion.

Grammar

A **linking verb** links the subject of a sentence to a noun or an adjective.

Grammar Handbook
See page 461.

turtles, had to be caught and cleaned by veterinarians before they were ← returned to the wild. Meanwhile, naturalists and ecologists had to clean the animals' habitats. It took a lot of scientists and volunteers to help the animals. Protecting animals and their environments was a huge job.

Sentence Structure
I used a variety of sentence types to keep readers interested.

Strong Conclusion
The last sentence of my paragraph sums up my response.

Your Turn

What contribution do you feel was most helpful in dealing with the Gulf crisis? Explain your response.

Go Digital!
Write your response online.
Use your editing checklist.

Essential Question

How do we explain what happened in the past?

Go Digital!

SL.5.lc See the California Standards section.

Pieces of the Puzzle

People like me all over the world excavate and study remnants of the past to learn where we came from.

▶ At the site of an ancient temple in Luxor, Egypt, I am trying to reconstruct a broken pottery plate.

▶ Artifacts like this help us understand how people lived, what technology they had, and what problems they may have experienced. From this, we may gain an insight into our own future!

Talk About It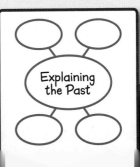

Write words you have learned about things that help us explain the past. Then talk about something in the past that you would like to have explained.

Explaining the Past

Vocabulary

Use the picture and sentences to talk with a partner about each word.

archaeologist

An **archaeologist** examines ancient places for clues about early cultures.

What early culture would you investigate if you were an archaeologist?

era

The people sitting for the photograph wore clothes from an earlier **era**.

If you could time-travel to another era, which would you choose?

fragments

The dropped pottery vase was in **fragments** on the floor.

What fragments of objects have you found?

historian

A good **historian** finds interesting stories by studying past objects and events.

What would a future historian tell about the time you live in?

intact

Cardboard cartons help protect eggs so they arrive at the store whole and **intact**.

What would you like to find intact after a storm or flood?

preserved

Foods from our garden have been **preserved** in jars for enjoying all year.

Which of your possessions would you want preserved in a time capsule?

reconstruct

A skilled craftsman can **reconstruct** broken china so that it looks like new.

What famous place would you like to reconstruct as a model?

remnants

Divers discovered the **remnants** of a sunken ship.

What could someone learn from the remnants of a meal?

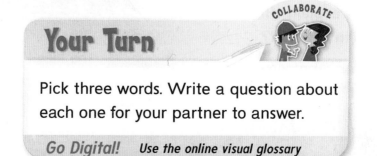

COLLABORATE

Your Turn

Pick three words. Write a question about each one for your partner to answer.

Go Digital!   *Use the online visual glossary*

(t to b) Antonio M. Rosario/Photographer's Choice/Getty Images; Robert George Young/Photographer's Choice RF/Getty Images; Michael Blann/Photodisc/ Getty Images; Franco Banfi/WaterFrame/Getty Images

Essential Question

How do we explain what happened in the past?

Read two different views about the uses of a mysterious object.

The Inca Empire was centered in what is now Peru. It was taken by Spanish conquest in the middle of the 16th century.

Nigel Smith/SuperStock/Corbis

What Was the Purpose of the Inca's STRANGE STRINGS?

String Theory

Was the quipu an ancient mathematical calculator?

Most of us do not do math problems without an electronic calculator. It would be even tougher without paper and pencil. Now imagine adding numbers with a device that looks like a mop! The quipu (pronounced KWEE-poo) was an invention of the Incas, an ancient civilization in South America. Most quipus were not **preserved**, but about 600 of them still remain **intact**.

Quipus are made of cotton and wool strings, sometimes hundreds of them, attached to a thicker horizontal cord. Both the **archaeologist** and the **historian** have tried to figure out how the quipu works. Here is their solution:

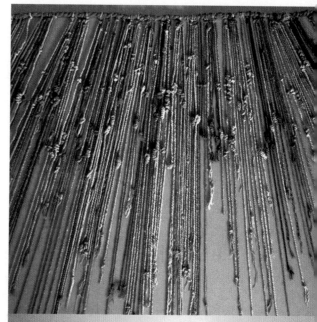

The quipu is an object that has baffled archaeologists for many years.

Knots were tied to the dangling strings to represent numbers.

The quipus were likely used by Inca officials to record and keep track of data, including statistics on anything from the number of crops produced by a village to the number of people living in a house.

Stuart Franklin/Magnum Photos

223

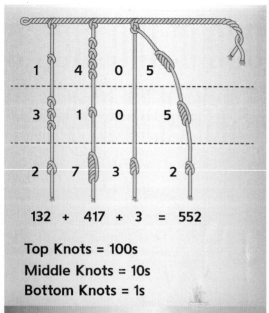

1	4	0	5
3	1	0	5
2	7	3	2

132 + 417 + 3 = 552

Top Knots = 100s
Middle Knots = 10s
Bottom Knots = 1s

Follow the illustration to understand how to count with a quipu.

Here is how a quipu would work: Each group of knots on a string represents a power of 10. Depending on their position, knots can stand for ones, tens, hundreds, and thousands. Clusters of knots increase in value the higher they are on the string. As a result, Incas with special training could add up the knots on a string to get the sum. They could also add up the total of many strings or even many quipus.

The patterns of the knots show repeating numbers. When you add it all up, it seems clear that the quipu was nothing less than an amazing low-tech calculator.

Spinning a Yarn

The Incas had a 3-D language written in thread!

Mystery surrounds the Inca civilization. In its peak **era**—the middle of the 1400s—the Incas built thousands of miles of roads over mountains, and yet they had no knowledge of the wheel. They made houses of stone blocks that fit together perfectly without mortar, a bonding material. The biggest mystery may be how the Incas kept their empire together without a written language.

The solution to the last mystery might be an odd-looking object called a quipu. Only a few hundred of these **remnants** of the Inca culture still exist.

Researchers discuss a quipu.

Quipus are made of wool strings that hang from a thick cord. On the strings are groups of knots. Many researchers believe the knots stand for numbers—even though no evidence supports this. But others make a strong case that the knots of the quipu were really language symbols, or a form of language.

Researchers found an identical three-knot pattern in the strings of seven different quipus. They think the order of the knots is code for the name of an Incan city. They hope to **reconstruct** the quipu code based on this and other repeating patterns of knots.

More conclusive proof that the quipu is a language comes from an old manuscript, a series of handwritten pages from the 17th century. It was found in a box holding **fragments** of a quipu. The author of the manuscript says the quipus were woven symbols. The manuscript even matches up the symbols to a list of words.

The Inca empire covered nearly 3,000 miles. Perhaps the strings of the quipu helped hold it together.

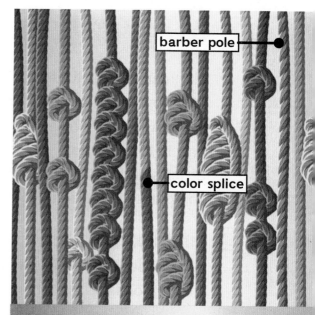

barber pole

color splice

Some experts now believe that the quipu's knots, colors, and patterns made it more than just a counting device. Decoding the quipu may reveal historical records.

Make Connections

Talk about what historians found by studying the ancient quipu. ESSENTIAL QUESTION

Think about an object that confused you the first time you saw it. How did you find out what it was for? TEXT TO SELF

Summarize

Summarizing persuasive articles as you read is a good way to keep track of how the authors make important points. Summarize sections as you read and then summarize the whole article to check your understanding. When reading multiple articles on the same topic, you can use your summaries to compare information.

Find Text Evidence

As you read "String Theory" on pages 223 and 224, summarize the author's theory of how the quipu might have been used.

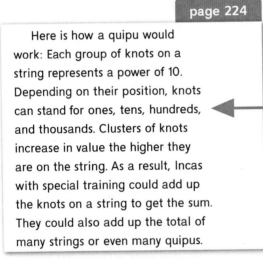

page 224

Here is how a quipu would work: Each group of knots on a string represents a power of 10. Depending on their position, knots can stand for ones, tens, hundreds, and thousands. Clusters of knots increase in value the higher they are on the string. As a result, Incas with special training could add up the knots on a string to get the sum. They could also add up the total of many strings or even many quipus.

The Incas' quipu had different patterns of knots on strings. Experts think the quipu may have been a calculator, and the patterns may have stood for numbers of different value.

Your Turn

COLLABORATE

Summarize the article "Spinning a Yarn." How does this summary compare with the summary of "String Theory"?

Author's Point of View

In arguing for or against an idea in a persuasive article, an author is giving his or her **point of view,** or position, about the topic. Supporting details such as word choice, evidence, and reasons give clues to the author's point of view.

 Find Text Evidence

I will read "Spinning a Yarn" to look for evidence of the author's point of view. Just below the title is this sentence: The Incas had a 3-D language written in thread! *It shows that the author supports a connection between the quipu and language. The author provides evidence to support the idea that the knots were language symbols.*

Details	Author's Point of View
"Incas had language in thread."	The author is in favor of quipu as a form of language.
knots may not mean numbers	
patterns may be symbols	
old manuscript shows a code	

Your Turn COLLABORATE

Identify important details in "String Theory" and place them in your graphic organizer. Then state the author's point of view.

Go Digital!
Use the interactive graphic organizer

Persuasive Article

"String Theory" and "Spinning a Yarn" are persuasive articles.

Persuasive articles:

- Try to persuade a reader to support a position or idea
- Include opinions that are supported with details, reasons, and evidence
- Include text features, such as diagrams

Find Text Evidence

I can tell that "String Theory" is a persuasive article. The article states an idea of how a quipu was used. Details about how the quipu worked and how the Incas used it support the idea. A diagram illustrates the information.

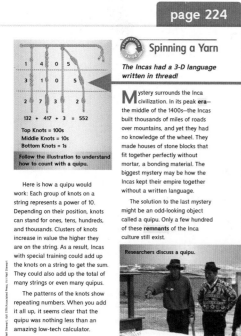

page 224

Spinning a Yarn

The Incas had a 3-D language written in thread!

M ystery surrounds the Inca civilization. In its peak **era**— the middle of the 1400s—the Incas built thousands of miles of roads over mountains, and yet they had no knowledge of the wheel. They made houses of stone blocks that fit together perfectly without mortar, a bonding material. The biggest mystery may be how the Incas kept their empire together without a written language.

The solution to the last mystery might be an odd-looking object called a quipu. Only a few hundred of these **remnants** of the Inca culture still exist.

Researchers discuss a quipu.

1	4	0	5
3	1	0	5
2	7	3	2

132 + 417 + 3 = 552

Top Knots = 100s
Middle Knots = 10s
Bottom Knots = 1s

Follow the illustration to understand how to count with a quipu.

Here is how a quipu would work: Each group of knots on a string represents a power of 10. Depending on their position, knots can stand for ones, tens, hundreds, and thousands. Clusters of knots increase in value the higher they are on the string. As a result, Incas with special training could add up the knots on a string to get the sum. They could also add up the total of many strings or even many quipus.

The patterns of the knots show repeating numbers. When you add it all up, it seems clear that the quipu was nothing less than an amazing low-tech calculator.

224

Diagram A diagram is a simple visual representation of an object, place, idea, or event. **Labels** show how parts relate to one another and to the whole.

COLLABORATE

Your Turn

Give two reasons that the diagram on page 224 supports the author's claim that the quipu was used as a calculator.

Context Clues

When you come across an unfamiliar or multiple meaning word, context clues found in the same sentence may help you learn its meaning. **Sentence clues** are words that help support the meaning of an unfamiliar word in the same sentence.

 Find Text Evidence

In the first paragraph of "String Theory" on page 223, I do not know the meaning of the word calculator. *The words* do math problems *and* electronic *in the sentence suggest that a calculator is a mini-computer that solves math problems.*

page 223

Most of us do not do math problems without an electronic calculator. It would be even tougher without paper and pencil.

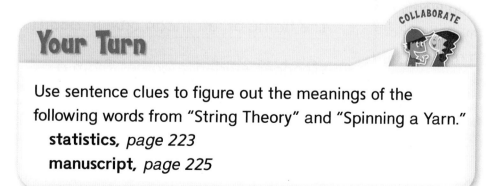

COLLABORATE

Your Turn

Use sentence clues to figure out the meanings of the following words from "String Theory" and "Spinning a Yarn."

statistics, *page 223*

manuscript, *page 225*

Stuart Franklin/Magnum Photos

Pages 222–225

Write About the Text

Marta

I answered the question: *What evidence exists to support the researchers' theory that quipus were a form of language?*

Student Model: *Informative Text*

One of the most important pieces of evidence researchers have to suggest quipus were a form of language is a similar pattern of knots found in many different quipus. These patterned knots have led researchers to believe these quipus have a code for the name of an Incan city. In addition, stronger evidence comes from a

Precise Language
I used a precise term to give readers concrete details.

Transitions
I used linking words to develop my topic and group two related facts from the text.

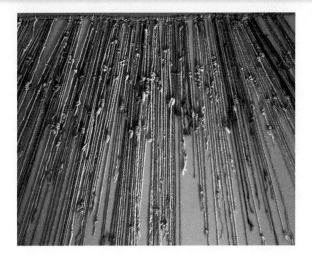

handwritten manuscript from the 17th century that was found with a piece of quipu. The manuscript states that quipus were woven symbols. It matches up these symbols to a list of words. These logical reasons suggest that researchers could be correct about the quipu.

Grammar

An **irregular verb** is a verb that does not add *-ed* to form the past tense.

Grammar Handbook
See page 462.

Reasons and Evidence

I included facts from the text to support my reasoning.

Your Turn

Explain how the quipu illustrations support the text.

Go Digital!
Write your response online.
Use your editing checklist.

231

Unit 4

IT'S UP TO YOU

A CLEAN MACHINE

So many options every day
to get me up and on my way:
To walk or drive or ride my bike—
It's clear to me which choice I like.

I keep my bike in tip-top shape
And ready for a quick escape
To get me where I want to go,
And show me all there is to know.

My heart grows full; my spirit, too.
I'm proud of what my legs can do
To pedal places, far and near
While keeping our skies clean and clear.

I ride because I love the Earth
And honor all it's truly worth.
My bike and I, together we
Explore our planet, strong and free.

—Hugh Coyle

THE BIG IDEA

How do we decide what's important?

Essential Question

What kinds of stories do we tell? Why do we tell them?

Go Digital!

Jim Wileman/Alamy

SL.5.lc See the California Standards section.

Show and Tell

Wherever we travel in the world, the words, "Once, long ago," let us know a story has begun.

▶ Some stories are written, some are told aloud, and still others are performed, as you see here, using puppets, light, and shadow.

▶ Whether stories teach lessons or entertain us with humor, exaggeration, or heroic adventure, they always help to show us who we are.

Talk About It

COLLABORATE

Write words you have learned about sharing stories. Then talk about one of your favorite stories and why you like to tell it.

Sharing Stories

Vocabulary

Use the picture and the sentences to talk with a partner about each word.

commenced

The horse race **commenced** on time and ended only three minutes later!

What is an antonym for commenced?

deeds

Doing good **deeds** for others can make us feel useful and happy.

What good deeds might you do to help a neighbor?

exaggeration

Dad's description of the giant fish must be an **exaggeration** since the fish in this lake are not that big.

How is an exaggeration like a lie?

heroic

The **heroic** acts of firefighters help save lives.

What heroic acts do police officers perform?

impress

Carolina hoped to **impress** the class with her amazing science project.

What might an athlete do to impress a coach?

posed

The family members stood very still as they **posed** for photographs.

Why do you think they stood still as they posed?

sauntered

We all enjoyed the sights as we slowly **sauntered** through the park.

What is a synonym for sauntered?

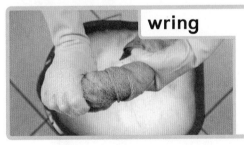

wring

After soaking a wash rag, **wring** it out to remove excess water.

When might you have to wring a towel?

Your Turn

COLLABORATE

Pick three words. Write three questions for your partner to answer.

Go Digital! *Use the online visual glossary*

(t to b) Ariel Skelley/Blend Images/Getty Images, Stewart Cohen/Taxi/Getty Images, Purestock/Getty Images, Jochen Tack/imagebroker/age fotostock

How Mighty Kate
Stopped the Train

Essential Question

What kinds of stories do we tell?
Why do we tell them?

Read a tall tale about a heroic young
girl who saves the day.

Chances are y'all have seen a railroad train passing through your neck of the woods. Some of you lucky critters may have even ridden one once or twice. But this here story takes place back in the days when railroads were still pretty new in the American South.

The star of this amazing tale is a young gal that folks around here call Mighty Kate. She got that name at birth, on account of how unbelievably strong she was. After the doctor weighed her on a scale, the tiny babe picked up the doc to see how much he weighed! **Deeds** like that proved just how mighty Kate was, and her nickname stuck like paper to glue.

Growing up, Mighty Kate continued to **impress** her family and neighbors with her great strength. When she went walking through the woods, if a boulder was in her path, she never stepped around it. She just picked up that rock, tossed it aside, and **sauntered** along her way! Once, her pappy's horse and buggy got stuck in a ditch. Mighty Kate stepped in and pulled them both out—with just one hand!

But let's not get "off track" from the amazing railroad story you really should hear now.

One night, when Mighty Kate was right near 15 years old, a powerful storm struck outside her home. The wind and rain raged so hard that homes shook in fear, and trees ran for their lives! From her window, Mighty Kate saw a work train crossing Creek Bridge. Suddenly, there was a thunderous crash. The loud noise caused the weeping willows to weep so hard that their tears flooded the entire area!

Mighty Kate ran outside to see what had happened. The bridge, whipped by the storm, had fallen into the creek. So had the train! Kate grabbed a long vine on a nearby plant and slid down to the crash site. She found two railroad workers trapped under a pile of twisted rails. With one push of her arm, she swept away all that mess. Whoosh!—the men were free. She yanked each man up with one hand and ascended the vine back up to land with the other hand—no **exaggeration**!

I reckon y'all may be guessing Mighty Kate was done with her **heroic** deeds for the night. But you'd be wrong. She knew the 10:30 local train, filled with passengers, would soon be rolling through the area. She had to tell workers at the nearest railroad station to hold the train, since the bridge was out. But the station was an hour away by foot. There was no time to waste!

With the wind and rain attacking her, Mighty Kate set out for the train station. Soon she came to River Bridge, which had somehow managed to stay up in the storm. Kate **commenced** to cross the bridge. Floodwaters rushed just beneath her feet. Suddenly, she spotted a huge log floating in the river. It was headed straight for the bridge—and for Kate!

Mighty Kate leaned over the railing. She stood still, as if **posed** for a photograph. As the log was about to strike, Kate grabbed it. She began to **wring** the wood with her bare hands. Pretty soon, that fat, wet log was nothing but a shriveled twig!

After crossing the bridge, Mighty Kate ran straight to the station. When she got there, the passenger train had already left. Kate raced after it along the tracks but couldn't catch up. Then she got an idea. She whistled loudly—so loudly that the engineer heard it and stopped the train.

Kate ran up and told him how Creek Bridge was out. The engineer hugged and thanked the brave young girl who had saved the day.

And because of Mighty Kate's mighty good idea, today we have whistles on trains to give warnings along the track!

Make Connections

Discuss the way the author told the story of Mighty Kate. Why do you think she told it this way? ESSENTIAL QUESTION

What stories do you most like to tell to people? How do you tell them? TEXT TO SELF

Jimmy Holder

Visualize

When you visualize a story, you form pictures of the characters, setting, and actions in your mind. To visualize, pay close attention to any descriptive words the author uses. Visualizing as you read a story can help you understand and remember it.

Find Text Evidence

As you read the third paragraph of "How Mighty Kate Stopped the Train" on page 239, you may need to visualize the scene to understand how powerful Kate is.

> **page 239**
>
> Growing up, Mighty Kate continued to **impress** her family and neighbors with her great strength. When she went walking through the woods, if a boulder was in her path, she never stepped around it. She just picked up that rock, tossed it aside, and **sauntered** along her way! Once, her pappy's horse and buggy got stuck in a ditch. Mighty Kate stepped in and pulled them both out—with just one hand!
>
> But let's not get "off track" from the amazing railroad story you really should hear now.
>
> One night, when Mighty Kate was right near 15 years old, a powerful storm struck outside her home. The wind and rain raged so hard that homes shook in fear, and trees ran for their lives! From her window, Mighty Kate saw a work train crossing Creek Bridge. Suddenly, there was a thunderous crash. The loud noise caused the weeping willows to weep so hard that their tears flooded the entire area!

The narrator says that Kate tossed a boulder and sauntered away. The verbs <u>tossed</u> *and* <u>sauntered</u> *help me visualize how easy this action is for her. By picturing this, I see the exaggeration in the scene.*

Your Turn

How did Kate save her pappy's horse and buggy? Use story details to help you picture it. As you read, use the strategy Visualize.

Jimmy Holder

Point of View

Point of view in a story refers to the way the story is being told. The voice that you hear in a story is the voice of the narrator, and told either in first-person or third-person. Details tell you what the narrator thinks about the characters and events.

Find Text Evidence

From the first page of "How Mighty Kate Stopped the Train," I see that the story is told from the third-person point of view. I can also tell that the narrator enjoys telling "this amazing tale" and admires Kate's strength, which is exaggerated.

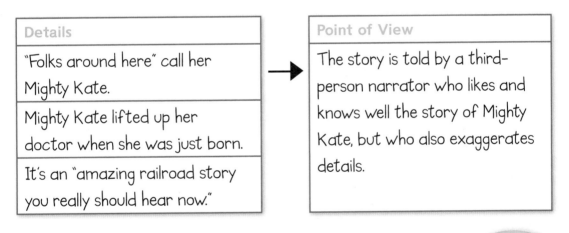

Details	Point of View
"Folks around here" call her Mighty Kate.	The story is told by a third-person narrator who likes and knows well the story of Mighty Kate, but who also exaggerates details.
Mighty Kate lifted up her doctor when she was just born.	
It's an "amazing railroad story you really should hear now."	

COLLABORATE

Your Turn

Reread the rest of "How Mighty Kate Stopped the Train." Record important details in the left column of the graphic organizer. In the right column, describe the point of view.

Go Digital! *Use the interactive graphic organizer*

Tall Tale

The selection "How Mighty Kate Stopped the Train" is a tall tale.

A **tall tale**:
- Has larger-than-life characters, including a hero
- Involves humorous exaggerations, or hyperbole
- Describes events that couldn't happen in real life

Find Text Evidence

I can tell that "How Mighty Kate Stopped the Train" is a tall tale. For example, a newborn baby could not possibly lift a person. The description of young Kate, the hero, easily tossing a boulder is also an exaggeration, or hyperbole.

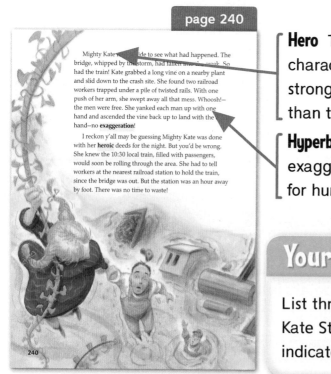

page 240

Mighty Kate ___ ide to see what had happened. The bridge, whipped by the storm, had fallen into the creek. So had the train! Kate grabbed a long vine on a nearby plant and slid down to the crash site. She found two railroad workers trapped under a pile of twisted rails. With one push of her arm, she swept away all that mess. Whoosh!— the men were free. She yanked each man up with one hand and ascended the vine back up to land with the other hand—no **exaggeration**!

I reckon y'all may be guessing Mighty Kate was done with her **heroic** deeds for the night. But you'd be wrong. She knew the 10:30 local train, filled with passengers, would soon be rolling through the area. She had to tell workers at the nearest railroad station to hold the train, since the bridge was out. But the station was an hour away by foot. There was no time to waste!

240

Hero The hero is the main character in a story and is stronger, braver, or more clever than the other characters.

Hyperbole Hyperbole is an obvious exaggeration. It is used in a story for humorous effect.

COLLABORATE

Your Turn

List three details in "How Mighty Kate Stopped the Train" that indicate that the story is a tall tale.

Synonyms and Antonyms

The relationship between synonyms or antonyms in a sentence or paragraph can help you better understand the meaning of each word. **Synonyms** are words with the same or similar meanings. **Antonyms** are words with opposite meanings.

Find Text Evidence

When I read the phrase <u>if a boulder was in her path,</u> *on page 239, I didn't know what* boulder *meant. In the next sentence I read,* she just picked up that rock. Rock *is a synonym for* boulder, *so since the story is exaggerated, a boulder must be a big rock.*

> When she went walking through the woods, if a boulder was in her path, she never stepped around it. She just picked up that rock, tossed it aside, and sauntered along her way!

COLLABORATE

Your Turn

Find a synonym or antonym to help you better understand the meaning of each of the following words in "How Mighty Kate Stopped the Train."

thunderous, *page 239*

ascended, *page 240*

shriveled, *page 241*

Jimmy Holder

Write About the Text

Pages 238–241

Karim

I responded to the prompt: *Write a narrative comparing Mighty Kate to an average person. Use figurative language.*

Student Model: *Narrative Text*

Style and Tone

I wrote in an informal voice to show that my writing is meant to be fun.

Grammar

The **pronoun** *she* takes the place of the **antecedent** *Mighty Kate.*

Grammar Handbook
See page 463.

Mighty Kate is much stronger

than the average person. As a baby,

she lifted her doctor off the ground.

What other baby can do that?

Only Mighty Kate can! Most people

would never think of moving boulders,

but Mighty Kate doesn't break a

sweat as she tosses them aside.

246

An average person would laugh at the idea of lifting a horse and buggy from a ditch, but Mighty Kate does this with one hand. She even squeezes water out of big, soggy logs as easily as wringing water from a wet washcloth. Mighty Kate has the strength of 10,000 men!

Sensory Details
I included words that describe the scene precisely.

Figurative Language
My conclusion uses hyperbole to reinforce Mighty Kate's strength.

Your Turn

Write a narrative describing a "mighty" action performed by Kate. Use figurative language.

Go Digital!
Write your response online.
Use your editing checklist.

W.5.3b, W.5.3d, L.5.5a See the California Standards section.

247

Jimmy Holder

Essential Question

What can you discover when you give things a second look?

Go Digital!

Look Between the Lines

Often we need to look at something a second time to see the whole picture.

▷ At first glance, this is a map of the United States. Now look again. See the trees? This map has been made in an unexpected place!

▷ As you reconsider this photo, notice the light green layer of lines beneath the big map. How do you interpret that picture?

Talk About It
COLLABORATE

Write words you have learned about what we discover from taking a second look. Then talk about the object on the map between California and Arizona.

Discoveries

249

Vocabulary

Use the picture and the sentences to talk with a partner about each word.

astounded

Jada was **astounded** by her high score on the computer game.

What experiences have astounded you?

concealed

The mask **concealed** the identity of the mysterious superhero.

What other ways have people concealed their identities?

inquisitive

Our new pet goldfish caused our cat to become **inquisitive**.

How might an inquisitive person find things out?

interpret

My sister is taking a class to learn to use and **interpret** sign language.

When might someone interpret for you?

perplexed

The complicated math problem **perplexed** Joshua for many hours.

What problems or puzzles have perplexed you the most?

precise

The nurse made a **precise** measurement of June's height.

What other tasks require someone to be precise?

reconsider

After Cara placed her chess piece, Greta had to **reconsider** her next move.

What else might make you reconsider a choice?

suspicious

Fluffy's owner grew **suspicious** when he saw paw prints leading to the chair.

What behavior might make you suspicious of something?

COLLABORATE

Your Turn

Pick three words. Write three questions for your partner to answer.

Go Digital! *Use the online visual glossary*

Where's Brownie?

CAST

SAM and **ALEX JENSEN:** Twin sisters with different personalities. SAM is athletic and outgoing. ALEX is quiet and studious.

NARRATOR: One of the sisters, ten years later.

EVAN: A classmate.

NICK: The building superintendent.

NICKY: Nick's young son.

Essential Question

What can you discover when you give things a second look?

Read about kids who piece together clues to find a missing pet.

Elizabeth Buttler

Scene One

Setting: A two-person bedroom in an apartment. SAM sits at a messy desk, creating a poster. EVAN works at a clean desk. Nearby are an empty terrarium and a paper bag that is wet and torn at the bottom.

Narrator: Whoever claimed that "two heads are better than one" never met my twin sister. Half the time, she makes problems worse rather than better. Like when we lost Brownie, our pet chameleon . . .

(ALEX enters. SAM and EVAN quickly cover up their work.)

Alex: How was the science fair? Did everyone like Brownie?

Sam: They did. Mr. Rollins was **astounded** that my exhibit was so good. *(SAM tries to hide the empty terrarium from ALEX.)*

Alex: So where's Brownie? And why is Evan here?

(EVAN and SAM begin texting on hand-held devices.)

Alex: How should I **interpret** this silence? You're making me feel **suspicious**. And where's Brownie?

Sam: Um, Brownie's missing. But look! Evan and I made these.

*(SAM pulls out a poster she had **concealed** on her desk.)*

Sam: We'll put them up at school tomorrow.

Alex: What makes you think Brownie's back at school?

Sam: Because that's the last place I saw him. In that bag.

Alex: Hey, the bottom of the bag is all wet.

Sam: Maybe it got wet in the lobby. Little Nicky was playing in the fountain with his foldy-paper boat thingies.

Alex: That's *origami*, to be **precise**. Hey! The bag has a rip.

Sam: Rip? I didn't see a rip. Oh, at the bottom.

Alex: Follow me. I think I know where Brownie is!

Narrator: We raced to the lobby. Brownie had been missing for over an hour, but better late than never!

Scene Two

Setting: The lobby of the apartment building. A tall, green, potted plant stands next to a small fountain, where NICKY is playing. ALEX, SAM, and EVAN talk to NICK near a bulletin board.

Nick: So these posters are about your lizard, Brownie. I'm still **perplexed** as to why you think he's down here.

Sam: Because we already checked upstairs.

Alex: Brownie's a chameleon. We think he escaped when Sam set the bag down near the fountain.

Nick: Hey, Nicky! Any brown lizards in the lobby?

Nicky: Nope.

Nick: Maybe you should **reconsider** this and try searching your apartment again.

Evan: Wait a minute. (*checks his device*) It says here that chameleons climb trees.

Nick: Nicky! Any brown lizards in that tree?

Nicky: Nope.

Evan: It also says that chameleons prefer running water, like that fountain.

Nick: Nicky! Any brown lizards in the fountain?

Nicky: Nope.

Nick: What else does that thing say?

Sam: Yeah, **inquisitive** minds want to know.

Alex: (*to SAM*) Don't you want to find Brownie, or are you thinking "out of sight, out of mind"?

Sam: He's just a lizard, Alex. I mean chameleon. It's not exactly "absence makes the heart grow fonder."

Evan: Listen to this! Chameleons change color to match their environments when they're confused or afraid.

Alex: Of course! Nicky, any GREEN lizards over there?

Nicky: (*points into the tree*) There's just that one.

Alex: It's Brownie!

Sam: (*confused*) Brownie has always been brown.

Alex: That's because we put only brown things in his cage, like branches and wood chips.

Evan: Maybe you should buy him a green plant.

Sam: And a little fountain.

Nicky: And boats to go sailing!

Narrator: Well, that's how we found our beloved Brownie, and all was well with the world once more!

Make Connections

How do Alex's and Evan's observations help them find Brownie? ESSENTIAL QUESTION

Think about a time in your life when you had to take a second look at someone or something. What changed between your first and second observations? TEXT TO SELF

Visualize

A play is written to be performed for an audience. When you read a play for the first time, visualizing, or picturing, the scene descriptions, characters, settings, and actions can be helpful.

 ## Find Text Evidence

When you read the setting description for Scene One of the play, "Where's Brownie?" on page 253, you may have to slow down and take time to picture what is happening.

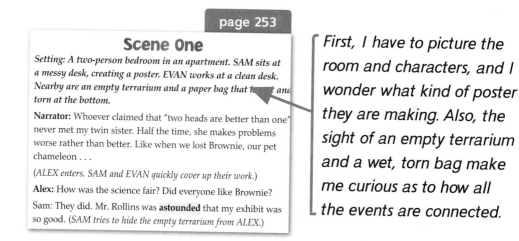

page 253

Scene One

Setting: A two-person bedroom in an apartment. SAM sits at a messy desk, creating a poster. EVAN works at a clean desk. Nearby are an empty terrarium and a paper bag that is wet and torn at the bottom.

Narrator: Whoever claimed that "two heads are better than one" never met my twin sister. Half the time, she makes problems worse rather than better. Like when we lost Brownie, our pet chameleon . . .

(ALEX enters. SAM and EVAN quickly cover up their work.)

Alex: How was the science fair? Did everyone like Brownie?

Sam: They did. Mr. Rollins was **astounded** that my exhibit was so good. *(SAM tries to hide the empty terrarium from ALEX.)*

First, I have to picture the room and characters, and I wonder what kind of poster they are making. Also, the sight of an empty terrarium and a wet, torn bag make me curious as to how all the events are connected.

Your Turn

COLLABORATE

Why is it important that Nicky is playing near the fountain in Scene Two? Visualize the events to help you. As you read, remember to use the strategy Visualize.

Point of View

In a play, a character who delivers a particular line of dialogue from his or her own point of view is called a **speaker**. In some plays, one speaker may be a **narrator**, who provides information from a point outside of the main action of the play.

 Find Text Evidence

From the first speech of "Where's Brownie?" on page 253, I see a narrator looking back in time to an experience involving her twin sister and a lost pet. This means that she has firsthand knowledge of what happened. I can probably trust what she has to say.

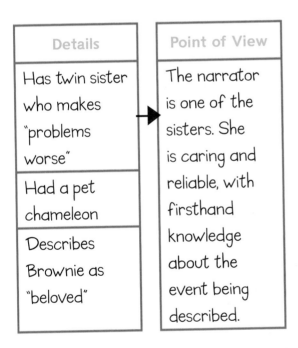

Details	Point of View
Has twin sister who makes "problems worse"	The narrator is one of the sisters. She is caring and reliable, with firsthand knowledge about the event being described.
Had a pet chameleon	
Describes Brownie as "beloved"	

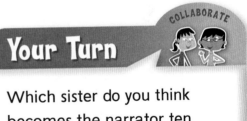

Your Turn

Which sister do you think becomes the narrator ten years after the events of the play? Select details that support your answer to place in your graphic organizer.

Go Digital!
Use the interactive graphic organizer

Mystery

The selection "Where's Brownie?" is a mystery play.

Mystery plays:

- Center on a mystery that must be solved using clues
- Are made up mostly of dialogue among characters
- Contain scenes, setting details, and stage directions

Find Text Evidence

I can tell that "Where's Brownie?" is a mystery play. It begins with a cast of characters and a description of the setting. It also includes stage directions that tell what the characters are doing. Through dialogue, the characters realize their pet is missing. They begin to look for clues to solve the mystery.

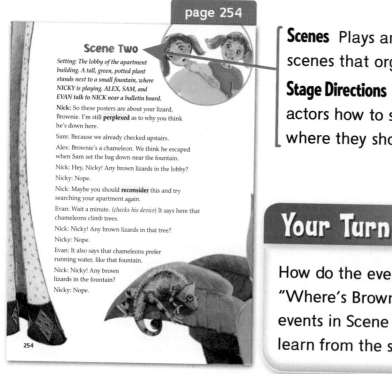

page 254

Scene Two

Setting: *The lobby of the apartment building. A tall, green, potted plant stands next to a small fountain, where NICKY is playing. ALEX, SAM, and EVAN talk to NICK near a bulletin board.*

Nick: So these posters are about your lizard, Brownie. I'm still **perplexed** as to why you think he's down here.

Sam: Because we already checked upstairs.

Alex: Brownie's a chameleon. We think he escaped when Sam set the bag down near the fountain.

Nick: Hey, Nicky! Any brown lizards in the lobby?

Nicky: Nope.

Nick: Maybe you should **reconsider** this and try searching your apartment again.

Evan: Wait a minute. *(checks his device)* It says here that chameleons climb trees.

Nick: Nicky! Any brown lizards in that tree?

Nicky: Nope.

Evan: It also says that chameleons prefer running water, like that fountain.

Nick: Nicky! Any brown lizards in the fountain?

Nicky: Nope.

254

Scenes Plays are often divided into scenes that organize the story.

Stage Directions Stage directions tell actors how to speak dialogue and where they should move.

COLLABORATE

Your Turn

How do the events in Scene 1 of "Where's Brownie?" lead to the events in Scene 2? What do you learn from the stage directions?

Adages and Proverbs

Adages and proverbs are traditional sayings that are often repeated. You can usually use surrounding words and sentences to help you understand the meaning of an unfamiliar saying.

 Find Text Evidence

On page 253, the narrator of "Where's Brownie?" disagrees with an adage, "Two heads are better than one." It must be a common saying. In this case, the "two heads" are her own and that of her twin. Since her twin "makes problems worse rather than better," the narrator probably prefers to figure out things on her own.

Narrator: Whoever claimed that "two heads are better than one" never met my twin sister.

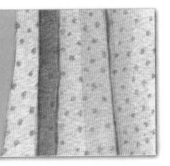

Your Turn COLLABORATE

Use context clues and other textual evidence to explain the meanings of the following adages and proverbs from "Where's Brownie?"

better late than never, *page 253*

out of sight, out of mind, *page 255*

absence makes the heart grow fonder, *page 255*

Elizabeth Buttler

Write About the Text

Reggie

I responded to the prompt: *Add additional dialogue between Sam and Alex into Scene One. Have them discuss their terrarium exhibit in more detail.*

Student Model: *Narrative Text*

Alex: So, what did Mr. Rollins like about your terrarium?

Sam: He liked the miniature waterfall and all of the different plants, rocks, and mosses.

Alex: It's like a playground for a chameleon.

Sam: Yep! Mr. Rollins wanted to know

Descriptive Details
I included concrete details to show how the terrarium looks.

Figurative Language
I used a simile to compare a terrarium with a playground.

how I came up with the idea. I told

him it was easy. I asked myself what I

would want if I were a chameleon.

Alex: Ha ha. You're hilarious.

Sam: He's getting his classroom a

terrarium and wants my help.

Alex: That's awesome! You may have

found your calling, Sam.

Grammar

This is an example of a **reflexive pronoun**.

Grammar Handbook
See page 463.

Develop Characters
I showed the friendship between Alex and Sam through dialogue.

Your Turn

Write a short Scene Three with Sam and Alex. Have them discuss a plan to keep track of Brownie in the future. Use details from the play.

Go Digital!
Write your response online.
Use your editing checklist.

Elizabeth Buttler

Essential Question

What can people do to bring about a positive change?

Go Digital!

MR. PRESIDENT
HOW LONG
MUST
WOMEN WAIT
FOR LIBERTY

U OF MO.

WASHINGTON
COLLEGE of LAW

LELAND
STANFORD

SL.5.1c See the California Standards section.

Everett Collection/SuperStock

Changing Times

Throughout history, outspoken citizens have challenged laws and practices they believe to be wrong and unfair. Many social movements have brought about positive changes.

▶ At one time, women in the United States did not have the right to vote in elections. They wanted to change this.

▶ For many years, women marched to defy the old law. Finally, in 1920, women won the right to vote!

Talk About It

Write words you have learned about taking action. Then talk about another way to bring about a positive change.

Take Action

Vocabulary

Use the picture and the sentences to talk with a
partner about each word.

anticipation

The goalie waited with **anticipation** as
the ball came toward her.

Describe something that you have
waited for with anticipation.

defy

If you **defy** a driving rule, a police
officer may give you a ticket.

Why might someone defy a rule or law?

entitled

The library card **entitled** Matt to check
out a book.

What phrase has the same meaning
as entitled?

neutral

An umpire must stay **neutral** when
making a call on a play.

Why must an umpire or referee stay
neutral during a game?

outspoken

Henry and Jake are **outspoken** about protecting the environment.

What word has the opposite meaning of outspoken?

reserved

Parking lots keep spaces **reserved** for handicapped parking.

What other kinds of things can be reserved?

sought

Josie's group **sought** the latest team rankings in the sports section.

Name something that you sought and were able to find.

unequal

The number of players on the tug-of-war teams was **unequal**.

If two teams are unequal, what might the game be like?

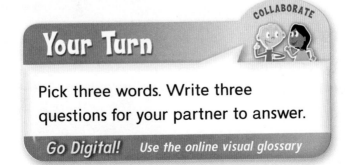

Your Turn

COLLABORATE

Pick three words. Write three questions for your partner to answer.

Go Digital! *Use the online visual glossary*

FREDERICK DOUGLASS

Freedom's Voice

Essential Question

What can people do to bring about a positive change?

Read about what Frederick Douglass did to bring about positive change for African Americans.

Growing Up with Slavery

When Frederick Douglass was growing up in Maryland, he never could have imagined that he would become a great civil rights leader. Born Frederick Bailey, he was enslaved, or living in slavery, until the age of twenty. Frederick's life was difficult. He never knew his father and was separated from his mother at a young age. If he dared to **defy** his "master" in any way, he was punished. One of the few bright spots of his youth was being taught to read by the wife of a slave holder. Perhaps it was his love of words, along with his courage, that inspired Frederick to reach for the kind of life he was **entitled** to have.

A Life-Changing Speech

In 1838 Frederick **sought** his freedom by escaping to the North. In New York City, he married Anna Murray. Then he and Anna moved to New Bedford, Massachusetts.

In New Bedford, Frederick changed his last name to Douglass to protect himself against slave catchers. That was just the first of many changes. He also discovered a group of people—abolitionists—who shared his hope of ending slavery. He had read about the abolition movement in William Lloyd Garrison's newspaper, *The Liberator*. Frederick devoured every issue because the ideas inspired him so much. Soon he began speaking against slavery at the church meetings he attended.

▼ This etching depicts a slave auction, a common event of the time.

New Opportunities

In 1841, The Massachusetts Anti-Slavery Society held a meeting in Nantucket. Frederick was eager to hear the abolitionist speakers and traveled to the meeting with **anticipation**. However, when he arrived, something totally unexpected happened. An abolitionist who had heard Frederick speak at a church meeting asked him to speak to this large gathering!

Frederick went to the front of the meeting hall, trembling with fright. At first, he spoke quietly and hesitantly. He felt anxious standing in front of so many people— especially white people! However, once he got started, his fear evaporated. He spoke from his heart, describing the horrors of slavery. Frederick was a stirring speaker, articulate and **outspoken**. At the end of his speech, the audience's reaction was spontaneous— suddenly everyone stood up and cheered! Among those cheering was none other than William Lloyd Garrison.

After the meeting, Garrison congratulated Frederick and offered him a job as a speaker for the Society. Frederick agreed and was hired as a full-time lecturer. He felt he had found a purpose for his life.

Frederick traveled through New England and the Midwest, giving passionate speeches that captivated audiences. It was impossible to listen to his powerful words and remain **neutral**. Frederick had a commanding presence and spoke with eloquence and dignity. He was making a name for himself.

Making His Mark

In addition to giving speeches, Frederick had time **reserved** for his writing. In 1845 he wrote an autobiography, *Narrative of the Life of Frederick Douglass, an American Slave.* The book became a huge success, making him even more famous.

In his autobiography, Frederick revealed that he was a fugitive. For his safety, friends suggested that he go on a speaking tour in Great Britain. Frederick was very popular there, and people lined up to hear him speak.

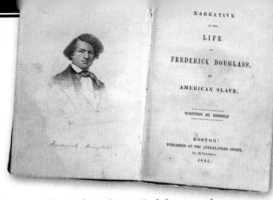

▲ Douglass's autobiography helped advance abolition.

In 1847 Frederick returned to the United States. By now, he had a family and missed them terribly. Upon his return, they moved to Rochester, New York, where Frederick started his own abolitionist newspaper. *The North Star* was an unusual newspaper. It published articles not only about the antislavery cause, but also about the **unequal** status of women. Frederick also worked tirelessly to end segregation in Rochester's schools.

THE NORTH STAR.

▲
The North Star was the newspaper published by Frederick Douglass and his wife.

Make Connections

Talk about what Frederick Douglass did to bring about positive change for African Americans. ESSENTIAL QUESTION

When have you worked to bring about positive change? What was the result? TEXT TO SELF

Summarize

When you summarize, you sort the most important ideas and key details and retell them in your own words. This helps you recognize and remember what you have learned. Summaries should include facts, and not opinions about the content.

Find Text Evidence

To make sure you understand the most important details of the first section of "Frederick Douglass: Freedom's Voice" on page 267, you can summarize the most important points.

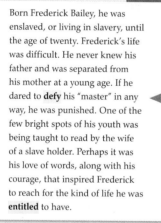

page 267

Born Frederick Bailey, he was enslaved, or living in slavery, until the age of twenty. Frederick's life was difficult. He never knew his father and was separated from his mother at a young age. If he dared to **defy** his "master" in any way, he was punished. One of the few bright spots of his youth was being taught to read by the wife of a slave holder. Perhaps it was his love of words, along with his courage, that inspired Frederick to reach for the kind of life he was **entitled** to have.

Frederick Douglass spent the first twenty years of his life in slavery. He was sent away from his mother at an early age, was punished by his "master," and was taught to read by a slave holder's wife. Learning to read inspired him.

Your Turn

COLLABORATE

Use the most important ideas and key details to summarize the rest of the biography. As you read other selections, remember to use the strategy Summarize.

Author's Point of View

An **author's point of view** is the author's attitude toward the person or subject he or she is writing about. You can figure out an author's point of view by looking at the details, descriptions, and the reasons and evidence for points the author makes.

 ## Find Text Evidence

On page 267, the author's words tell that she thinks highly of Frederick. She says that coming from slavery and learning to read are two reasons that he became a great civil rights leader.

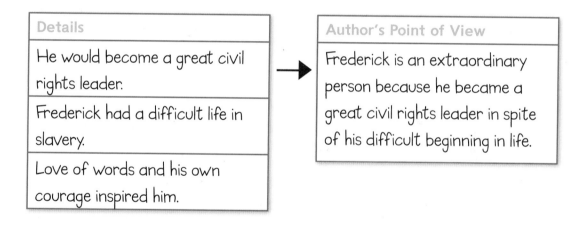

Details
He would become a great civil rights leader.
Frederick had a difficult life in slavery.
Love of words and his own courage inspired him.

Author's Point of View
Frederick is an extraordinary person because he became a great civil rights leader in spite of his difficult beginning in life.

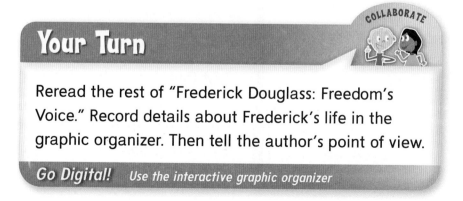

COLLABORATE

Your Turn

Reread the rest of "Frederick Douglass: Freedom's Voice." Record details about Frederick's life in the graphic organizer. Then tell the author's point of view.

Go Digital! *Use the interactive graphic organizer*

Biography

"Frederick Douglass: Freedom's Voice" is a biography.

A biography:
- Tells facts about the life of a real person
- Describes the person's talents and achievements
- Is often written in logical order
- Often includes photographs and captions

Find Text Evidence

I can tell that "Frederick Douglass: Freedom's Voice" is a biography. Frederick Douglass was a real person, and the photographs show real people and events. The selection tells about his talents and achievements, and the events are told in a logical order.

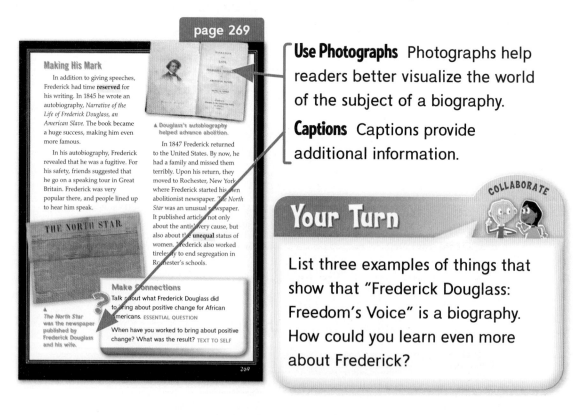

page 269

Making His Mark

In addition to giving speeches, Frederick had time **reserved** for his writing. In 1845 he wrote an autobiography, *Narrative of the Life of Frederick Douglass, an American Slave.* The book became a huge success, making him even more famous.

In his autobiography, Frederick revealed that he was a fugitive. For his safety, friends suggested that he go on a speaking tour in Great Britain. Frederick was very popular there, and people lined up to hear him speak.

▲ Douglass's autobiography helped advance abolition.

In 1847 Frederick returned to the United States. By now, he had a family and missed them terribly. Upon his return, they moved to Rochester, New York, where Frederick started his own abolitionist newspaper. *The North Star* was an unusual newspaper. It published articles not only about the antislavery cause, but also about the **unequal** status of women. Frederick also worked tirelessly to end segregation in Rochester's schools.

The North Star was the newspaper published by Frederick Douglass and his wife.

Make Connections

Talk about what Frederick Douglass did to bring about positive change for African Americans. ESSENTIAL QUESTION

When have you worked to bring about positive change? What was the result? TEXT TO SELF

269

Use Photographs Photographs help readers better visualize the world of the subject of a biography.

Captions Captions provide additional information.

COLLABORATE

Your Turn

List three examples of things that show that "Frederick Douglass: Freedom's Voice" is a biography. How could you learn even more about Frederick?

Prefixes and Suffixes

Prefixes are added to the beginnings of words and change their meanings. The prefix *un-* means "not," as in *unsure*. The prefix *en-* means "to make," as in *enlarge*. **Suffixes** are added to the ends of words and change their meanings. For example, the suffix *-ly* means "in a specified manner," as in *slowly*. The suffixes *-er* and *-or* mean "a person who," as in *writer* and *actor*.

 Find Text Evidence

When I read the word enslaved *in the first paragraph of "Frederick Douglass: Freedom's Voice" on page 267, I can use the prefix* en- *to figure out the meaning of the word. Since* en- *means "to make,"* enslaved *must mean "made a slave."*

> "Born Frederick Bailey, he was enslaved, or living in slavery, until the age of twenty."

COLLABORATE

Your Turn

Use the prefix or suffix as a clue to help you figure out the meanings of the following words from "Frederick Douglass: Freedom's Voice."

Liberator, *page 267*
unexpected, *page 268*
hesitantly, *page 268*

Write About the Text

Pages 266–269

Brandon

I answered the question: *Why did the author write this text using sequence as the primary text structure?*

Grammar

The **pronoun-verb contraction** *he'd* is a combination of the words *he* and *had*.

Grammar Handbook
See page 464.

Student Model: *Informative Text*

The author used sequence to show how Frederick Douglass's life changed as he grew older. As a child, Frederick lived in slavery. He escaped enslavement in 1838. Many changes followed, and in 1841 he'd given an abolitionist speech that led to a job as a full-time lecturer.

Develop a Topic
I included facts and details from the text.

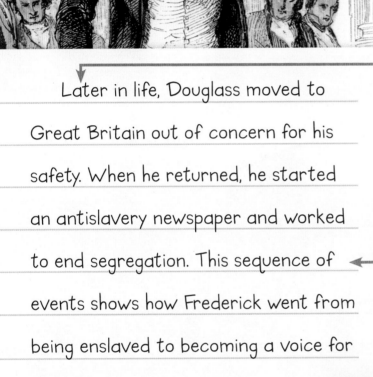

Later in life, Douglass moved to Great Britain out of concern for his safety. When he returned, he started an antislavery newspaper and worked to end segregation. This sequence of events shows how Frederick went from being enslaved to becoming a voice for African American freedom.

Logical Order
I used signal words to show the sequence of events.

Strong Conclusion
My last sentence summarizes my response and restates the main idea.

Your Turn

How did the events in Frederick Douglass's early life shape his adult life? Use text evidence.

Go Digital!
Write your response online.
Use your editing checklist.

North Wind Picture Archives/Alamy

SL.5.lc See the California Standards section.

Essential EARTH

Water. Trees. Land. Oil. Minerals. These are just a few of the earth's valuable natural resources.

▶ Salt is one of our most important natural resources. In this salt marsh, people work to extract salt from the water.

▶ Natural resources are a necessity for us, but many are limited. As people use natural resources, they must remember to conserve and protect them, too.

Talk About It

Talk about words you have learned about the value of natural resources. Then talk about a natural resource you could not live without.

Natural Resources

Vocabulary

Use the picture and the sentences to talk with a partner about each word.

absorb

A sponge will **absorb**, or soak up, the spilled coffee.

What else will absorb the liquid?

affect

Adding honey will **affect** the sweetness of the cereal.

How will adding salt affect a food?

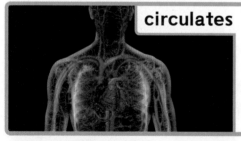

circulates

Blood **circulates** from the heart through the body and back to the heart.

What else do you know of that circulates?

conserve

I **conserve** energy by turning off lights when I leave a room.

What is an antonym for conserve?

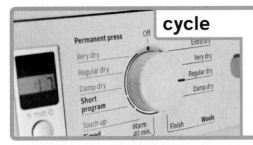

cycle

When the dryer completes its **cycle**, I will remove the clothes.

What other kinds of cycles can you think of?

glaciers

Huge **glaciers** made of thick ice can be found in freezing waters.

What would happen if the glaciers melted?

necessity

A guide dog or cane is a **necessity** to help visually impaired people cross a street.

What tool is a necessity for helping deaf people communicate?

seeps

The latex from the rubber tree **seeps**, or flows slowly, into a bucket.

If water seeps up from the ground, how quickly will it spread?

COLLABORATE

Your Turn

Pick three words. Write three questions for your partner to answer.

Go Digital! *Use the online visual glossary*

Power from NATURE

Wind turbines are placed in open areas.

? **Essential Question**

Why are natural resources valuable?

Read about the ways natural resources provide energy.

Renewable and Nonrenewable Energy

Click! You just turned on a lamp. A faraway power plant most likely supplied the electricity for that lamp by burning coal. Coal, which has to be extracted from deep within the earth, is a natural resource.

Natural resources are nature's gifts, the riches that exist in the natural world. They include metals and minerals, along with vegetation, soil, and animals in the wild. They include the things that are a **necessity** for all life—water, air, and sunlight.

One important use for natural resources is to provide energy. Energy makes things work. It runs our cars, computers, heating and cooling systems, kitchen appliances, telephones, televisions, and industrial machinery. Where do we get all this energy? Natural resources serve as energy sources.

Energy sources are divided into two categories. Renewable energy sources—such as sunlight and wind—can be renewed, or continuously refilled. They do not run out. In contrast, nonrenewable energy sources can be depleted, or used up. Coal, natural gas, and oil—also called petroleum—fall into this category. Only a limited amount of these substances, called fossil fuels, exists. Nuclear energy is also nonrenewable because it requires uranium. Amounts of uranium are finite, or limited.

Cooling towers at a nuclear facility

A natural gas pipeline

From the start of human history, people used renewable energy. For example, sails captured wind to move ships, and wood was burned to cook food. Then, about 150 years ago, human energy needs exploded. New machines required more energy. New ways to harness, or control, energy for use had to be developed. From the 19th century on, most energy has come from nonrenewable sources.

Challenges and Problems

Nonrenewable energy has filled our needs on a huge scale. However, satisfying our energy hunger has been challenging. Supplies of coal, natural gas, oil, and uranium are buried underground. They must be discovered and extracted. Also, human technology is needed to transform natural resources into usable forms of energy. For example, gasoline has to be manufactured from oil and then delivered to customers.

Although nonrenewable energy sources have filled our needs, continuing to use them poses problems. They not only can run out but also can pollute the environment. Burning coal produces gases that can poison the air. Some scientists argue that these gases have heated up our atmosphere. They say global warming will **affect** our climate so dramatically that **glaciers** will melt and sea levels will rise.

In addition, it is not just our atmosphere that can be polluted. Oil from spills often **seeps** into the ocean. Extracting natural gas can pollute a site's surroundings. Nuclear energy creates dangerous waste.

U.S. Energy Use from 1949–2010

Types of Energy, Percentage of Energy Used by Year (approximate)

SOURCE OF ENERGY	1949	1969	1989	2010
Fossil Fuels	91%	93%	86%	83%
Nuclear Power	0%	1%	6%	9%
Renewable Energy	9%	6%	8%	8%

What are solutions to our energy challenges? We must find some answers. One possibility is a return to renewable energy, which generally causes less pollution than fossil fuels. However, renewable energy is currently expensive and complex to harness on a large scale.

Solutions for the Future

Solar power, or power from the sun, shows promise. Solar panels on houses can **absorb** the sun's energy to provide heat. Nonetheless, because Earth rotates on its axis and **circulates** in a yearly **cycle** around the sun, the sun's energy is less available at certain times and seasons and in different places. It will take innovation and investment to maximize our use of solar power and other renewable energy.

Solar panels on the roof help provide heat and electricity.

We also can learn to use nonrenewable energy more wisely. Government and private industry have a role to play in protecting our natural resources and in reducing pollution. Moreover, individuals can try to **conserve** energy. We can remember to turn off lights, TVs, computers, and other devices when we are not using them. Small personal efforts can add up to big changes in our energy future.

Oil rigs for drilling oil are often found offshore.

Make Connections

Talk about some of the ways natural resources are valuable. **ESSENTIAL QUESTION**

What ways does the text suggest that individuals can save energy? What are some other things you can do personally to save energy? **TEXT TO SELF**

(bkgd) morkeman/Vetta/Getty Images; (t) David J. Green/Alamy

Summarize

To summarize a text, include the most important ideas and key details, use your own words, and organize information in a logical way. Summaries do not include your own opinions or unimportant details. Summarizing helps you check your understanding and remember what you read.

 Find Text Evidence

You can check your understanding of the section "Renewable and Nonrenewable Energy" on page 281 by summarizing.

> **page 281**
>
> Natural resources are nature's gifts, the riches that exist in the natural world. They include metals and minerals, along with vegetation, soil, and animals in the wild. They include the things that are a **necessity** for all life—water, air, and sunlight.

First, I'm going to identify the section's main idea. I see that all the sentences are about natural resources and energy. Next, I see the key details are about renewable and nonrenewable sources.

Your Turn

COLLABORATE

With a partner, summarize the information in the first paragraph of "Challenges and Problems" on page 282.

Author's Point of View

Understanding an author's point of view on a topic can help you understand the author's purpose for writing. Details and word choice can give you clues to the author's position. You can also ask: *What reasons and evidence does the author use?*

 Find Text Evidence

In the section "Challenges and Problems" on page 282, the author talks about our energy hunger. Hunger *is a powerful word that suggests how much we want energy. The author's point of view is stated directly:* Continuing to use nonrenewable energy sources poses problems. *Evidence about coal and oil supports this.*

Details
Burning coal poisons the air.
Oil spills can seep into the ocean.

➡

Author's Point of View
There are problems with using nonrenewable energy sources.

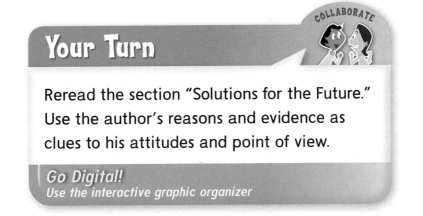

Your Turn

COLLABORATE

Reread the section "Solutions for the Future." Use the author's reasons and evidence as clues to his attitudes and point of view.

Go Digital!
Use the interactive graphic organizer

Expository Text

The selection "Power from Nature" is an expository text.

Expository text:
- Explains a topic
- Supports specific points with reasons and evidence
- Presents information in a logical order
- May include text features such as charts

Find Text Evidence

I can tell "Power from Nature" is an expository text. The selection explains why natural resources are valuable, especially as an energy source. It supports particular points in a logical way with reasons and evidence. A chart adds information.

page 282

From the start of human history, people used renewable energy. For example, sails captured wind to move ships, and wood was burned to cook food. Then, about 150 years ago, human energy needs exploded. New machines required more energy. New ways to harness, or control, energy for use had to be developed. From the 19th century on, most energy has come from nonrenewable sources.

Challenges and Problems

Nonrenewable energy has filled our needs on a huge scale. However, satisfying our energy hunger has been challenging. Supplies of coal, natural gas, oil, and uranium are buried underground. They must be discovered and extracted. Also, human technology is needed to transform natural resources into usable forms of energy. For example, gasoline has to be manufactured from oil and then delivered to customers.

Although nonrenewable energy sources have filled our needs, continuing to use them poses problems. They not only can run out but also can pollute the environment. Burning coal produces gases that can poison the air. Some scientists argue that these gases have heated up our atmosphere. They say global warming will **affect** our climate so dramatically that **glaciers** will melt and sea levels will rise.

In addition, it is not just our atmosphere that can be polluted. Oil from spills often seeps into the ocean. Extracting natural gas can pollute a site's surroundings. Nuclear energy creates dangerous waste.

U.S. Energy Use from 1949–2010

Types of Energy, Percentage of Energy Used by Year (approximate)

SOURCE OF ENERGY	1949	1969	1989	2010
Fossil Fuels	91%	93%	86%	83%
Nuclear Power	0%	1%	6%	9%
Renewable Energy	9%	6%	8%	8%

282

Chart A chart presents facts visually to allow readers to compare and contrast information, reading from top to bottom and from left to right. A title tells what the chart is about.

COLLABORATE

Your Turn

Use the chart's title, headings, and numbers to figure out its purpose. How has the use of renewable energy changed over time?

Context Clues

When you read an unfamiliar or multiple meaning word, sometimes a **definition** or **restatement** of the word appears in the same sentence or in a nearby sentence. A comma followed by *or* can be a clue to an upcoming definition or restatement.

Find Text Evidence

In the section "Renewable and Nonrenewable Energy," the words renewable, renewed, *and* nonrenewable *are unfamiliar. I notice that a comma and the words* or continuously refilled *follow the word* renewed. *This can help me define all three words.*

Energy sources are divided into two categories. Renewable energy sources—such as sunlight and wind—can be renewed, or continuously refilled.

Your Turn

COLLABORATE

Use context clues to figure out the meaning of the following words in "Power from Nature":

depleted, *page 281*
finite, *page 281*
harness, *page 282*

John A. Karachewski

Write About the Text

Natalie

I answered the question: *What is the best solution for our future energy needs? Use text evidence.*

Student Model: *Opinion*

I think the best solution for our future energy needs is to use solar and wind power. Both sunlight and wind are renewable energy sources that will not run out. In contrast, nonrenewable energy sources, such as coal and oil, must be located and extracted from underground.

Strong Opening
My first sentence clearly states my opinion.

Transitions
I included the phrase *in contrast* to signal a difference between the two types of energy.

Mark Bowden/iStock/360/Getty Images

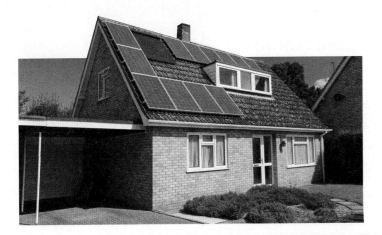

Supplies of nonrenewable energy resources are limited and can run out. They create pollution, poison the air, and may cause global warming. Solar and wind power do not cause these problems, and their supplies refill every day! They are the best solution for our future energy needs.

Reasons and Evidence

I used facts and details from the text.

Grammar

A **possessive pronoun** shows who or what owns something.

Grammar Handbook See page 465.

Your Turn

Did the author do a good job convincing readers that we need to use renewable sources of energy? Use text evidence.

Go Digital!
Write your response online.
Use your editing checklist.

David J. Green/Alamy

Essential Question

How do you express something that is important to you?

Go Digital!

COLOR YOUR WORLD

Writing, acting, painting, dancing, playing music—these are all ways you express things that are meaningful to you.

▶ Drawing and painting are my favorite forms of expression.

▶ I wanted to share my ideas about life in a way that others could enjoy. It's amazing how much one picture can say!

Talk About It

Write words you have learned about expressing yourself. Then talk about how you have expressed something that is important to you.

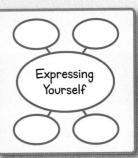

Expressing Yourself

Vocabulary

Use the picture and the sentences to talk with a
partner about each word.

barren

We traveled across **barren** land without
seeing a single tree or bush.

What is another word or phrase for
barren?

expression

James wrote songs as an **expression** of
his beliefs about friendship.

Name another form of artistic
expression.

meaningful

The students had a **meaningful** discussion
about how to protect the environment.

What meaningful discussions have you
had?

plumes

Each year, peacocks shed their beautiful
tail **plumes** and grow new ones.

What beautiful plumes you have seen?

Poetry Terms

lyric

Some poets write **lyric** poetry that describes their feelings about nature and seasons.

Would you prefer to read a lyric poem about spring or fall?

alliteration

"Lou's lamb" shows **alliteration** because the same consonant sound begins two or more words.

Give another example of alliteration, using any consonant.

meter

Rita tapped her fingers in rhythm to the **meter** of the poem as she read it aloud.

Tap out the meter of the nursery rhyme, "Jack and Jill."

stanza

In some poems, each **stanza** may have four lines.

Recite a stanza from a favorite poem or song.

Your Turn

COLLABORATE

Pick three words and write a question about each for your partner to answer.

Go Digital!   *Use the online visual glossary*

How Do I Hold the Summer?

The sun is setting sooner now,
   My swimsuit's packed away.
How do I hold the summer fast,
   Or ask it, please, to stay?

The lake like cold, forbidding glass—
   The last sailboat has crossed.
Green leaves, gone gold, fall, float away—
   Here's winter's veil of frost.

Essential Question

How do you express something that is important to you?

Read three ways that poets express what matters to them.

I thought of ice and barren limbs—
    Last winter's snow so deep!
I know I cannot ball up light,
    And green grass just won't keep,

So I'll search for signs of summer,
    Hold memories of each—
Soft plumes of brown pressed in a book,
    The pit of one ripe peach,

Each instance of a cricket's chirp,
    And every bird's sweet call,
And store them up in a poem to read
    When snow begins to fall.

— Maya Jones

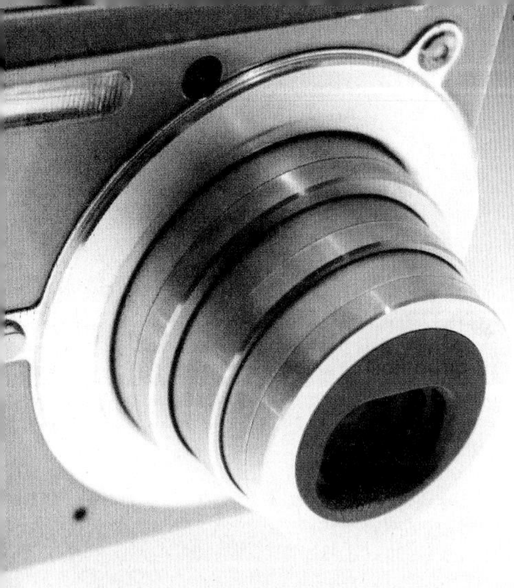

Catching a Fly

It lighted, uninvited
upon the china plate
next to the peas.

No hand I raised
nor finger flicked
but rather found a lens

framed, focused,
zoomed in, held
the hands, still–

the appearance of hands,
like two fine threads, caught
plotting, planning–

greedy goggle eyes, webbed wings
like me, invading–
but no time to pause, he'd go–

and right at the last
instead of a swat,
I snapped!

– Ken Kines

(t) Perry Hanson Concepts/Alamy; (bl) Stockbyte/Getty Images; (br) Noam Armonn/Alamy

WHEN I DANCE

Always wanna break out,
   use my arms and legs
     to shout!

On any dark day
   that doesn't go
     exactly my way—

I bust a move,
   get a groove,
     feet feel the ground—

That slap's
   the only sound
     slap, pound

my body needs to charge,
   I play my tracks,
     I make it large

to take myself away!
   Nothing else
     I need to say.

— T. C. Arcaro

Make Connections

Talk about what the speaker of each poem wants to express. How does each express it? ESSENTIAL QUESTION

Compare the forms of expression in the poems to the way you express what is important to you. TEXT TO SELF

Tiffani Bearup/Flickr/Getty Images

Lyric and Free Verse

Lyric poetry: • Expresses the poet's thoughts and feelings, often in a regular meter, or pattern of sounds. • May be arranged in stanzas • May contain rhyme and alliteration.

Free verse: • Expresses a poet's ideas and feelings with carefully chosen words. • Has no set rhyming pattern, meter, or line length. • May include alliteration and stanzas.

Find Text Evidence

I can tell that "How Do I Hold the Summer?" is a lyric poem because it expresses the poet's thoughts and feelings. It also includes rhyme, a regular meter, stanzas, and alliteration.

page 294

CCSS Shared Read ⟩ Genre • Poetry

How Do I Hold the Summer?

The sun is setting sooner now,
My swimsuit's packed away.
How do I hold the summer fast,
Or ask it, please, to stay?

The lake like cold, forbidding glass—
The last sailboat has sailed.
Green leaves, gone gold, fall, float away—
Here's winter's veil of frost.

Essential Question
How do you express something that is important to you?
Read three ways that poets express what matters to them.

The poem expresses feelings and includes rhyme.

The poem contains alliteration, with words that begin with the consonants g and f.

COLLABORATE

Your Turn

Reread the poems "Catching a Fly" and "When I Dance." Decide whether each poem is an example of lyric or free verse poetry. What elements do you see in each?

Theme

The **theme** of a poem is the message, or big idea, that the poet wishes to communicate. Identifying poetic elements and key details can help you determine a poem's theme.

Find Text Evidence

All three poems have speakers who express something important to them, but each poem has a specific theme. I'll reread "How Do I Hold the Summer?" and look for key details to determine its theme.

> **Detail**
>
> How do I hold the summer fast,
> Or ask it, please, to stay?

⬇

> **Detail**
>
> So I'll search for signs of summer,

⬇

> **Detail**
>
> And store them up in a poem to read/When snow begins to fall.

⬇

> **Theme**
>
> Good memories can be saved and revisited by recording our feelings about them in a poem.

Your Turn

Reread the poem "When I Dance." List key details in the graphic organizer. Use the details to figure out the theme of the poem.

Go Digital!
Use the interactive graphic organizer

Stanza and Meter

Poets often arrange their poems into **stanzas**, or groups of lines. Each stanza is a unit, or section, of the poem that expresses a key idea. Together these ideas help form a poem's main message. Poets may also use **meter**, also called rhythm, which is a regular pattern of sounds in a line.

 Find Text Evidence

Reread the poem "How Do I Hold the Summer?" on pages 294 and 295. Identify the stanzas in the poem and think about how they are alike.

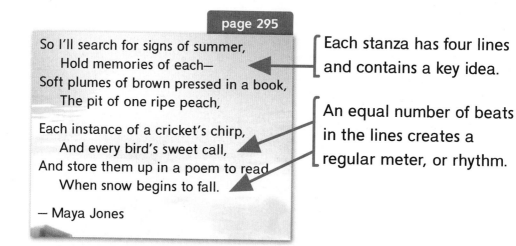

page 295

So I'll search for signs of summer,
　Hold memories of each—
Soft plumes of brown pressed in a book,
　The pit of one ripe peach,

Each instance of a cricket's chirp,
　And every bird's sweet call,
And store them up in a poem to read
　When snow begins to fall.

— Maya Jones

Each stanza has four lines and contains a key idea.

An equal number of beats in the lines creates a regular meter, or rhythm.

Your Turn

COLLABORATE

Identify the key idea of each stanza of "How Do I Hold the Summer?" How do these ideas help form the poem's main message?

Simile and Metaphor

A **simile** makes a comparison, using the words *like* or *as*: "legs like sticks." A **metaphor** makes a comparison without using the words *like* or *as*: "stick legs."

 Find Text Evidence

The fourth stanza of "Catching a Fly" has a simile using the word like: hands, like two fine threads. *The fly's front legs appear to be like long, thin hands. In the fifth stanza, the metaphor "greedy goggle eyes" compares the fly's eyes to goggles, focused on food.*

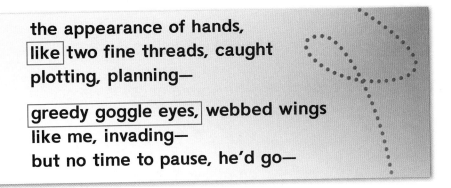

the appearance of hands,
⬚like⬚ two fine threads, caught
plotting, planning—

⬚greedy goggle eyes,⬚ webbed wings
like me, invading—
but no time to pause, he'd go—

 **Your Turn**

COLLABORATE

Read the following simile and metaphor from "How Do I Hold the Summer?" What comparison does the simile make? What picture does the metaphor create?

The lake like cold, forbidding glass, *page 294*
Here's winter's veil of frost. *page 294*

Pages 294–297

Write About the Text

Esther

I responded to the prompt: *Write a free-verse poem about your favorite season. Include several descriptive adjectives in your poem.*

Student Model: *Narrative Text*

Sensory Language
I used vivid words to create a concrete image in readers' minds.

Grammar

This is an example of a **homophone**.

Grammar Handbook See page 465.

Spring Is My Thing

I hear the birds begin to sing,

and know that spring is here.

The young grass is as green

as it's ever been,

or at least in about a year!

Cold winter, hot summer, chilly fall

are just so-so with me, all in all.

It's the blue, spring skies ◄

that are my invite

to watch festive, fabulous flowers ◄

bloom and delight.

Your Turn

Write a free-verse poem about your favorite after-school activity. Include several descriptive adjectives in your poem.

Go Digital!
Write your response online.
Use your editing checklist.

Tiffani Bearup/Flickr/Getty Images

What's Next?

The BIG Idea

In what ways can things change?

surprising sunlight—
yesterday a maple tree
where my father stands

metamorphosis—
look, caterpillar, how much
we will learn today

the longer you look
at the meadow, the more birds
you will hear singing

—Jean LeBlanc

Essential Question

What experiences can change the way you see yourself and the world around you?

Go Digital!

SL.5.lc See the California Standards section.

Alan Schein Photography/Terra/Corbis

The View from Here

When you walk down the street, a city like this appears one way. When you go high up, your perspective of the same city changes.

▶ From the top of this skyscraper in New York City, a visitor can see how tall, vast, and bustling with people this big city is!

▶ In the transition back to the ground, you may see the city streets in a whole new way, too!

Talk About It

COLLABORATE

Write words you have learned about how you can change your perspective. Then talk about one experience that made you see the world in a new way.

New perspectoves

Vocabulary

Use the picture and the sentences to talk with a
partner about each word.

disdain

Rebecca likes to eat many vegetables,
but she always shows **disdain** for
broccoli.

What is a synonym for disdain?

focused

Ellie pays attention and stays **focused**
during class discussions.

What is an antonym for focused?

genius

My sister is a **genius** when it comes to
fixing computer problems.

How might a mechanical genius help
other people?

perspective

Binoculars gave Kyle a closer
perspective of the boat in the harbor.

How does a telescope affect your
perspective of the moon?

prospect

Gillian was happy at the **prospect** of traveling to Paris next year.

Why might the prospect of moving be both exciting and scary?

stunned

Luis was **stunned** by the unexpected test grade.

What kinds of events have stunned you?

superb

The cooking teacher praised his student for the **superb** dish.

What is a synonym for superb?

transition

Max was afraid to make the **transition** from walking to riding a bus to school.

How might you prepare a young child for this transition?

COLLABORATE

Your Turn

Pick three words. Write three questions for your partner to answer.

Go Digital! *Use the online visual glossary*

Miguel in the Middle

Essential Question

What experiences can change the way you see yourself and the world around you?

Read about what causes the title character to change his view of himself.

Rogerio Soud

For as long as I can remember, I've always been in the middle. I'm the middle child in my family. I've always sat in the middle of the classroom in school. Even my first and last names, Miguel Martinez, start with an M—the middle letter of the alphabet.

Luckily, I'm also in the middle of a large circle of friends. Most of them are classmates in school—well, at least they were until now. You see, I started middle school in September, and the **transition** from elementary school caused some painful changes for me. All of my closest friends go to a different middle school in the area, because of the way our school district is mapped out. The only classmate I know from my old school is Jake, who's a **genius** in math, but since it's not my favorite subject, we never became friends.

Another big change is that I'm no longer situated in the middle of the classroom. My seat is now in the front row. Also, my new teachers shovel tons more homework at us (especially in math) than we used to get. So you can imagine why my heart wasn't exactly dancing when middle school began.

By the end of October, Jake and I had become good friends. It happened because I was so hopeless trying to do my math homework. I have a **disdain** for math—especially fractions. To me, fractions are a foreign language—I may as well be trying to learn Greek or Latin. So one day, I approached Jake after school.

"Hey, Jake," I began, "I was wondering if you could—"

"Help you with the math homework, right?" he said, completing my sentence. "Sure, I'd be happy to help you, Miguel."

I was **stunned** because, to be truthful, I wasn't sure until that moment if Jake even knew my name. And yet here he was, happy to save me from drowning in my sea of math problems.

That night, Jake and I had a study session, and it was time well spent. I must admit that Jake's a **superb** math teacher. He used slices of a pizza pie to explain the idea of eighths and sixteenths, and by the end of the night, I finally understood why eight-sixteenths is the same as one-half!

The next day in class, I was even able to answer one of the math problems our teacher put on the chalkboard. She was surprised when I raised my hand, and guess what—so was I!

They say time flies when you're having fun, and I guess it's really true. I can't believe winter vacation is almost here! The school days have been flying by like a jet plane. I suppose it's because I'm a much more **focused** student—especially in math—than I ever was before. Until this year, I always looked forward to the **prospect** of a school break. Now, I actually feel sad that I'll be away from middle school for two weeks.

The other day, the most amazing thing happened when our teacher gave us a math brainteaser. She asked, "If you wrote all the numbers from one to one hundred, how many times would you write a nine?" The question was harder than it seemed.

Most of the students said ten, although some clever kids said eleven, because they realized that ninety-nine has two nines, not just one. But Jake and I were the only students with the correct answer—twenty! Everyone else forgot to count all the nineties.

Jake and I plan to hang out together during winter break. He promised to show me the Math Museum downtown. It won't just be us, however, since all my new friends from middle school will come, too. You see, even though I now have a completely different **perspective** on math, some things haven't changed. I'm still in the middle of a large circle of friends!

Make Connections

Discuss the ways that Miguel changed after entering middle school. What caused him to change? ESSENTIAL QUESTION

When has a new place changed the way you see yourself or the world around you? TEXT TO SELF

Make Predictions

When you **make predictions** as you read text, you use text details to help you think about what might happen next. You can confirm your predictions if they are correct. If they are not correct, you can revise them.

 Find Text Evidence

When you read the second paragraph of "Miguel in the Middle" on page 311, you might make a prediction about how Miguel will feel in his new school.

> **page 311**
>
> For as long as I can remember, I've always been in the middle. I'm the middle child in my family. I've always sat in the middle of the classroom in school. Even my first and last names, Miguel Martinez, start with an M—the middle letter of the alphabet.
>
> Luckily, I'm also in the middle of a large circle of friends. Most of them are classmates in school—well, at least they were until now. You see, I started middle school in September, and the **transition** from elementary school caused some painful changes for me. All of my closest friends go to a different middle school in the area, because of the way our school district is mapped out. The only classmate I know from my old school is Jake, who's a **genius** in math, but since it's not my favorite subject, we never became friends.

When I read that all of Miguel's friends had gone to a different school, I predicted that Miguel will be unhappy in his new school. When Miguel mentioned Jake, I revised this by predicting that Jake may become a friend.

Your Turn

COLLABORATE

What did you predict would happen after the first page? Point to the text evidence that supported your prediction. As you read, use the strategy Make Predictions.

Compare and Contrast

When you **compare and contrast settings** in a story, you figure out how the places and times are alike and different. In a story with more than one setting, you can compare and contrast the effects of the different settings on the characters.

Find Text Evidence

By contrasting the settings in "Miguel in the Middle" on page 311, I find that Miguel was happy in his old school and unhappy in the new one. However, he wants to have friends no matter where he is.

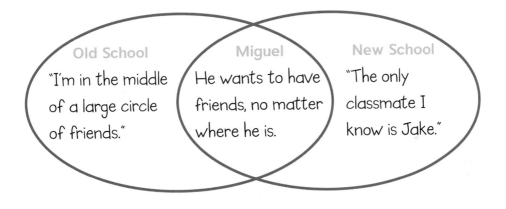

Old School

"I'm in the middle of a large circle of friends."

Miguel

He wants to have friends, no matter where he is.

New School

"The only classmate I know is Jake."

COLLABORATE

Your Turn

Reread the rest of "Miguel in the Middle." Record details about Miguel's old school and new school in the graphic organizer. In the center, describe how Miguel remains the same in both places.

Go Digital! *Use the interactive graphic organizer*

Realistic Fiction

The selection "Miguel in the Middle" is realistic fiction.

Realistic fiction:
- Has characters and settings that could actually exist
- May have a first-person narrator
- May include figurative language, such as hyperbole and metaphor

Find Text Evidence

I see that "Miguel in the Middle" is realistic fiction. Miguel attends middle school. When Miguel says that teachers shovel tons more homework, he is using hyperbole, as people do. Shovel is used as a metaphor to show how the homework seems to be assigned.

page 311

For as long as I can remember, I've always been in the middle. I'm the middle child in my family. I've always sat in the middle of the classroom in school. Even my first and last names, Miguel Martinez, start with an M—the middle letter of the alphabet.

Luckily, I'm also in the middle of a large circle of friends. Most of them are classmates in school—well, at least they were until now. You see, I started middle school in September, and the **transition** from elementary school caused some painful changes for me. All of my closest friends go to a different middle school in the area, because of the way our school district is mapped out. The only classmate I know from my old school is Jake, who's a **genius** in math, but since it's not my favorite subject, we never became friends.

Another big change is that I'm no longer situated in the middle of the classroom. My seat is now in the front row. Also, my new teachers shovel tons more homework at us (especially in math) than we used to get. So you can imagine why my heart wasn't exactly dancing when middle school began.

Narrator The narrator is the person who tells the story.

Figurative Language Figurative language paints a word picture. Hyperbole exaggerates, and metaphors compare unlike things.

Your Turn

How does the narrator's point of view affect "Miguel in the Middle"? Point out any figurative language.

Context Clues

When you find an unfamiliar or multiple meaning word in a sentence, you can look for sentence clues such as **comparisons** to help you figure out the meaning.

 Find Text Evidence

When I read the second paragraph of "Miguel in the Middle," I can use the comparison a different middle school in the area *to figure out the meaning of* district *in* school district. District *must mean the same as "area."*

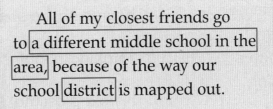

All of my closest friends go to a different middle school in the area, because of the way our school district is mapped out.

Your Turn

Use context clues to figure out the meanings of the following words in "Miguel in the Middle."

situated, *page 311*

session, *page 312*

brainteaser, *page 313*

Rogerio Soud

Write About the Text

Pages 310–313

Gilbert

I answered the question: *In your opinion, was Miguel well prepared for middle school? Use details from the story to support your reasons.*

Student Model: *Opinion*

There is no way Miguel was prepared for middle school! In the beginning, he spent way too much time thinking about elementary school and his old classmates. Then he admitted his heart wasn't in it when middle school began. He also spoke about his disdain for math. This shows that

Strong Opening
My first sentence grabs readers' attention with a strong opinion.

Supporting Details
I included evidence from the text to strengthen my opinion.

he didn't have the best attitude and

wasn't prepared.

    By the end of October, Miguel

became friends with Jake, and his math

skills improved. However, these things

could have happened sooner if he had

been ready for new challenges.

Linking Words

I used the word *however* to show contrast between ideas.

Grammar

A **dependent clause** is introduced by a subordinating conjunction such as *if*.

Grammar Handbook See page 453.

Your Turn

In your opinion, what qualities allowed Miguel to finally adjust to middle school? Use details from the story to support your reasons.

Go Digital!
Write your response online.
Use your editing checklist.

Rogerio Soud

? Essential Question

How do shared experiences help people adapt to change?

Go Digital!

SL.5.lc See the California Standards section.

Through Thick and Thin

When times get tough, people have to rely on each other to help them adapt to changing situations. Even small gestures can help.

During the Great Depression, many businesses closed, causing widespread unemployment.

In cities like this one, supportive groups gave unemployed people free soup, coffee, and doughnuts as they waited for work. The shared meal helped them not feel so alone.

Talk About It  COLLABORATE

Write words you have learned about how people help each other adapt to change. Then talk about a time that other people helped you adapt to a change.

Adapting to Change Together

Vocabulary

Use the picture and the sentences to talk with a
partner about each word.

assume

Caitlyn could only **assume** the cat broke
the flower pot.

What might you assume if you awaken to
snow on a school day?

guarantee

With such dark clouds approaching,
Henrik can **guarantee** that it will rain soon.

When else might you guarantee
something?

nominate

The team will **nominate** the best
candidates to run for class president.

Why might you nominate a particular
person for a task or position?

obviously

The hand-knitted scarf was **obviously**
too long for Marta's little brother.

What kinds of clothes are obviously
wrong for a cold day?

rely

To make a basket, Calvin must **rely** on the skills his coaches taught him.

When have you had to rely on someone else?

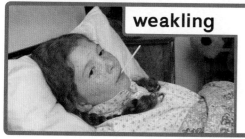

supportive

The audience's **supportive** applause boosted Clare's energy.

In what other ways can you be supportive of a performer on stage?

sympathy

Erik's dad offered **sympathy** when his team lost the game.

When else might you express sympathy to someone?

weakling

Being tired and ill in bed made Emily feel like a **weakling**.

At what other times might you feel like a weakling?

Your Turn

COLLABORATE

Pick three vocabulary words. Then write three questions for your partner to answer.

Go Digital! *Use the online visual glossary*

L.5.6 See the California Standards section.

The Day the Rollets
Got Their Moxie Back

Essential Question

How do shared experiences help people adapt to change?

Read about how a family comes together during a period of great hardship in the United States.

Ron Mazellan

324

Sometimes, the thing that gets you through hard times comes like a bolt from the blue. That's what my older brother's letter was like, traveling across the country from a work camp in Wyoming. It was 1937, and Ricky was helping to build facilities for a new state park as part of President Roosevelt's employment program. Though the program created jobs for young men like Ricky, it hadn't helped our dad find work yet.

I imagined Ricky looking up at snow-capped mountains and sparkling skies, breathing in the smell of evergreens as his work crew turned trees into lumber and lumber into buildings. It almost made an 11-year-old **weakling** like me want to become a lumberjack.

Back in our New York City apartment, the air smelled like meatloaf and cabbage. Dad sat slant-wise in his chair by the window, **obviously** trying to catch the last rays of sunlight rather than turn on a light. My older sister Ruth and I lay on the floor comparing the letters Ricky had sent us. "Shirley, Ricky says they had a talent show, and he wore a grass skirt and did a hula dance while playing the ukulele!" Ruth reported with delight. "I'll bet he was the cat's pajamas!"

"It'd be swell to have our own talent show!" I replied.

"Should I start sewing grass skirts?" Mom asked from the kitchen, which was just the corner where someone had plopped down a stove next to a sink and an icebox. "Now come set the table. Dinner's almost ready."

Dad stayed where he was, sullen and spent. "Any jobs in the paper?" Mom asked, her voice rich with **sympathy**. Dad shook his head no. He had worked as an artist in the theater for years, but most productions were still strapped for cash. Dad sketched posters for shows that did get the green light, just to keep his skills sharp. He even designed posters for "Rollet's Follies," with Ruth and me depicted in watercolor costumes.

For dinner, Mom served a baked loaf of whatever ingredients she had that worked well together. From the reddish color, I could **assume** that she had snuck in beets. "I **guarantee** you'll like these beets," she said, reading my frown. "It's beet loaf, the meatless meat loaf," she sang as she served up slices.

Ruth fidgeted in her seat, still excited about the talent show. Though calm on the outside, inside I was all atwitter, too.

Over the next week, Ruth and I practiced our Hawaiian dance routine. Our parents worried about heating bills as cold weather settled in. One Saturday, my father decided to grin and bear it, and grab some hot coffee at the local soup kitchen, where he hoped to hear about available jobs. Ruth and I begged to go along. Since the kitchen offered doughnuts and hot chocolate on weekends, he agreed.

Ron Mazellan

Most everyone in line was bundled up against the cold. Many of us had to **rely** on two or three threadbare layers. Like many other men, Dad bowed his head as if in shame.

The line moved slowly. Bored, Ruth began practicing her dance steps. I sang an upbeat tune to give her some music. Around us, downturned hats lifted to reveal frowns becoming smiles. Soon, folks began clapping along. Egged on by the **supportive** response, Ruth twirled and swayed like there was no tomorrow.

"Those girls sure have moxie!" someone shouted.

"They've got heart, all right!" offered another. "Why, they oughta be in pictures!"

"With performances like that, I'd **nominate** them for an Academy Award!" a woman called out.

"Those are my girls!" Dad declared, his head held high.

Everyone burst into applause. For those short moments, the past didn't matter, and the future blossomed ahead of us like a beautiful flower. I couldn't wait to write Ricky and tell him the news.

Make Connections

Talk about ways that Ricky, Ruth, and Shirley helped each other adapt to the times. ESSENTIAL QUESTION

Think about a time when others helped you adapt to a new situation. How did your experience compare with the Rollet family's? TEXT TO SELF

Make Predictions

As you read a story, clues in the text can help you predict what will happen next. Making predictions helps you read with purpose. As you continue to read, you can find out if your predictions are correct. If they are not correct, you can revise them.

Find Text Evidence

You can make predictions about the story "The Day the Rollets Got Their Moxie Back," beginning with the title on page 324.

page 324

CCSS Shared Read   Genre • Historical Fiction

The Day the Rollets
Got Their Moxie Back

From the title, I predict that the main characters in the story will be the Rollets. I don't know what Moxie *means, but the story will probably have a positive ending since the Rollets will get back something that they have been missing.*

COLLABORATE

Your Turn

Based on the girls' reactions to the letters from their older brother, Ricky, what did you predict might happen next? As you read, use the strategy Make Predictions.

Compare and Contrast

The characters in a story may be similar to or different from one another in their traits, actions, and responses to events. You **compare and contrast characters** to help you better understand how their personalities and actions affect events, or are changed by events.

Find Text Evidence

When I reread the dinner scene on page 326 of "The Day the Rollets Got Their Moxie Back," I can use text details to compare each family member's different responses to their difficult situation.

Mother
sings, tries to make the best of things

Father
sullen, shakes head, tired

Event
Dinner at the Rollets'

Ruth
excited and fidgety, dreaming of show

Shirley
quiet yet excited, dreaming of show

COLLABORATE

Your Turn

In the graphic organizer, record the feelings of the characters outside the soup kitchen at the start of the scene. How do their feelings change by the story's end?

Go Digital!
Use the interactive graphic organizer

Historical Fiction

The selection "The Day the Rollets Got Their Moxie Back" is historical fiction.

Historical fiction:

- Features events and settings typical of the time period in which the story is set
- Includes characters who act like and speak the dialect of people from a particular place in the past

🔍 Find Text Evidence

I can tell that "The Day the Rollets Got Their Moxie Back" is historical fiction. The year is 1937, and President Roosevelt was real. Rollet family members are fictional but use dialect of the time.

page 325

Sometimes, the thing that gets you through hard times comes like a bolt from the blue. That's what my older brother's letter was like, traveling across the country from a work camp in Wyoming. It was 1937, and Ricky was helping to build facilities for a new state park as part of President Roosevelt's employment program. Though the program created jobs for young men like Ricky, it hadn't helped our dad find work yet.

I imagined Ricky looking up at snow-capped mountains and sparkling skies, breathing in the smell of evergreens as his work crew turned trees into lumber and lumber into buildings. It almost made an 11-year-old **weakling** like me want to become a lumberjack.

Back in our New York City apartment, the air smelled like meatloaf and cabbage. Dad sat slant-wise in his chair by the window, **obviously** trying to catch the last rays of sunlight rather than turn on a light. My older sister Ruth and I lay on the floor comparing the letters Ricky had sent us. "Shirley, Ricky says they had a talent show, and he wore a grass skirt and did a hula dance while playing the ukulele," Ruth reported with delight. "I'll bet he was the cat's pajamas!"

"It'd be swell to have our own talent show!" I replied.

"Should I start sewing grass skirts?" Mom asked from the kitchen, which was just the corner where someone had plopped down a stove next to a sink and an icebox. "Now come set the table. Dinner's almost ready."

325

Dialect Characters sometimes use dialect, which is speech typical of a place or time. Dialect may include words, phrases, and idioms that might sound unfamiliar.

COLLABORATE

Your Turn

List two examples of dialect in "The Day the Rollets Got Their Moxie Back." Why might an author include dialect in historical fiction?

Idioms

An **idiom** is an expression that cannot be defined by the words in it. Surrounding words and sentences can offer context clues to help you understand the meaning of an idiom.

 Find Text Evidence

I'm not sure what the idiom a bolt from the blue *means on page 325. When I think of a "bolt," I think of lightning and how quickly and unpredictably it can strike. Letters often come unexpectedly, as if out of nowhere. That must be the meaning.*

> Sometimes, the thing that gets you through hard times comes like a bolt from the blue. That's what my older brother's letter was like, traveling across the country from a work camp in Wyoming.

Your Turn

COLLABORATE

Use context clues to explain the meanings of the following idioms from "How the Rollets Got Their Moxie Back."

the cat's pajamas, *page 325*
get the green light, *page 326*
grin and bear it, *page 326*
like there was no tomorrow, *page 327*

Ron Mazellan

CCSS Write to Sources

Write About the Text

Bree

I responded to the prompt: *Add an event to the story. Write about the family as they ate their beet loaf dinner. Include dialogue in your scene.*

Grammar

This is an example of a **complex sentence.**

Grammar Handbook See page 453.

Figurative Language

I included a simile to help readers think about familiar ideas in a new way.

Student Model: *Narrative Text*

While Ruth and I were not thrilled with the idea of beet loaf, it smelled great. My stomach was rumbling like a truck grinding gears, and I took a bite. I could tell Ruth was waiting to see what I thought before trying it herself. "Wow!" I said, surprised. "This is delicious."

"Shirley is absolutely correct,"

Dad added, with a rare smile. "You're a kitchen magician. What will you think of next?"

"Well," Mom said, "funny you should ask. For dessert, I made zucchini bread with apple icing, but it's only for the 'clean-plate club.'"

"We're in that club!" Ruth and I exclaimed.

Develop Characters

I included sensory details to help readers picture the event.

Transitions

I used a signal word to connect two separate ideas.

Your Turn

Add an event to the story. Write about the father telling the mother about what the girls did at the soup kitchen. Use details from the story.

Go Digital!
Write your response online.
Use your editing checklist.

W.5.3b, W.5.3c, W.5.3d See the California Standards section.

333

Ron Mazellan

Essential Question

What changes in the environment affect living things?

Go Digital!

SL.5.lc See the California Standards section.

A Change in the Air

Earth is in a constant state of change. Some changes, such as a volcano erupting, may happen quickly. Other changes are gradual.

▷ One change scientists study is the impact of seasons on animals and plants.

▷ Each winter, for example, these Monarch butterflies migrate south to Mexico. They live in colonies like this one before heading north in the spring, when food is plentiful.

Talk About It COLLABORATE

Write words you have learned about the changing Earth. Then talk about one change you have wondered about.

Changing Earth

Vocabulary

Use the picture and the sentences to talk with a partner about each word.

atmosphere

Clouds form in our **atmosphere**, the layer of gases around Earth.

Why is the Earth's atmosphere important?

decays

When fruit **decays**, or rots, it is not very tasty and should not be eaten.

What does a banana look like as it decays?

gradual

The release of sand in an hourglass is **gradual**, so that it takes one hour.

What is a gradual event or change you have seen?

impact

A veterinarian has a big **impact** on the health of a pet.

Who has had an important impact on your life?

noticeably

José's hair was **noticeably** shorter after his haircut.

What is a synonym for noticeably?

receding

As I drove away, the mountain seemed to be **receding** in the distance.

If it was receding, was it getting close?

stability

While his sprained leg healed, Stephan used crutches for **stability** when walking.

If a thing has stability, is it shaky or steady?

variations

In the valley, there are many **variations** in the color green.

Where might you see variations in the color blue?

Your Turn

COLLABORATE

Pick three words. Write three questions for your partner to answer.

Go Digital! *Use the online visual glossary*

Forests on Fire

?

Essential Question

What changes in the environment affect living things?

Read about the effects of forest fires on plants, animals, and people.

A few years ago, several red squirrels—an endangered species—had a temporary home at the Phoenix Zoo. Rescued from a ravaging wildfire that had already destroyed thousands of acres of land, the squirrels were waiting for the fire to be extinguished before being returned to the wild. Forest fires are part of nature, so it is important for us to understand not only how to fight fires, but also why they occur.

Destructive and Productive

Like rainstorms, wildfires are a force of nature. However, unlike rainstorms, wildfires are almost always destructive. They consume everything in their way, including plants, trees, and animals. Sometimes, they take human lives and homes as well.

Like a big storm, the destructive power of wildfires is terrifying. On the other hand, naturally occurring wildfires are also productive forces. Whether their flames race through a forest, a prairie, or acres of brush, these fires produce necessary changes in their environment. Like rain, they can allow new life to flourish.

Benefits of Naturally Occurring Wildfires

A naturally occurring wildfire, sometimes called a forest fire, happens without any human cause. Three factors must be present for one to burn. These include fuel, such as dry grasses; oxygen, which is in our **atmosphere**; and a heat source to ignite the fuel. A lightning strike usually sparks a naturally occurring wildfire. The danger of fire is highest during a drought, when an area has experienced little rain.

Wildfires have happened throughout history, and they help to regenerate Earth and its species. When vegetation **decays**, wildfires clear it away so that new plant life can grow.

Open cone

New seedling

A young forest

The black spruce tree needs a fire's heat to cause its cones to open and scatter seeds. Eventually, seedlings sprout, and a new forest will grow.

Fire also releases nutrients back into the soil, making it more fertile. And by eliminating leafy canopies of mature trees, fire allows nourishing sunlight to reach a forest floor.

Often, this new plant life will be better adapted to fire than what existed before. Some species will have fire-resistant roots, leaves, or bark. Other species will actually depend on fire to reproduce and thrive.

Stability and Diversity

Among its benefits, fire promotes **stability**. By eliminating invasive species that can take over an area, fire encourages the healthy growth of a region's own vegetation.

At the same time, fire promotes diversity. It ensures that plant life will exist at different stages of development. For example, a forest recently struck by fire will have new seedlings. Not far away, in a forest struck by fire twenty years earlier, there may be small trees. And nearby, there may be a forest of mature trees, untouched by fire for years.

These **variations** in plant life provide food and habitats for different kinds of insects, birds, and mammals. Woodpeckers eat insects in burned-out trees. Sparrows depend on seeds for food. Predators such as foxes are drawn by small prey. Forests at different stages attract a diversity of animals to a region.

The Human Factor

Although wildfires have benefits, they also are feared and misunderstood. As a result, our government tried to suppress them completely throughout the 20th century. This policy had a negative **impact** on the environment. The **gradual** buildup of decayed vegetation provided more fuel to feed fires. Consequently, wildfires became **noticeably** fiercer.

More recently, the government has used two different strategies to manage wildfires. One is to try to limit fires before they burn out of control. The other is to set small "prescribed" fires to reduce the amount of fuel in the environment. Hopefully, the danger of catastrophic fires is now **receding**.

Unfortunately, human carelessness, such as a campfire left to smolder, also can start a fire. While a natural or prescribed wildfire can be beneficial, this is not true of fires that result from malice or mistakes. These happen at times and places that may cause irreparable damage to plant, animal, and human life. Fires cannot control themselves, so humans will always have to figure out how best to handle them.

Whether wildfires are small or large, firefighters are needed to help contain them.

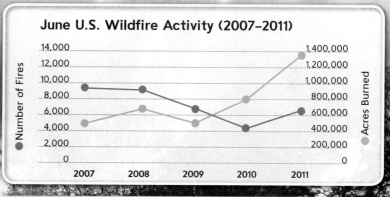

June U.S. Wildfire Activity (2007–2011)

Number of Fires: 14,000 / 12,000 / 10,000 / 8,000 / 6,000 / 4,000 / 2,000 / 0

Acres Burned: 1,400,000 / 1,200,000 / 1,000,000 / 800,000 / 600,000 / 400,000 / 200,000 / 0

2007 2008 2009 2010 2011

Make Connections

Talk about how wildfires change the environment for plants. ESSENTIAL QUESTION

Why is it important for you to be careful around a fire of any kind, even in a home? TEXT TO SELF

Ask and Answer Questions

To be sure you understand what you read, ask questions about the text. If you have trouble answering the question, reread the section. At the end of an expository text, ask: *What is the main idea?* Then find details to support your answer.

 Find Text Evidence

To check your understanding of the section "Destructive and Productive" on page 339, you might ask yourself, *What is the main idea?*

page 339

Like a big storm, the destructive power of wildfires is terrifying. On the other hand, naturally occurring wildfires are also productive forces. Whether their flames race through a forest, a prairie, or acres of brush, these fires produce necessary changes in their environment. Like rain, they can allow new life to flourish.

The main idea is that wildfires are both destructive and productive. Details such as how wildfires in a forest or prairie produce necessary changes help support the main idea.

Your Turn

COLLABORATE

Ask and answer a question about the information in the section "Benefits of Naturally Occurring Wildfires" on page 339. Use this strategy as you read.

Compare and Contrast

Writers may organize a text to show how an idea is similar to or different from another idea. To figure out if a writer is using a compare-and-contrast structure, look for signal words and phrases such as *however, on the other hand,* and *just as.*

 ## Find Text Evidence

The first section tells how wildfires are both like storms and unlike storms. This comparison helps me understand that both forces of nature have uses. Wildfires may be mostly destructive, but, like storms, they can be useful, too.

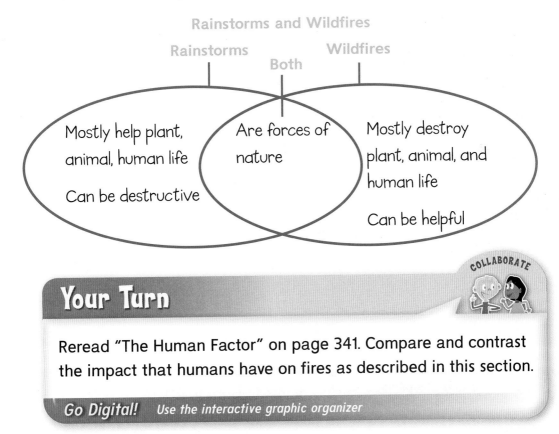

Rainstorms and Wildfires

Rainstorms | Both | Wildfires

Mostly help plant, animal, human life

Can be destructive

Are forces of nature

Mostly destroy plant, animal, and human life

Can be helpful

COLLABORATE

Your Turn

Reread "The Human Factor" on page 341. Compare and contrast the impact that humans have on fires as described in this section.

Go Digital! *Use the interactive graphic organizer*

Expository Text

The selection "Forests on Fire" is expository text.

Expository text:

- Gives information about a topic
- Develops the topic with facts, examples, and explanations
- May include graphs and photographs

Find Text Evidence

I can tell that "Forests on Fire" is expository text. The selection gives facts about the causes of wildfires and explains more about them. Photographs, captions, and a graph add information.

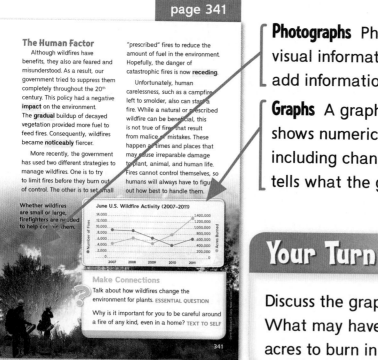

page 341

The Human Factor
    Although wildfires have benefits, they also are feared and misunderstood. As a result, our government tried to suppress them completely throughout the 20th century. This policy had a negative **impact** on the environment. The **gradual** buildup of decayed vegetation provided more fuel to feed fires. Consequently, wildfires became **noticeably** fiercer.
    More recently, the government has used two different strategies to manage wildfires. One is to try to limit fires before they burn out of control. The other is to set small

"prescribed" fires to reduce the amount of fuel in the environment. Hopefully, the danger of catastrophic fires is now **receding**.
    Unfortunately, human carelessness, such as a campfire left to smolder, also can start a fire. While a natural or prescribed wildfire can be beneficial, this is not true of fires that result from malice or mistakes. These happen at times and places that may cause irreparable damage to plant, animal, and human life. Fires cannot control themselves, so humans will always have to figure out how best to handle them.

Whether wildfires are small or large, firefighters are needed to help contain them.

June U.S. Wildfire Activity (2007–2011)

Make Connections
Talk about how wildfires change the environment for plants. ESSENTIAL QUESTION

Why is it important for you to be careful around a fire of any kind, even in a home? TEXT TO SELF

341

Photographs Photographs provide visual information. **Captions** also add information.

Graphs A graph is a diagram that shows numerical information, including changes over time. A title tells what the graph will show.

COLLABORATE

Your Turn

Discuss the graph on page 341. What may have caused so many acres to burn in 2011?

Context Clues

Sometimes you can figure out the meaning of unfamiliar or multiple meaning words by looking for **clues in the paragraph**. You may see a synonym, an antonym, or a comparison that can help you define a word that puzzles you.

 ## Find Text Evidence

When I read "Stability and Diversity" on page 340, the phrases new seedlings *and* small trees *refer to trees in early life. Since* mature trees *have been* untouched by fire for years, *the word* mature *must mean "fully grown or developed."*

For example, a forest recently struck by fire will have new seedlings. Not far away, in a forest struck by fire twenty years earlier, there may be small trees. And nearby, there may be a forest of mature trees, untouched by fire for years.

Your Turn

Use context clues to figure out the meaning of the following words in "Forests on Fire":

productive, *page 339*

regenerate, *page 339*

diversity, *page 340*

Write About the Text

Pages 338–341

Jane

I responded to the prompt: *Explain the relationship between wildfires and habitats. Use details from the text.*

Student Model: *Informative Text*

Wildfires change habitats in ways that are destructive and productive. They destroy everything in their way, such as plants and animals. However, in environments such as prairies and forests, the effect of wildfires helps new plant life thrive. They burn away rotten vegetation so new plants can grow, and they make soil more

Topic Sentence
My first sentence introduces the focus of the paragraph.

Develop a Topic
I used facts and details from the text to develop the topic.

Text Structure
I included text evidence to explain the cause-and-effect relationship between wildfires and habitats.

fertile by putting nutrients back into it.

Wildfires also get rid of invasive

plants and allow for different stages

of plant life. These different stages

provide food and habitats for many

kinds of animals. Wildfires can damage

an environment, but they can also

renew Earth and its

different species.

Grammar

This is an example of a descriptive **adjective**.

*Grammar Handbook
See page 466.*

Your Turn

Compare and contrast the negative and positive effects of wildfires. Provide examples from the text.

Go Digital!
Write your response online.
Use your editing checklist.

Joe Bator/Corbis

Essential Question

How can scientific knowledge change over time?

Go Digital!

Going Deeper

Learning about the ocean is one of our greatest challenges. As researchers design new technologies and evaluate new ideas, our criteria for knowledge changes.

▶ Compare the modern research submersible on the left with the early diving suit on the right.

▶ The diving suit weighed 190 pounds, and the metal helmet allows almost no visibility! It's easy to see how today's technology allows scientists to learn so much more.

Talk About It

Write words you have learned about changes in scientific knowledge over time. Then talk about a scientific idea you would like to know more about.

Scientific Knowledge

Vocabulary

Use the picture and the sentences to talk with a partner about each word.

approximately

The recipe called for **approximately** two cups of oil, so I did not measure exactly.

What is an antonym for approximately?

astronomical

The space exhibit included amazing **astronomical** instruments to study stars.

Besides stars, what are astronomical instruments used to study?

calculation

Mina did a quick **calculation** to figure out if she had enough money for six tickets.

What kinds of skills help with a calculation?

criteria

Blood pressure is one of the **criteria** doctors use for evaluating your health.

What other criteria help doctors to check your health?

diameter

The large pizza pan has a **diameter** of fourteen inches.

How would you measure the diameter of a pan?

evaluate

Reading food labels can help you **evaluate** the nutritional value.

What questions might help you evaluate a restaurant?

orbit

It takes a year for the Earth to **orbit** the sun, and a month for the moon to orbit the Earth.

What objects in space orbit the sun?

spheres

Basketballs, soccer balls, and baseballs are **spheres**, but footballs are not.

What other objects are spheres?

COLLABORATE

Your Turn

Pick three words. Write three questions for your partner to answer.

Go Digital! *Use the online visual glossary*

CHANGING VIEWS OF
EARTH

NASA-GFSC Image created by Reto Stockli with the help of Alan Nelson, under the leadership of Fred

Essential Question

How can scientific knowledge change over time?

Read about how our understanding of Earth has changed along with scientific developments over time.

On the Ground, Looking Around

No matter where on Earth you go, people like to talk about the weather. This weekend's forecast may provide the main criteria for planning outdoor activities. Where does all that information about the weather come from? The ability to predict storms and droughts required centuries of scientific innovation. We had to look up at the skies to learn more about life here on Earth.

Long ago, humans based their knowledge on what they experienced with their eyes and ears. If people could heighten their senses, they might not feel so mystified by the events confronting them daily. For example, something as simple as the rising sun perplexed people for centuries.

They believed that the Earth stayed in place while the Sun moved around it. This was called the geocentric model.

In the early 1600s, an Italian named Galileo pointed a new tool called the telescope toward the night sky. As a result of his heightened vision, he could see stars, planets, and other celestial spheres with new clarity. Each observation and calculation led him to support a radical new model of the solar system. In the heliocentric version proposed by the scientist Copernicus, the Sun did not orbit the Earth. The Earth orbited the Sun.

Galileo's telescope helped prove that Copernicus's heliocentric view was correct. ▶

These diagrams show the geocentric (Earth in the center), and the heliocentric (sun in the center) views of the solar system.

Earth   Sun

Sun   Earth

In the Sky, Looking Down

New technology allowed scientists to evaluate theories better than ever. Measuring devices such as the thermometer and barometer offered new insights into weather patterns. However, people were still limited to ground-based learning. What if they could travel into the sky, where the weather actually happened?

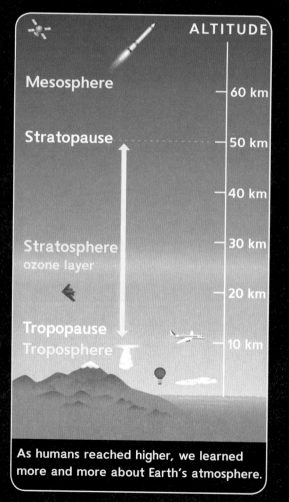

ALTITUDE

Mesosphere

Stratopause — 50 km

— 60 km

— 40 km

Stratosphere
ozone layer — 30 km

— 20 km

Tropopause
Troposphere — 10 km

As humans reached higher, we learned more and more about Earth's atmosphere.

In the mid-1700s, some scientists sent measurement devices higher and higher. At first they used kites. Before long, hot-air balloons offered new ways to transport the tools—and sometimes scientists themselves—into the sky.

However, scientists were not satisfied studying the lower layers of Earth's atmosphere. The more they learned, the higher they wanted to go. They also wanted to obtain information more quickly and accurately. Kites and balloons were hard to control. As a result, they occasionally veered off course or got lost, taking their data with them.

The development of aircraft in the early 1900s promised safer ways to observe Earth's surface and the atmosphere above it. Kites and balloons could reach altitudes of approximately three kilometers. By comparison, airplanes lifted scientists to a height of five kilometers and more. Radio technology allowed scientists to transmit data from the air to the ground, where other scientists analyzed and compared information. Breakthroughs came fast and furiously. Still, scientists dreamed of reaching ever higher.

Out in Space, Looking Back Home

In the late twentieth century, advances in aeronautics led to more powerful rockets that lifted satellites into orbit around Earth. From these heights, scientists could study the composition and relative thinness of our layered atmosphere. Since meteorologists could analyze multiple factors at once, the accuracy of their weather predictions improved dramatically.

NASA launched dozens of satellites into orbit in the following years. Some stared back at Earth, while others peered deep into endless space. They gathered astronomical data about the ages of planets and galaxies. Sensors and supercomputers measured things such as Earth's diameter with incredible accuracy. Because of this technology, scientists could develop more reliable models about Earth's systems. For example, they could form theories to show how climate might change over time.

Space missions continue to venture farther from home. Even so, nothing compares to seeing Earth the old way, with our own eyes. Views of our planet from space inspire awe in nearly all people who have seen them, even in photographs. "With all the arguments . . . for going to the Moon," said astronaut Joseph Allen, "no one suggested that we should do it to look at the Earth. But that may in fact be the most important reason."

Satellites launched into orbit only last for a limited number of years and then must be replaced.

Make Connections

What were some effects of flight on our knowledge about Earth? **ESSENTIAL QUESTION**

How has your knowledge of Earth changed over time? What effect has this change had on you? **TEXT TO SELF**

Brand X Pictures/PunchStock

355

Ask and Answer Questions

Asking and answering questions as you read helps you stay focused. Try it with "Changing Views of Earth." Think about each question the author asks, and form your own questions, too. Then read on for the answers.

 Find Text Evidence

In the first paragraph on page 353, the author asks a question: *Where does all that information about the weather come from?* This may lead you to another question.

page 353

No matter where on Earth you go, people like to talk about the weather. This weekend's forecast may provide the main criteria for planning outdoor activities. Where does all that information about the weather come from?

I think about what I already know—that weather forecasters use scientific instruments. So I ask myself, "What kinds of instruments do scientists use to make forecasts?" I will read on to find the answer.

Your Turn

COLLABORATE

Reread "Out in Space, Looking Back Home" on page 355. Ask a question and then read to find the answer. Use the strategy Ask and Answer Questions as you read.

Cause and Effect

Science and history authors want you to know not just *what* happens but *why* it happens. They show that one event is the **cause** of another event, called the **effect**. Cause-and-effect relationships often form a chain, with the effect of one event becoming the cause of another event.

Find Text Evidence

In the section "On the Ground, Looking Around" on page 353, I read that people once believed the sun orbits Earth. I learn the cause of this mistake: people had only their eyes for viewing the skies. The invention of the telescope had an important effect—the discovery that Earth actually orbits the sun.

Cause →	Effect
Long ago, people had only their eyes to see the skies.	They thought the sun orbited Earth.
The telescope was invented.	People could see the stars and planets more clearly.
People could see the stars and planets more clearly.	They found out that Earth orbits the sun.

Your Turn

COLLABORATE

Reread the rest of "Changing Views of Earth." Show important connections between certain events by recording causes and effects in your own graphic organizer.

Go Digital!
Use the interactive graphic organizer

Expository Text

The selection "Changing Views of Earth" is an expository text.

Expository text:

- Presents information and facts about a topic in a logical order
- Supports specific points with reasons and evidence
- May include text features, such as subheadings, photos, and diagrams

 Find Text Evidence

"Changing Views of Earth" is an expository text. The facts about inventions are given in a logical order. The author backs up her points with evidence, including a diagram.

page 354

In the Sky, Looking Down

New technology allowed scientists to evaluate theories better than ever. Measuring devices such as the thermometer and barometer offered new insights into weather patterns. However, people were still limited to ground-based learning. What if they could travel into the sky, where the weather actually happened?

In the mid-1700s, some scientists sent measurement devices higher and higher. At first they used kites. Before long, hot-air balloons offered new ways to transport the tools—and sometimes scientists themselves—into the sky.

However, scientists were not satisfied studying the lower layers of Earth's atmosphere. The more they learned, the higher they wanted to go. They also wanted to obtain information more quickly and accurately. Kites and balloons were hard to control. As a result, they occasionally veered off course or got lost, taking their data with them.

The development of aircraft in the early 1900s promised safer ways to observe Earth's surface and the atmosphere above it. Kites and balloons could reach altitudes of approximately three kilometers. By comparison, airplanes lifted scientists to a height of five kilometers and more. Radio technology allowed scientists to transmit data from the air to the ground, where other scientists analyzed and compared information. Breakthroughs came fast and furiously. Still, scientists dreamed of reaching ever higher.

Diagrams A diagram is a drawing that shows the different parts of something and how they relate to each other. A title tells what the diagram illustrates, and labels identify each main part.

Your Turn

COLLABORATE

List three other examples of things in "Changing Views of Earth" that show that this is expository text.

Greek Roots

Many English words contain Greek roots. For example, the Greek root *meter* means "measure," so any English word containing *meter* (*thermometer, barometer, kilometer*) usually has to do with measuring something.

Find Text Evidence

On page 354 of "Changing Views of Earth," I come across the word thermometer. *The Greek root* therm *has to do with heat. Since I know that* meter *means "measure," I can figure out that a thermometer is something that records or measures temperature.*

Measuring devices such as the
thermometer and barometer
offered new insights into
weather patterns.

Your Turn

Use the Greek roots below to figure out the meanings of two words from "Changing Views of Earth":

Greek Roots: *geo* = earth   *helio* = sun   *centr* = center
  geocentric, *page 353*
  heliocentric, *page 353*

Write About the Text

Pages 352–355

April

I answered the question: *How have scientific advances in observing Earth benefited humans? Provide examples.*

Student Model: *Informative Text*

Advances in observing Earth

have benefited humans by allowing

them to forecast events such as

droughts and storms. Long ago, people

only had their eyes and ears to predict

the weather. As technology improved,

so did our understanding of weather

patterns. Kites and balloons were used to

study Earth's lower atmosphere, and the

Domain-Specific Language

I included vocabulary related to the subject area, such as *droughts.*

Strong Paragraphs

I included transitions and relevant facts in order to write strong paragraphs.

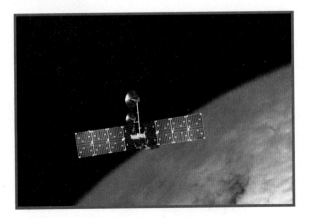

development of aircraft led to an even

bigger breakthrough.

   Forecasts became more accurate in

the late 20th century as meteorologists

studied data collected from satellites

in orbit above Earth. It is a safe bet

that further advances will continue

to help us prepare for changes to

Earth's climate.

Grammar

This is an example of a **comparative adjective**.

Grammar Handbook See page 467.

Figurative Language

I used the phrase *safe bet* to show the strong likelihood that forecasting technology will continue to improve.

Your Turn

Explain the meaning of Joseph Allen's quote on page 355. Use text evidence to support your answer.

Go Digital!
Write your response online.
Use your editing checklist.

Weekly Concept Scientific Viewpoints

Essential Question

How do natural events and human activities affect the environment?

Go Digital!

(bkgd) Adrian Dennis/AFP/Getty Images; (inset) Don Farrall/Photodisc/Getty Images

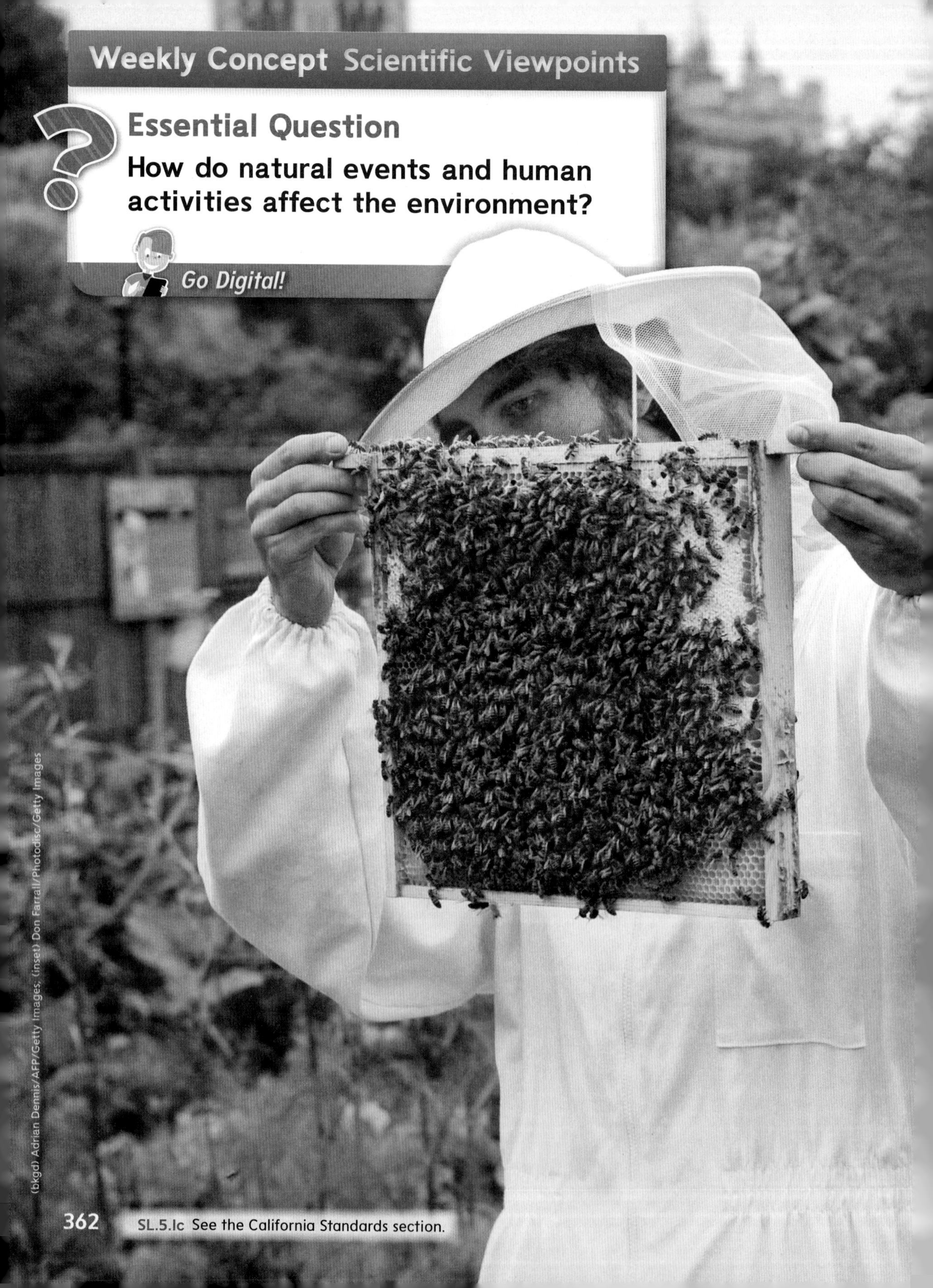

 SL.5.1c See the California Standards section.

Friend or Foe?

We are surrounded by many species of plants and animals that are not native to the area they live in.

▶ Beekeeping is not just an agricultural activity. I keep honey bees in the heart of a busy city!

▶ Bees can thrive in this unusual setting, and I enjoy the honey they produce.

Talk About It

COLLABORATE

Write words you have learned about activities that affect an environment. Then talk about an activity you have done that affected the environment.

Affecting the Environment

Vocabulary

Use the picture and the sentences to talk with a partner about each word.

agricultural

Sam and Gina gathered apples and other **agricultural** products for the market.

How do agricultural products make a difference in your life?

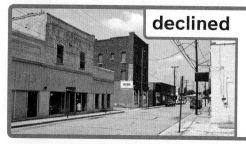

declined

Because many businesses closed, the town had clearly **declined** over the years.

What actions can a restaurant take when its profits have declined?

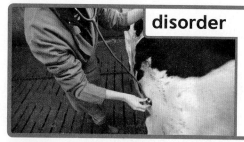

disorder

The veterinarian examined the cow for a stomach **disorder**.

What kind of medical disorder might keep you home from school?

identify

People are able to **identify** my dog not only by his dog tag, but by his smile.

How would you identify your best friend in a crowd?

probable

The **probable** cause of the shattered window was Jake and his soccer ball.

What type of weather is most probable in the winter where you live?

thrive

Some plants manage to grow and **thrive** even in snow.

What would you do to help a pet thrive?

unexpected

As the wildebeests drank at the river, the crocodile's arrival was **unexpected**.

How might an unexpected event change your plans?

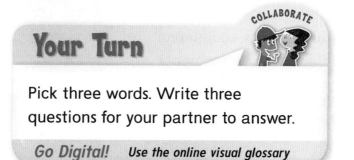

widespread

Starlings, introduced from England, are now a **widespread** bird species.

What is a good example of a widespread fad?

Your Turn

COLLABORATE

Pick three words. Write three questions for your partner to answer.

Go Digital! **Use the online visual glossary**

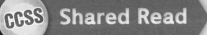
Eddie/Photodisc/Getty Images

Essential Question

How do natural events and human activities affect the environment?

Read two different views on the arrival of new species into the United States.

It's hard to imagine life without oranges and chickens, which are examples of nonnative species.

Should Plants and Animals from Other Places Live Here?

POINT COUNTERPOINT

New Arrivals Welcome

Nonnative species are good for the economy—and they taste good, too!

Some of America's most important immigrants are plants and animals. Called *nonnative species,* these creatures arrive here from other regions or countries. Nonnative species are known as *invasive* when they harm the environment, our health, or the economy. Invasive species often take over a **widespread** area and overwhelm native wildlife. The population of some native species has **declined** because of a few newcomers, but the news is not all bad. We would be a lot worse off without some of them.

In Florida, for example, about 2,000 species of familiar plants and animals are nonnative. These include oranges, chickens, and sugarcane. In fact, 90 percent of farm sales can be traced directly to nonnative species.

Nonnative species help to control insects and other pests that harm crops. Some scientists **identify** a pest's natural enemy and bring in nonnative enemy species, such as insects, to kill the pests. Killing the pests is a good thing, and an even better result is that pesticide use is reduced. Vedalia beetles were transported here from Australia to eat insects that killed citrus fruit. The beetles completed their mission without any side effects. They also help keep citrus farmers in business!

Not all new arrivals benefit humans. However, many nonnative species are just what the doctor ordered. Many of the dogs and cats we love so much originated in other parts of the world. Would you want to ban Labrador retrievers and Siamese cats? Creatures like these surely make our lives and our nation better!

Gary John Norman/Digital Vision/Getty Images

367

A Growing Problem

Thousands of foreign plant and animal species threaten our country.

Visitors to the Florida Everglades expect to see alligators, not pythons. These huge snakes are native to Southeast Asia. But about 150,000 of the reptiles are crawling through the Everglades. The **probable** reason they got there is that pet owners dumped the snakes in the wild. Now the nonnative pythons have become a **widespread** menace, threatening to reduce the population of endangered native species.

Some nonnative species may be useful, but others are harmful to the nation. It costs the U.S. $137 billion each year to repair the damage these species cause to the environment. The trouble occurs when nonnative species become invasive. Invasive species are a nuisance just about everywhere in the nation. For example, the Asian carp, which was introduced unintentionally to the U.S., has been able to **thrive** in the Mississippi River and now threatens the Great Lakes ecosystem. Because of its large appetite, the population of native fish has gone down.

Some germs are also invasive species, and they are especially harmful to humans. One, the avian influenza virus, came to the U.S. carried by birds. This microbe can cause a serious lung **disorder** in infected people.

Some **agricultural** experts have introduced nonnative species on purpose to improve the environment. However, this can sometimes create **unexpected** problems. A hundred years ago, melaleuca trees were brought to Florida from Australia to stabilize swampy areas. Now millions of the trees blanket the land, crowding out native plants and harming endangered plants and animals.

The facts about this alien invasion lead to one conclusion: We must remove invasive species and keep new ones from our shores.

Jeff Greenberg/Alamy

Nonnative Species: Benefits and Costs

Over the years, about 50,000 nonnative species have entered the U.S. These four examples show the positive and negative impacts they can have.

SPECIES	NATIVE LAND	WHEN AND HOW INTRODUCED TO U.S.	POSITIVE IMPACT	NEGATIVE IMPACT
Horse	Europe	Early 1500s, on purpose	Used for work, transportation, and recreation	Made large-scale wars possible
Kudzu	Asia	Early 1800s, on purpose	Stops soil erosion	Crowds out native plants
Olives	Middle East and Europe	Early 1700s, on purpose, cultivation began in 1800s	Major food and cooking oil source, important industry in California	Most olives must be imported because they do not grow everywhere.
Mediterranean Fruit Fly	Sub-Saharan Africa	1929 (first recorded), accidentally	May be a food source for creatures such as spiders	Destroys 400 species of plants, including citrus and vegetable crops

(t to b) Ingram Publishing; Matt Meadows/Peter Arnold/Getty Images; Emilio Simion/Photodisc/Getty Images; Jack Dykinga/USDA

This community is trying to control the invasive melaleuca plant that has taken over this marsh.

Make Connections

Talk about the uses and harmful effects of species introduced into the United States.
ESSENTIAL QUESTION

Would you give up eating or using a species if you discovered it was nonnative? Explain your reasons. TEXT TO SELF

CAUTION
MELALEUCA CONTROL PROJECT
IN MARSH AREAS

369

Ask and Answer Questions

To check your understanding of a persuasive article, pause at different points and ask yourself questions about what you have read so far. Then look for answers. You can also ask questions about the whole text when you have finished.

 Find Text Evidence

After you read the article "New Arrivals Welcome" on page 367, you might ask yourself, *What is the main idea of this article?*

> page 367
>
> In Florida, for example, about 2,000 species of familiar plants and animals are nonnative. These include oranges, chickens, and sugarcane. In fact, 90 percent of farm sales can be traced directly to nonnative species.

When I reread, I learn the answer to my question. The main idea is that many species in the United States are nonnative, but can be very useful to us. Examples such as oranges and sugarcane support this.

 **Your Turn**

Ask and answer a question about "A Growing Problem" on page 368. As you read, use the strategy Ask and Answer Questions.

Author's Point of View

In a persuasive article, the author's **point of view** is the author's position on a topic. To identify an author's point of view, look for the author's word choices, reasons, and factual evidence used to explain the argument for or against an idea.

 ## Find Text Evidence

I see from the title "A Growing Problem" on page 368 that the author might have a negative point of view toward nonnative species. The word threaten *expresses a negative emotion, and the facts about pythons support a negative viewpoint.*

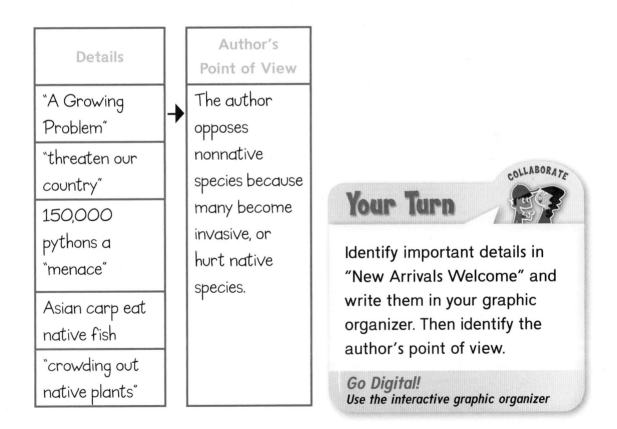

Details	Author's Point of View
"A Growing Problem"	The author opposes nonnative species because many become invasive, or hurt native species.
"threaten our country"	
150,000 pythons a "menace"	
Asian carp eat native fish	
"crowding out native plants"	

COLLABORATE

Your Turn

Identify important details in "New Arrivals Welcome" and write them in your graphic organizer. Then identify the author's point of view.

Go Digital!
Use the interactive graphic organizer

Persuasive Article

"New Arrivals Welcome" and "A Growing Problem" are persuasive articles.

Persuasive articles:
- Persuade a reader to support an idea or viewpoint
- Include facts and evidence that support opinions
- May include text features, such as charts and headings

Find Text Evidence

"New Arrivals Welcome" and "A Growing Problem" are persuasive articles. The titles reveal the authors' opinions about nonnative species. Facts and evidence support their opinions. A chart has headings and information for comparing the two points of view.

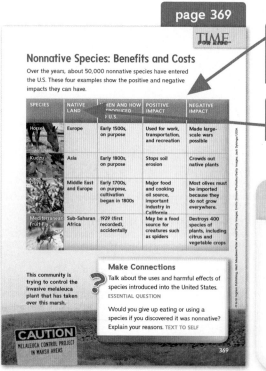

page 369

Chart A chart organizes data so that information can be easily analyzed and compared.

Headings Headings identify the main categories of information.

Your Turn

Analyze the information in the chart on page 369. Identify a species that has a mostly positive impact and one that has a mostly negative impact. Explain your conclusions.

COLLABORATE

Root Words

A **root word** is the basic word part that gives a word its main meaning. Knowing the meaning of a root is a key to recognizing and understanding many words that share that root.

 Find Text Evidence

In the first paragraph of "New Arrivals Welcome" on page 367, I read the word invasive. *It has the same root as* invade: vas *and* vad *both come from a Latin word meaning "to go." Something* invasive *goes into areas beyond its boundaries.*

page 367

Nonnative species are known as *invasive* when they harm the environment, our health, or the economy.

COLLABORATE

Your Turn

Use the roots below to figure out the meanings of words from "New Arrivals Welcome" and "A Growing Problem." List other words you know that contain those roots.

Roots: *nativus* = to be born   *spec* = appearance, kind
         avis = bird

nonnative, *page 367*   **avian,** *page 368*
species, *page 367*

Matt Meadows/Peter Arnold/Getty Images

Pages 366–369

Write About the Text

Vince

I answered the question: *In your opinion, do the benefits of purposely introducing a nonnative species outweigh the risks?*

Student Model: *Opinion*

Transitions

I used the phrase *for instance* to introduce an example that supports my opinion.

Reasons and Evidence

I developed my topic using facts and details from the text.

I think the benefits of purposely

introducing nonnative species into

an environment outweigh the risks.

For instance, without the introduction

of vedalia beetles into Florida's citrus

crops, many citrus farmers could have

faced a bad situation.

The beetles ate the insects that

were killing the citrus plants and did

laflor/iStock/360/Getty Images

so without any bad side effects or the need for additional pesticides. They kept the citrus healthy, the environment clean, and the farmers employed. The beetles were the best solution. With smart planning, purposely bringing nonnative species into certain areas has more advantages than disadvantages.

Grammar

The **adjective** *best* is used to compare more than two people, places, or things.

Grammar Handbook See page 467.

Strong Conclusion
My final sentence summarizes my response.

Your Turn

In your opinion, what has been the most helpful nonnative species brought to the United States? Explain your answer.

Go Digital!
Write your response online.
Use your editing checklist.

Kirk Weddle/Photodisc/Getty Images

Unit 6

Linked In

The BIG Idea

How are we all connected?

Peace can be made and kept only by the united determination of free and peace-loving peoples who are willing to work together — willing to help one another — willing to respect and tolerate and try to understand one another's opinions and feelings.

— **FRANKLIN D. ROOSEVELT,** President of the United States, 1933-1945, from *State of the Union Address, January 6, 1945*

Essential Question

How do different groups contribute to a cause?

Go Digital!

Giving Our All

When the United States joined the fight in World War II, people all over the country were called on to make contributions to the war effort.

▶ Many factories had to convert from making their usual products and start producing war equipment, such as airplanes.

▶ When men went off to war, women went to work! The women pictured here are putting rivets into an airplane wing.

Talk About It COLLABORATE

Write words you have learned about contributing to a cause. Then talk about a time that you joined others to help contribute to a cause.

Contributing to a Cause

Vocabulary

Use the picture and the sentences to talk with a
partner about each word.

bulletin

Kip posted a **bulletin** in the neighborhood
about his missing dog.

Why else might you post a bulletin?

contributions

The school art exhibit will feature
contributions from many student artists.

What other events rely on contributions
from others?

diversity

There was a great **diversity** of breeds at
the dog show.

Where else might you see a wide
diversity of animals?

enlisted

Citizens who have **enlisted** in the military
are sworn in before training begins.

Why have people enlisted for military
duty?

intercept

I jumped up to **intercept** the pass and prevent a touchdown by the other team.

In what other sports might you intercept a ball?

operations

The crew of workers began **operations** to clean up after the disaster.

What other operations might help in a disaster?

recruits

The officer addressed the **recruits** as they prepared for training.

What kinds of services look for new recruits?

survival

A first aid kit, a blanket, and water are important for **survival** in an emergency.

What other items are important for survival in an emergency?

Your Turn

COLLABORATE

Pick three words. Write three questions for your partner to answer.

Go Digital! *Use the online visual glossary*

(t to b) Juice Images/Alamy; CW Images/Alamy; PJF News/Alamy; ©Syracuse Newspapers/G. Wright/The Image Works

SHIPPED OUT

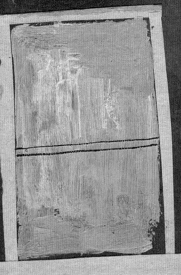

Essential Question

How do different groups contribute to a cause?

Read about how a young girl learns how to contribute to the war effort during World War II.

My name is Libby Kendall, and I am a prisoner of war. Well, not really, but some days it feels that way. Just like my dad, I've packed up my things and shipped out. Unlike my dad, however, nothing I do will ever help the Allies win World War II.

My father is a mechanic on a battleship in the Pacific Ocean. I'm trapped in a little apartment above my Aunt Lucia's bakery downtown. Mom says it's just for a few months while she works double shifts at the clothing factory. She makes uniforms, mostly sewing pockets on jackets. I asked her once if she snuck things into the pockets for soldiers to find, like little poems written in calligraphy. She said soldiers wore jackets with pockets to hold tools they might need for war **survival**, not silly things like poetry.

It seems no one appreciates my creative **contributions** to the war effort, but Aunt Lucia says my help to her is important, since both her workers joined the army.

On my first day with Aunt Lucia, she explained the daily **operations** of the bakery. First, we get up before dawn to knead the dough. Next, we bake breads and muffins. Then,

while I help customers, Lucia makes cakes and cookies for sale in the afternoon. Whenever the phone rings, she races from the back room to **intercept** the call. She's always worried that it might be bad news, so she wants to be the first to hear it.

After dinner, Aunt Lucia invites neighbors over to listen to the radio. Some are immigrants from a wide **diversity** of backgrounds. Lucia and others help translate the news into several languages for everyone to understand. I always listen closely for any **bulletin** about fighting in the Pacific.

Sean Qualls

I remember how intently my parents read reports about the war, which I rarely understood. They often whispered to one another, and I'd shout out something like, "Speak up! I can't hear you!" They'd frown and leave me alone to talk in private.

One night, they came into the living room and turned off the radio. At first I was angry, but they had serious expressions on their faces. "Our country's at war," Dad said. "The military will be looking for new **recruits**. I know something about boats and ship engines, so I intend to join the navy."

My face grew hot, but my hands felt cold. "You can't just leave," I said. I stomped on the floor for emphasis and stormed off to my bedroom. Looking back on that now, I feel ashamed of how selfishly I had acted.

This morning, Aunt Lucia can tell I'm feeling down. She asks me to help her decorate cupcakes for a fundraiser tonight. At first I'm not interested. I just slather on frosting and plop a berry on top. Then I realize that I can make red stripes out of strawberries and a patch of blue from blueberries. Soon I have a whole tray of cupcakes decorated like flags to show Aunt Lucia.

Sean Qualls

384

"These are wonderful!" Lucia says. "I'm sure they'll sell better than anything else!"

For the first time in weeks, I feel like I've done something right. I think of all the money we might make at the sale, and how it may buy supplies for my father.

"I **enlisted** in the navy to help restore democracy in the world," my dad said on the day he left. "Now you be a good navy daughter and sail straight, young lady." I promised I would. As he went out the door, I slipped a little poem into his coat pocket. "Here's a little rhyme to pass the day," it said. "I love you back in the U.S.A.!"

I look at the cupcakes and wish I could send one to my dad. Instead, I'll draw a platter on which they're piled high and send the picture off to the Pacific with a letter. That way, my dad will have plenty to share with everyone there.

Make Connections

What kinds of contributions to the war effort do characters make in this story? **ESSENTIAL QUESTION**

Think about an event in your own life that required contributions from others. How did they all work together? **TEXT TO SELF**

Summarize

Summarizing can help readers remember details as they read. You may want to summarize the important details at the beginning of a story that help you understand the setting and plot events. Remember that a summary should not include your opinions.

Find Text Evidence

Summarizing the opening paragraphs of "Shipped Out" on page 383 may help you understand the setting and plot of the story.

page 383

My name is Libby Kendall, and I am a prisoner of war. Well, not really, but some days it feels that way. Just like my dad, I've packed up my things and shipped out. Unlike my dad, however, nothing I do will ever help the Allies win World War II.

My father is a mechanic on a battleship in the Pacific Ocean. I'm trapped in a little apartment above my Aunt Lucia's bakery downtown. Mom says it's just for a few months while she works double shifts at the clothing factory. She makes uniforms, mostly sewing pockets on jackets. I asked her once if she snuck things into the pockets for soldiers to find, like little poems written in calligraphy. She said soldiers wore jackets with pockets to hold tools they might need for war **survival**, not silly things like poetry.

while I help customers, Lucia makes cakes and cookies for sale in the afternoon. Whenever the phone rings, she races from the back room to **intercept** the call. She's always worried that it might be bad news,

The first paragraphs introduce Libby Kendall, a girl living during World War II. Because her father has gone off to war and her mother must work long hours, Libby has been sent to live with her Aunt Lucia. I can infer that the war has caused many changes.

Your Turn

COLLABORATE

Summarize Libby's experiences at her aunt's bakery. Include details showing the war's effect on events.

Theme

To identify a story's **theme**, or overall message, consider what the characters say and do, and how their behavior affects the events and other characters. Finally, think about how characters change as a result of what happens to them.

 Find Text Evidence

On page 383 of "Shipped Out," Libby says that she feels like a prisoner of war at her aunt's apartment. This is because her father has gone to war and her mother has had to go to work. Libby feels her war efforts are not appreciated, but Aunt Lucia needs her help. These events will help me identify the theme.

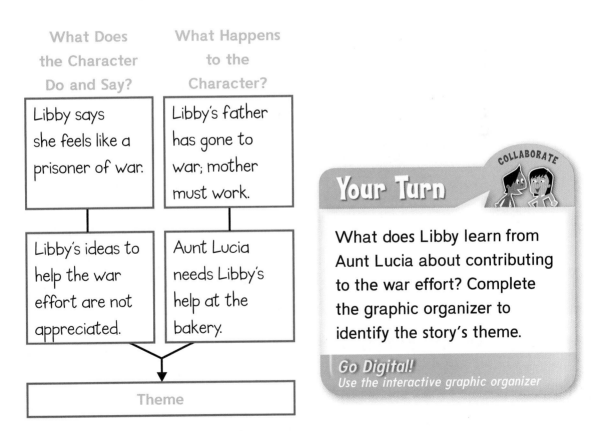

What Does the Character Do and Say?	What Happens to the Character?
Libby says she feels like a prisoner of war.	Libby's father has gone to war; mother must work.
Libby's ideas to help the war effort are not appreciated.	Aunt Lucia needs Libby's help at the bakery.

Theme

Your Turn COLLABORATE

What does Libby learn from Aunt Lucia about contributing to the war effort? Complete the graphic organizer to identify the story's theme.

Go Digital!
Use the interactive graphic organizer

Historical Fiction

The selection "Shipped Out" is historical fiction.

Historical fiction:
- Features events and settings typical of the period in which the story is set
- Features realistic characters who speak and act like people from a particular time and place in the past
- May include flashback

Find Text Evidence

I can tell that "Shipped Out" is historical fiction. The first paragraph mentions a real event, World War II. In flashback, we learn why Libby, the main character, has to live with her aunt.

page 384

I remember how intently my parents read reports about the war, which I rarely understood. They often whispered to one another, and I'd shout out something like, "Speak up! I can't hear you!" They'd frown and leave me alone to talk in private.

One night, they came into the living room and turned off the radio. At first I was angry, but they had serious expressions on their faces. "Our country's at war," Dad said. "The military will be looking for new **recruits**. I know something about boats and ship engines, so I intend to join the navy."

My face grew hot, but my hands felt cold. "You can't just leave," I said. I stomped on the floor for emphasis and stormed off to my bedroom. Looking back on that now, I feel ashamed of how selfishly I had acted.

This morning, Aunt Lucia can tell I'm feeling down. She asks me to help her decorate cupcakes for a fundraiser tonight. At first I'm not interested. I just slather on frosting and plop a berry on top. Then I realize that I can make red stripes out of strawberries and a patch of blue from blueberries. Soon I have a whole tray of cupcakes decorated like flags to show Aunt Lucia.

384

Flashback Flashbacks describe events and actions that occurred before the main action of the story. Key words, such as *once* or *I remember*, may show a character remembering past events.

Your Turn

COLLABORATE

Find another example of a flashback in "Shipped Out." Why might an author use flashbacks in a work of historical fiction?

Homophones

Sometimes when you read, you come across **homophones**, or words that sound the same but are spelled differently and have different meanings. Surrounding words and sentences can help you figure out the meaning of a homophone.

 Find Text Evidence

In "Shipped Out" on page 383, I see the words war *and* wore, *which are pronounced the same. From the surrounding words, I can tell that* war *means a large conflict, and that* wore *is the past tense of the verb* wear, *which means to have clothing on.*

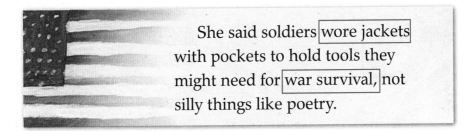

She said soldiers wore jackets with pockets to hold tools they might need for war survival, not silly things like poetry.

 COLLABORATE

Your Turn

Use context clues to distinguish between the meanings of the following homophones from "Shipped Out."

need and **knead,** *page 383*
read and **red,** *page 384*
sale and **sail,** *page 385*

Sean Qualls

Write About the Text

Pages 382–385

Roberto

I responded to the prompt: *Add an event to this story. Write a flashback from Libby's point of view about what life was like before the war.*

Student Model: *Narrative Text*

Life was great before the war.

On the first Sunday of each month,

Dad and I would go to the zoo to see

the "big cat" exhibits. One time, Dad

wanted to take my picture standing in

front of a group of lions. I posed with

a huge smile on my face. Then right

Sequence
I used time-order words to show when events happened.

Develop Character
I added descriptive details to develop the character.

before Dad snapped the photo, a lion

let out a huge roar. I jumped so high I

nearly hit the moon! Dad laughed so

hard that his eyes watered. I'll never

forget the sight of him laughing as if he

had no cares in the world.

Figurative Language
I included hyperbole to make my story more entertaining.

Grammar

An **adverb** can tell how, when, where, or how often an action can happen.

Grammar Handbook
See page 469.

Your Turn

Imagine that Libby received a letter from her father regarding her poem. Add an event to the story from Libby's point of view describing her reaction to the letter.

Go Digital!
Write your response online.
Use your editing checklist.

Sean Qualls

Essential Question

What actions can we take to get along with others?

Go Digital!

SL.5.1c See the California Standards section.

BernardBreton/iStock 360/Getty Images

Trying to
Fit In

It's a big crowded world out there, and we must work to figure out ways to live together. What can we do to get along well with others?

▶ This beach crowd consists of a colony of King Penguins and their chicks, and Southern Elephant Seals. Somehow they make it work!

▶ Part of getting along is learning to resolve a conflict when it arises. If we cannot resolve it, someone else may need to intervene.

Talk About It

Write words you have learned about how to get along with others. Then talk about a time you did not get along with someone and how you handled it.

Getting Along

Vocabulary

Use the picture and the sentences to talk with a
partner about each word.

abruptly

Playing in the park ended **abruptly**
because of a sudden rainstorm.

What else might cause an activity to
end abruptly?

ally

My little brother says that a dog is the
best **ally**, even for a superhero.

When might an ally be important?

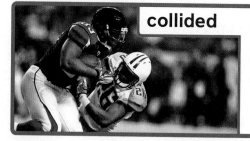

collided

The players **collided** on the field, and
both fell down.

What could happen if two cars collided?

confident

The more you practice a song before a
concert, the more **confident** you will feel.

How might practicing a lot make you feel
more confident?

conflict

To resolve their **conflict** over who would use the remote control, the sisters finally agreed to take turns.

What else can cause a conflict?

intervene

When the referee saw the players arguing, he had to **intervene** to stop them.

When else might a person need to intervene?

protective

Every bicycle rider should always wear a **protective** helmet.

How is an umbrella protective?

taunting

Outside the window, a squirrel seemed to be **taunting** my cat.

When have you seen people taunting other people?

Your Turn

COLLABORATE

Pick three words. Write three questions for your partner to answer.

Go Digital! *Use the online visual glossary*

The Bully

? Essential Question

What actions can we take to get along with others?

Read about how one student tries to deal with a bully.

Michael saw the trouble coming from all the way at the end of the school hallway. There standing by the stairs was J.T., the school bully who enjoyed **taunting** anyone he felt like at any given moment. J.T. was tall and strong, so few of his victims were willing to stand up to him and defend themselves. Michael hated the idea that he let J.T. get away with these offenses. Yet like most of the other kids who were picked on, he just took it quietly and waited for the unpleasant moment to pass.

J.T. walked directly toward Michael, his eyes locked on the books that Michael carried under his arms. When they met in the middle of the hallway, J.T. stopped **abruptly** and snapped at Michael, "Hey, let me see those books!" A group of students watched as Michael held out the books he was carrying, trying not to tremble to reveal how nervous he was.

J.T. grabbed a math book, looked inside for a second, and then shoved the book at Michael, who dropped all the books he held. "Hey, those books are school property," J.T. barked, "so don't let them fall to the floor!" Then he walked away, laughing loudly.

Michael, his cheeks turning red, half kicked the fallen books. Suddenly a hand appeared beside Michael and picked up an adventure novel as it slid away. "You look like you could use an **ally**," a friendly voice said with a laugh.

Marcelo Baez

397

Michael turned around and saw that it was Ramon. He was the school's star baseball player, basketball player, and everything-else-player you could name. Michael couldn't believe that Ramon was stopping to help him. The two had barely spoken to each other since the school year began.

"Thanks," Michael sighed with relief. "It's so confusing. I don't know what his problem is."

"I've been watching you in the halls," Ramon said, "and as I see it, you need to find a way to end this **conflict** with J.T." Michael nodded, stuck for what to say. "Well," Ramon continued, "I can tell you what my grandmother used to tell me whenever I had a problem with someone. She'd say, 'You can catch more flies with honey than with vinegar.'"

Looking puzzled, Michael asked, "What does that mean?"

"It means that being kind to your enemies may be more effective than being angry at them," Ramon explained.

"What if you just **intervene** and tell J.T. to stop picking on me?" Michael suggested. "I think he'd leave me alone if you threatened him."

"That's vinegar," Ramon laughed as he walked away. "Try honey instead."

That night, Michael thought about the advice that Ramon had given him. It sounded like a good plan, but deep down Michael wasn't very **confident** that it would actually work with J.T.

The next day in school brought Michael's usual misery. There stood J.T., and Michael knew it would be just a matter of seconds before the two of them **collided** in the middle of the hall.

As J.T. came nearer, Michael wished he had Ramon's **protective** arm to stop the bully from attacking. Then, suddenly, the unexpected happened. J.T. accidentally tripped. He fell down, and his own armful of books went flying across the floor.

For a moment, all was silent. The crowd of students in the hallway froze, waiting to see what J.T. would do next. As J.T. slowly stood up, Michael had an idea. He bent down, quickly picked up J.T.'s books from the floor, and offered them to him.

Michael said, "You look like you could use an ally."

J.T. was speechless, completely thrown by Michael's act of kindness. He took the books and muttered quickly, "Uh, thanks."

As J.T. walked away, Michael caught Ramon in the corner of his eye. Ramon gave him a big smile and a "thumbs-up." "My grandmother would be proud of you," Ramon said.

"It's just honey," Michael grinned. "I hope it sticks."

Make Connections

Talk about how Ramon's advice affected Michael's problem with J.T. ESSENTIAL QUESTION

What advice would you give to someone being bullied? Give reasons to support your opinion. TEXT TO SELF

Summarize

When you summarize a story, you include the most important details. As you read, you can decide which details are most important by asking yourself, *Would I understand the story without this detail?* If the answer is no, the detail is important.

🔍 Find Text Evidence

To help your understanding of the first part of "The Bully" on page 397, you can identify the important details and summarize that section.

page 397

Michael saw the trouble coming from all the way at the end of the school hallway. There standing by the stairs was J.T., the school bully who enjoyed **taunting** anyone he felt like at any given moment. J.T. was tall and strong, so few of his victims were willing to stand up to him and defend themselves. Michael hated the idea that he let J.T. get away with these offenses. Yet like most of the other kids who were picked on, he just took it quietly and waited for the unpleasant moment to pass.

J.T. walked directly toward Michael, his eyes locked on the books that Michael carried under his arms. When they met in the middle of the hallway, J.T. stopped **abruptly** and snapped at Michael, "Hey, let me see those books!" A group of students watched as Michael held out the books he was carrying, trying not to tremble to reveal how nervous he was.

J.T. grabbed a math book, looked inside for a second, and then shoved the book at Michael, who dropped all the books he held. "Hey, those books are school property," J.T. barked, "so don't let them fall to the floor!" Then he walked away, laughing loudly.

I read that J.T. picks on kids in school, including Michael. The text then says that Michael just took it quietly and waited for the unpleasant moment to pass. These seem like important details, so I will use them as I summarize.

Your Turn

COLLABORATE

Use the most important details to summarize the rest of "The Bully." As you read, use the strategy Summarize.

Theme

The **theme** of a story is the message or truth about life that the author wants readers to understand. To identify the theme, think about what the characters do and say and what happens to them. Then decide what lessons or truths about life can be learned from the events.

 Find Text Evidence

When I read the first page of "The Bully," I learned that Michael is regularly bullied by J.T. Because J.T. is taller and stronger, Michael is afraid to do anything to stop J.T. from bullying him.

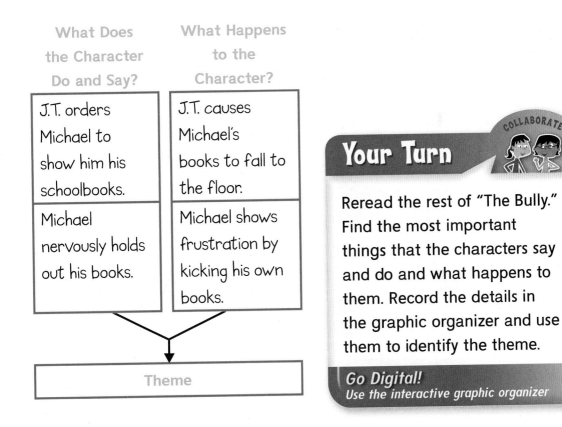

What Does the Character Do and Say?

J.T. orders Michael to show him his schoolbooks.

Michael nervously holds out his books.

What Happens to the Character?

J.T. causes Michael's books to fall to the floor.

Michael shows frustration by kicking his own books.

Theme

Your Turn COLLABORATE

Reread the rest of "The Bully." Find the most important things that the characters say and do and what happens to them. Record the details in the graphic organizer and use them to identify the theme.

Go Digital!
Use the interactive graphic organizer

Realistic Fiction

The selection "The Bully" is realistic fiction.

Realistic fiction:

- Is set in places and times that could actually exist
- Has characters and events like those found in real life
- Includes descriptive details and appropriate pacing

Find Text Evidence

I can tell that "The Bully" is realistic fiction. For example, Michael attends a school like those found in the real world. Being bullied is a real problem that some students face in school. Descriptive details and pacing help to make events of the story seem realistic.

page 397

Michael saw the trouble coming from all the way at the end of the school hallway. There standing by the stairs was J.T., the school bully who enjoyed **taunting** anyone he felt like at any given moment. J.T. was tall and strong, so few of his victims were willing to stand up to him and defend themselves. Michael hated the idea that he let J.T. get away with these offenses. Yet like most of the other kids who were picked on, he just took it quietly and waited for the unpleasant moment to pass.

J.T. walked directly toward Michael, his eyes locked on the books that Michael carried under his arms. When they met in the middle of the hallway, J.T. stopped **abruptly** and snapped at Michael, "Hey, let me see those books!" A group of students watched as Michael held out the books he was carrying, trying not to tremble to reveal how nervous he was.

J.T. grabbed a math book, looked inside for a second, and then shoved the book at Michael, who dropped all the books he held. "Hey, those books are school property," J.T. barked, "so don't let them fall to the floor!" Then he walked away, laughing loudly.

Michael, his cheeks turning red, half kicked the fallen books. Suddenly a hand appeared beside Michael and picked up an adventure novel as it slid away. "You look like you could use an **ally**," a friendly voice said with a laugh.

397

Descriptive Details Descriptive details tell you more about the setting, characters, and events.

Pacing Authors deliver details at a pace, or rate, that creates effects such as suspense or excitement.

COLLABORATE

Your Turn

List three other details in "The Bully" that indicate how the characters, problems, and story events are similar to those found in real life.

Connotation and Denotation

Every word has a dictionary meaning, or **denotation**. The same word may also have a **connotation**—a feeling the word suggests. Connotations are often negative or positive. Paying attention to word connotations as well as denotations will increase your understanding of a text.

Find Text Evidence

I read The crowd of students in the hallway froze *and realized that the word* froze *was another way of saying that the crowd stopped moving. The connotation of* froze, *however, suggests that they stopped out of fear and could not move at all.*

> For a moment, all was silent. The crowd of students in the hallway froze, waiting to see what J.T. would do next. As J.T. slowly stood up, Michael had an idea.

Your Turn

COLLABORATE

Decide whether each of the following words from "The Bully" has a positive or negative connotation. Then tell what each word means in the story.

tremble, *page 397*
barked, *page 397*
muttered, *page 399*

Write About the Text

Pages 396–399

Paco

I answered the question: *In your opinion, should Ramon have confronted J.T. when he saw Michael being bullied? Explain your answer.*

Student Model: *Opinion*

Strong Opening
My first sentence clearly states my opinion.

> Even though he helped Michael, I think Ramon should have said something to J.T. right when he saw him bullying Michael. This way Michael would not have been embarrassed by dropping his books. Ramon is very popular, so J.T. would have probably listened to him.
>
> Ramon could have first approached

Time-Order Words
I included time-order words to show how events could occur in this situation.

both of them to ask if they needed

help with anything. Then he could have

stood closer to Michael to show that

he is friends with him. Finally, he could

have asked Michael if he wanted to

grab lunch in the cafeteria later.

This would have sent the message

that Michael is a cool guy, and

J.T. should stop picking on him.

Strong Conclusion
My final sentence sums
up my thoughts.

W.5.ld See the California Standards section.

This is an example
of an **adverb that
compares.**

*Grammar Handbook
See page 470.*

Your Turn

In your opinion, how do you think
Michael and J.T. will interact the
next few times they see each
other? Explain your answer.

Go Digital!
Write your response online.
Use your editing checklist.

Marcelo Baez

Essential Question

How are living things adapted to their environment?

Go Digital!

Creature Comforts

Every living thing, including human beings, has developed ways to live in its environment.

▶ Take me, for example. I'm an Australian lizard called a Thorny Devil. My thorns protect me from predators. Also, I can duck my head, and up pops a "false head" at the back of my neck!

▶ I have another adaptation so I can get water from wherever it touches my body: Grooves on my body move water up into my mouth!

Talk About It 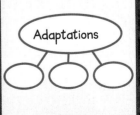 COLLABORATE

Write words you have learned about adapting to an environment. Then talk about an animal you know about and how it has adapted.

Adaptations

Words to Know

Vocabulary

Use the picture and the sentences to talk with a partner about each word.

adaptation

Changing color is an **adaptation** some lizards have made to their environment.

How is fur an example of an adaptation?

agile

Kim was such an **agile** gymnast, she could do a back bend on a balance beam.

Why should athletes be agile?

cache

My parents **cache** jewelry and other treasures in an old wooden chest.

Where else might people cache special things?

dormant

The guide explained that the volcano was **dormant**, so we felt safe standing near it.

Why is it safe to visit a dormant volcano?

forage

When winter comes, elk, deer, and other animals often have to **forage** for food.

Why is it hard to forage for food during winter?

frigid

We drank a hot beverage to warm up after being outside on that **frigid** day.

Do you usually wear shorts in frigid weather?

hibernate

Some animals, such as the dormouse, **hibernate** in some way during the winter.

Why do some animals hibernate in winter?

insulates

My coat **insulates** my body against the cold.

What kind of coat insulates a cat?

COLLABORATE

Your Turn

Pick three words. Write three questions for your partner to answer.

Go Digital! *Use the online visual glossary*

Mysterious Oceans

Essential Question

How are living things adapted to their environment?

Read about the adaptation of sea creatures to the deep ocean.

Deep Diving

It has no mouth, eyes, or stomach. Its soft body is encased in a white cylinder and topped with a red plume. It can grow to be eight feet tall. It is a sea creature known as a giant tube worm, and it lives without any sunlight on the deep, dark ocean floor.

What we sometimes call the deep ocean, in contrast to shallow waters, covers almost two-thirds of Earth's surface. On average, oceans are about two miles deep. However, the deepest point known on Earth, Challenger Deep, descends nearly seven miles.

◀ Some deep ocean fish are swimming among tube worms. New ocean species are being discovered all the time.

The ocean's floor is varied, consisting of vast plains, steep canyons, and towering mountains. It includes active, **dormant**, and extinct volcanoes. This undersea world is a harsh environment because of its **frigid** temperatures and lack of sunshine.

The deep ocean is also a mysterious environment that remains largely unexplored. Little is known about it or its creatures. Do any of them **cache** food the way land animals do? Do any ocean species **hibernate**? As one example among countless mysteries, not a single, live giant squid had ever been spotted until a few years ago. We knew they existed only because their corpses had been found.

The Challenger Deep is located in an undersea canyon called the Mariana Trench.

The Deepest Known Point on Earth

CHINA

JAPAN

PACIFIC OCEAN

N
W E
S

Hawaii
(U.S.)

PHILIPPINES

0 km   1,000
0 miles   1,000
Miller Projection

Key

Mariana Trench
1,554 miles long
and 44 miles wide

● Challenger Deep

INDIAN
OCEAN

AUSTRALIA

Dr. Ken MacDonald/Science Photo Library

This fish, the striated frogfish, lures prey. The nose is an adaptation to life in the deep ocean.

A basket starfish rests in a deep-sea coral reef.

Amazing Adaptations

When a submersible, or submarine, was invented that could descend farther than any other craft, scientists were then able to make the odyssey to the deep ocean floor. However, exploration remains difficult, and they have since seen merely five percent of the underwater world.

As scientists anticipated, life generally seems sparse at the bottom of the deep ocean. Few creatures can survive there. Food sources that sea creatures depend on, such as dead plants and animals, rarely drift down from the ocean's surface. As a result, animals have to adapt to an environment that is not only frigid and dark but also has little food.

One example of an **adaptation** to this environment is seen in the starfish. Deep sea starfish grow larger and more aggressive than their shallow water relatives. They can't afford to wait for an occasional snail to pass by. Instead, deep sea starfish are predators that actively **forage** for food. They reach up their five arms, which have pincers at the ends, to catch meals of **agile**, fast-moving shrimp.

Anglerfish also are adapted to the herculean task of finding scarce food. Each has a bioluminous, or naturally glowing, lure on the top of its head. This shining pole is sensitive to vibrations and allows them to attract other fish. With their huge jaws, they quickly seize their prey.

Heated Habitats

What has truly surprised scientists, however, is the discovery of another, very different type of environment on the deep ocean floor. They found that cracks, or vents, in Earth's surface exist underwater, just as they do on dry land. Sea water rushes into these vents, where it mingles with chemicals. The water is also heated by magma, or hot melted rock. When the water from the vent bursts back into the ocean, it creates geysers and hot springs.

To scientists' amazement, the habitats around these vents teem with life. In addition to tube worms, there are huge clams, eyeless shrimp, crabs, and mussels, along with many kinds of bacteria. One odd creature is the Pompeii worm. It has a fleece of bacteria on its back that, as far as scientists can determine, **insulates** it from heat.

How can so much life exist where there is so little food or sunlight? Scientists have discovered that many creatures transform the chemicals from the vents into food. The process is called chemosynthesis. Because of this process, animals are able to flourish in these remarkable habitats. Creatures that don't use chemosynthesis for food, such as crabs, eat the ones that do.

There are many mysteries to be found and solved at the bottom of the deep sea. In the last few decades alone, scientists have discovered more than 1,500 ocean species! If scientists continue sea exploration, they are bound to discover many more.

Make Connections

Talk about the ways some sea creatures adapt to the deep ocean. **ESSENTIAL QUESTION**

Compare one sea creature adaptation to that of another animal you have seen. **TEXT TO SELF**

Mussels, worms, and spider crabs live near heated vents.

OAR/National Undersea Research Program (NURP)/Texas A&M Univ./NOAA

Ask and Answer Questions

Asking and answering questions can help you check your understanding of complex scientific text. You can ask yourself what the main ideas are, or whether you need to reread a section of text.

 Find Text Evidence

The last paragraph in the section "Deep Diving" on page 411 of "Mysterious Oceans" asks several questions about oceans. You may wonder how to find the answers.

> **page 411**
>
> The deep ocean is also a mysterious environment that remains largely unexplored. Little is known about it or its creatures. Do any of them **cache** food the way land animals do? Do any ocean species **hibernate**? As one example among countless mysteries, not a single, live giant squid had ever been spotted until a few years ago. We knew they existed only because their corpses had been found.

There must be reasons why we know so little about ocean life. I'm going to ask myself, "Why is the deep ocean so mysterious?" I will reread the section to try to answer this question.

Your Turn

COLLABORATE

Use the information in the first two paragraphs of "Deep Diving" on page 411 to begin to answer the question "Why is the deep ocean so mysterious?"

Cause and Effect

To figure out cause and effect relationships in a text, first look for an event or action that makes something happen. This is the **cause**. Then look for what happens as a result of that cause. This is the **effect**. Words and phrases such as *because of, as a result, if/then,* or *when* can signal cause and effect.

 Find Text Evidence

In the first paragraph of the section "Amazing Adaptations" on page 412 of "Mysterious Oceans," the author explains that a new type of submersible was invented. The word when *signals a cause and effect relationship. This invention caused something else to happen.*

Cause   ➡️   Effect

Invention of submersible   ➡️   Exploration of ocean floor

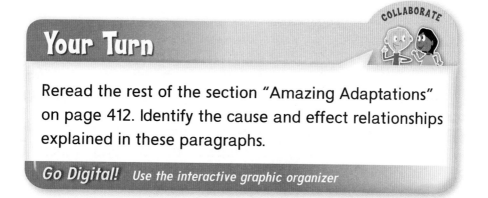

COLLABORATE

Your Turn

Reread the rest of the section "Amazing Adaptations" on page 412. Identify the cause and effect relationships explained in these paragraphs.

Go Digital!   *Use the interactive graphic organizer*

Expository Text

The selection "Mysterious Oceans" is expository text.

Expository text:

- Presents information about a topic, with main ideas and key details
- May be organized to show cause and effect relationships
- May include text features such as photos and maps

Find Text Evidence

I can tell "Mysterious Oceans" is expository text. The text gives information about oceans and includes main ideas and cause and effect relationships. A map gives visual information.

page 411

Deep Diving

It has no mouth, eyes, or stomach. Its soft body is encased in a white cylinder and topped with a red plume. It can grow to be eight feet tall. It is a sea creature known as a giant tube worm, and it lives without any sunlight on the deep, dark ocean floor.

What we sometimes call the deep ocean, in contrast to shallow waters, covers almost two-thirds of Earth's surface. On average, oceans are about two miles deep. However, the deepest point known on Earth, Challenger Deep, descends nearly seven miles.

◀ Some deep ocean fish are swimming among tube worms. New ocean species are being discovered all the time.

The ocean's floor is varied, consisting of vast plains, steep canyons, and towering mountains. It includes active, **dormant**, and extinct volcanoes. This undersea world is a harsh environment because of its **frigid** temperatures and lack of sunshine.

The deep ocean is also a mysterious environment that remains largely unexplored. Little is known about it or its creatures. Do any of them **cache** food the way land animals do? Do any ocean species **hibernate**? As one example among countless mysteries, not a single, live giant squid had ever been spotted until a few years ago. We knew they existed only because their corpses had been found.

The Challenger Deep is located in an undersea canyon called the Mariana Trench.

The Deepest Known Point on Earth

CHINA JAPAN *PACIFIC OCEAN*

Hawaii (U.S.)

PHILIPPINES

INDIAN OCEAN

AUSTRALIA

Key
🔺 Mariana Trench 1,554 miles long and 44 miles wide
● Challenger Deep

411

Map A map is a flat picture of an area. Most maps have a title, a scale to show how many miles are represented by an inch, a compass rose to show directions, and a key that explains colors or symbols.

COLLABORATE

Your Turn

Study the map on page 411. What is the approximate length and width of the Mariana Trench? How does the map help you visualize it?

Context Clues

If you read an unfamiliar or multiple meaning word that puzzles you, you can look for clues to its meaning as you read the paragraph in which it appears. Clues to a word's meaning can be found in the beginning, middle, or end of a paragraph.

Find Text Evidence

In first paragraph of "Mysterious Oceans" on page 411, I see the word cylinder. *I'm not sure what* cylinder *means. Since the creature being discussed is called a tube worm, I think that a cylinder may refer to the tube around the worm.*

It has no mouth, eyes, or stomach. Its soft body is encased in a white cylinder and topped with a red plume. It can grow to be eight feet tall. It is a sea creature known as a giant tube worm, and it lives without any sunlight on the deep, dark ocean floor.

Your Turn

COLLABORATE

With a partner, use context clues to figure out the meaning of the following words in "Mysterious Oceans." Remember, you may find context clues in the beginning, middle, or end of a paragraph.

sparse, *page 412*
aggressive, *page 412*
predators, *page 412*

Pages 410–413

Write About the Text

Ana

I answered the question: *Why are deep-sea creatures forced to adapt? Use evidence from the text.*

Student Model: *Informative Text*

Deep-sea creatures are forced to adapt because there is not enough food at depths below two miles. These environments are dark and cold. Starfish, for example, adapt by growing larger and becoming aggressive hunters, while anglerfish rely on a bioluminous lure to attract prey.

Grammar

Only use one negative within a sentence. Avoid **double negatives**.

Grammar Handbook See page 470.

Develop a Topic

I included facts and text evidence to support my writing.

Similarly, animals that live near heated vents in the ocean floor also experience a lack of food. Some adapt by changing chemicals from the vents into food through a process called chemosynthesis. Deep-sea creatures in every environment must adapt to feed themselves and survive.

Sentence Structure
I used a transition to show how different creatures are alike.

Strong Conclusion
My final sentence summarizes the most important information.

Your Turn

Why does deep-sea exploration remain difficult? Use evidence from the text.

Go Digital!
Write your response online.
Use your editing checklist.

Lophelia II 2009 Expedition, NOAA-OER

Essential Question

What impact do our actions have on our world?

Go Digital!

Penny Tweedie/Corbis

SL.5.1c See the California Standards section.

Show How You Care

Human beings influence events all over the world. When human actions have a negative impact on the environment, many people must work to help restore it. Their actions can make a big difference.

▶ I always wanted to take care of animals, so I studied to be a veterinarian. My studies led me to a special interest in chimpanzees.

▶ Working to protect this species is one way I can have a positive impact on the world.

Talk About It

Write words you have learned about making a difference. Then talk about actions you have taken that have had an impact on the world.

Making a Difference

Vocabulary

Use the picture and the sentences to talk with a
partner about each word.

export

Ships transport many goods made for
export overseas.

What goods might be produced
for export to other countries?

glistening

The **glistening** wrapping paper made
the gift look really special.

What other materials create a glistening
effect?

influence

Mrs. Garcia pointed out information that
could **influence** Anna's voting decision.

Who might influence your decisions
each day?

landscape

From our cabin, we see a **landscape** of
mountains, trees, and a clear blue lake.

What landscape would you like to visit?

native

Penguins are **native** to Antarctica.

What animals are native to your state or area?

plantations

Flying over the land, we had a view of farms and **plantations** below.

What kinds of things are grown on plantations?

restore

The upholsterer worked to **restore** the antique chair to its original condition.

What else might you restore by repairing?

urged

My mom **urged** my baby brother to eat his food.

What kinds of foods are growing children urged to eat?

Your Turn

COLLABORATE

Pick three words. Write three questions for your partner to answer.

Go Digital!   *Use the online visual glossary*

Words to Save the World

The Work of Rachel Carson

Essential Question

What impact do our actions have on our world?

Read about how the biologist Rachel Carson used the power of writing to change the world.

Sometimes, the quietest voice can spark the most clamorous outrage. Combining her love of nature with a belief in scientific accuracy, the soft-spoken writer Rachel Carson raised awareness about environmental issues. As a result, the U.S. government strengthened the rules and regulations regarding the use of chemical pesticides. Many people consider Rachel's book *Silent Spring* the foundation of today's environmental movement.

Early Influences

Rachel was born in Springdale, Pennsylvania, in 1907. Throughout her childhood, her mother encouraged her to explore the **landscape** surrounding the family's farm. Often equipped with binoculars, Rachel developed a love of nature that affected many of her decisions. For example, she first chose to study English literature and writing when she went to college. However, she later decided to study biology. While studying at a marine laboratory, she became fascinated by the **glistening** and shimmering seascape.

From an early age, Rachel had loved to write. These writing skills proved useful to her career. She began by creating radio programs for the U.S. Bureau of Fisheries. She then became an editor and librarian for the agency. While she was working, she submitted her own articles to newspapers and magazines. Rachel eventually published three books about the ocean and its **native** plants and animals. This trilogy included *Under the Sea-Wind, The Sea Around Us,* and *The Edge of the Sea.*

Rachel supported her ideas with well-researched facts.

◀ **Rachel preferred working alone as she gathered information.**

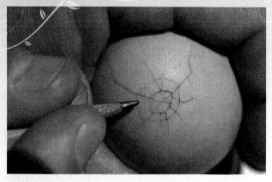

Rachel Carson's research revealed that DDT caused damage to birds and eggs.

A Call to Action

The success of Rachel's books allowed her to devote more time to her own projects. She built a cottage close to the sea on the coast of Maine. Soon, however, a letter arrived from some old friends, Olga and Stuart Huckins. They described problems resulting from the spraying of DDT on their private wildlife sanctuary. Chemical companies had developed DDT as an effective solution to crop-eating insects on farms and **plantations**. At the Huckins's sanctuary, however, the chemical also seemed to be harming birds.

In response, Rachel hired assistants to help research the Huckins's claim. Worried by the slow pace of their work, she decided to continue alone. By publishing her findings, she hoped to warn about the dangers of these new chemicals. In order to dramatize the situation, she **urged** readers to imagine a world without songbirds. The book's title, *Silent Spring,* describes this possible result of pesticide abuse.

Silent Spring prompted readers to raise their voices in unison against the chemical corporations. They demanded an investigation into pesticides and implored the government to restrict their use. In response, President John Kennedy created a Congressional committee to study the matter. Rachel testified before this group and provided facts and information to **influence** its decisions.

Though a pesticide may target insects, animals can also feel its effects.

Sample Food Chains

TROPHIC LEVEL	GRASSLAND BIOME	OCEAN BIOME
Primary Producer	grass	phytoplankton
Primary Consumer	grasshopper	zooplankton
Secondary Consumer	rat	fish
Tertiary Consumer	snake	seal

A Strong Reaction

Meanwhile, the chemical companies struggled to counter Rachel's claims. Despite her reasonable approach to the problem, they tried to depict her accusations as irrational. They published articles and reports that mocked her writing style and belittled her ideas. Advertisements on television proclaimed the safety of their products. When these ads did not change public opinion, they pulled financial support from programs that featured Rachel.

Rachel worried that once pesticides poisoned an area, it might be impossible to **restore** the environment to its original state. "Man's attitude toward nature is today critically important simply because we have now acquired a fateful power to alter and destroy nature," she said in an interview. Her testimony led to restrictions on certain pesticides in the United States. Even so, chemical companies continued to produce them for **export** to other countries.

Rachel Carson died shortly after *Silent Spring* was published, but her voice survives within her books. Her love of nature endures, along with her quiet desire to preserve and protect the natural world.

Carson understood the power her words had to educate others, especially children.

Make Connections

What impact did the publication of *Silent Spring* have on the makers of pesticides such as DDT? ESSENTIAL QUESTION

Think about a time when you wrote or spoke about something that needed to change. What impact did your words have? TEXT TO SELF

Ask and Answer Questions

Readers ask themselves questions about the text before, during, and after their reading. Asking and answering questions helps you focus, as well as check your understanding of a text.

Find Text Evidence

As you read "Words to Save the World" on page 425, you can ask yourself questions about Rachel Carson and the effects she had on the world around her.

---

page 425

Sometimes, the quietest voice can spark the most clamorous outrage. Combining her love of nature with a belief in scientific accuracy, the soft-spoken writer Rachel Carson raised awareness about environmental issues. As a result, the U.S. government strengthened the rules and regulations regarding the use of chemical pesticides. Many people consider Rachel's book *Silent Spring* the foundation of today's environmental movement.

Early Influences

Rachel was born in Springdale, Pennsylvania, in 1907. Throughout

laboratory, she became fascinated by the **glistening** and shimmering seascape.

From an early age, Rachel had loved to write. These writing skills proved useful to her career. She began by creating radio programs for the U.S. Bureau of Fisheries. She then became an editor and librarian for the agency. While she was working, she submitted her own articles to newspapers and magazines. Rachel eventually published three books about the ocean and its **native** plants and animals. This trilogy included *Under the Sea-Wind, The Sea Around Us,* and *The Edge of the Sea.*

I read that Rachel Carson was a writer whose work had major effects on our country. I ask myself, "What did she write about? Why did her books have influence?" I will read on to find answers.

COLLABORATE

Your Turn

Reread the section "A Call to Action" on page 426. Form questions about possible responses to Rachel's book. Then look for answers. Use the strategy Ask and Answer Questions as you read.

Problem and Solution

Presenting **problems and solutions** is one way of organizing information in a biography. The author may describe problems encountered by subject of the text and then explain any solutions that resulted. As you read, try to identify problems and the actions taken to solve them.

Find Text Evidence

In the section "A Call to Action" on page 426, Rachel receives information about a problem with dying birds. As she attempts solutions, she finds other problems she needs to address. I can record her problem and solution process in my graphic organizer.

Problem	Solution
Rachel gets a letter about bird deaths due to pesticides.	She hires assistants to help research the claim.
The research goes too slowly.	Rachel decides to work alone.

Your Turn

Continue to reread the section "A Call to Action" on page 426. Record the other problems and solutions in your graphic organizer.

Go Digital!
Use the interactive graphic organizer

Biography

"Words to Save the World: The Work of Rachel Carson" is a biography.

A **biography:**
- Tells the true story of someone else's life
- May be about someone who lived in the past or is living today, written in the third-person
- May include text features such as illustrations

Find Text Evidence

I can tell that "Words to Save the World: The Work of Rachel Carson" is a biography. It tells about her childhood, life, and work. The illustration helps me understand why her work was important.

page 426

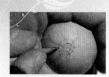

Rachel Carson's research revealed that DDT caused damage to birds and eggs.

A Call to Action

The success of Rachel's books allowed her to devote more time to her own projects. She built a cottage close to the sea on the coast of Maine. Soon, however, a letter arrived from some old friends, Olga and Stuart Huckins. They described problems resulting from the spraying of DDT on their private wildlife sanctuary. Chemical companies had developed DDT as an effective solution to crop-eating insects on farms and **plantations**. At the Huckins's sanctuary, however, the chemical also seemed to be harming birds.

In response, Rachel hired assistants to help research the Huckins's claim. Worried by the slow pace of their work, she decided to continue alone. By publishing her findings, she hoped

to warn about the dangers of these new chemicals. In order to dramatize the situation, she **urged** readers to imagine a world without songbirds. The book's title, *Silent Spring*, describes this possible result of pesticide abuse.

Silent Spring prompted readers to raise their voices in unison against the chemical corporations. They demanded an investigation into pesticides and implored the government to restrict their use. In response, President John Kennedy created a Congressional committee to study the matter. Rachel testified before this group and provided facts and information to **influence** its decisions.

Though a pesticide may target insects, animals can also feel its effe...

Sample Food Chains

TROPHIC LEVEL	GRASSLAND BIOME	OCEAN BIOME
Primary Producer	grass	phytoplankton
Primary Consumer	grasshopper	zooplankton
Secondary Consumer	rat	fish
Tertiary Consumer	snake	seal

426

Use Illustrations An illustration is a picture or diagram that clarifies information. The illustrations in a biography may help the reader understand key concepts related to the life or work of the subject.

Your Turn

COLLABORATE

List three details in "Words to Save the World: The Work of Rachel Carson" that help you understand the subject of this biography.

Synonyms and Antonyms

Synonyms are words that have the same, or almost the same, meaning. **Antonyms** are words that have the opposite, or nearly the opposite, meaning. The relationship between synonyms or antonyms in the same sentence or paragraph can help you better understand the meaning of each word.

Find Text Evidence

In the first sentence of "Words to Save the World: The Work of Rachel Carson" on page 425 most clamorous *must be an antonym of* quietest. *The word* clamorous *helps show that her quiet voice provoked a noisy, loud response from others.*

> Sometimes, the quietest voice can spark the most clamorous outrage.

Your Turn

Find a synonym or antonym in the same sentence or paragraph as each of the following words in "Words to Save the World." Explain how the meanings are the same or different.

regulations, *page 425*
reasonable, *page 427*
mocked, *page 427*

Pages 424–427

Write About the Text

Yasmine

I answered the question: *In your opinion, does the author show any bias about the use of pesticides? Use text evidence.*

Student Model: *Opinion*

Strong Opening

My paragraph begins by clearly stating my opinion in response to the question.

> I don't think the author shows any bias about the use of pesticides. The author tells how Rachel Carson worked to warn people about the effects of pesticides on nature. The author never states that pesticides are bad.

Transitions

I connected my opinion to relevant evidence.

> Instead, the author tells how Rachel researched the damage pesticides could cause. Then the author describes

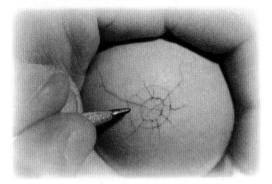

how Rachel issued a call to action by writing a book, asking people to think about a life without birds, and speaking before Congress. The government, not the author, decided to restrict or ban some pesticides in the United States. If these chemicals weren't harmful, the government wouldn't have done this.

Grammar

This **prepositional phrase** begins with the **preposition** *without* and ends with the noun *birds*.

Grammar Handbook See page 472.

Focus on a Topic
I provided logical reasons to support my opinion.

Your Turn

In your opinion, should all pesticides be banned? Use text evidence.

Go Digital!
Write your response online.
Use your editing checklist.

James P. Blair/National Geographic/Getty Images

Essential Question

What can our connections to the world teach us?

Go Digital!

Keeping in Touch

As we go out into the world, we find ways to stay connected to our friends, families, and countries.

▶ Sitting within sight of the famous Taj Mahal in India, I can keep a connection with others using my cell phone and laptop.

▶ As we exchange the stories of our adventures, I feel I am a part of the larger world.

Talk About It

Write words you have learned about connections to the world. Then talk about one thing you have learned from a connection to a person or place.

World Connections

Vocabulary

Use the picture and the sentences to talk with a partner about each word.

blares

When a trumpet or other loud instrument **blares**, Frankie covers his ears.

What might be the reason why a car horn blares?

connection

Ron feels a strong **connection** to the players on his soccer team.

How would you establish a connection with a new friend?

errand

My mom sent me on an **errand** to the cereal aisle of the grocery store.

What errand would you do for a relative?

exchange

Milo and his brothers were paid ten dollars in **exchange** for shoveling snow.

What favor might you do in exchange for free movie tickets?

Poetic Terms

personification

Poets use **personification** to make objects, animals, or ideas resemble people.

How might personification help describe a thunderstorm?

assonance

A poem using **assonance** includes words with the same vowel sound.

List three words that have assonance with the word moon.

consonance

A poem using **consonance** includes words with the same middle or final consonant sound.

Name three words that have consonance with the word buzz.

imagery

With **imagery**, poets use words to create a vivid picture that the reader can imagine.

What imagery might you use to describe a specific rainy day?

COLLABORATE

Your Turn

Pick three words. Write three questions for your partner to answer.

Go Digital! *Use the online visual glossary*

To Travel!

To travel! To travel!
To visit distant places;
To leave my corner of the world
To seek new names and faces.
Adventure! Adventure!
Exploring foreign lands;
If I can leap across the globe,
My universe expands!

A novel waves her arms to me,
"Come read! Come read!" she cries.
Her pages dance with ancient tales,
A feast for hungry eyes!
The paintings on museum walls
Are begging me to tour:
"Leave your home and live our scenes,
A grand exchange for sure!"

To travel! To travel!
Through timeless books and art,
I enter and experience
A life so far apart.

Essential Question

What can our connections to the world teach us?

Read two poems about connecting with other cultures and with nature.

I sail across the seven seas,
My heart soars like a bird.
And soon I'm hearing languages
I've never, ever heard.

Far across the seven seas,
Aromas fill the air.
Foods I've never, ever tried
Are eaten everywhere!
Music blares a different tune,
And strange, new clothes are worn.
Parents pass on customs
To the young ones who are born.

I've traveled! I've traveled!
It's left me more aware;
A valuable connection
To the universe we share.
By reading books and viewing art,
I've learned a thing or two:
The world was made not just for me,
But made for me and you!

— Jad Abbas

Wild Blossoms

One bright summer morning, my grandmother asked me to help her plant some flowers. I pedaled my bike downtown, wheels weaving between sunbeams. In the sky, clouds exchanged greetings, their language inaudible, while I, on my errand, brought a long list of seeds to the store. Back on my bike, I followed the same sensible route I always took to Grandmother's house. I watched with surprise as she tore off the tops of the seed packets and shook them willy-nilly around the backyard, then told me to do the same.

"I thought we were planting a garden," I told her,
"with row after row of flowers." She said, "Oh, no!
I prefer a mountain meadow, one with plenty
of variety." As she talked, bees buzzed about
in excitable flight, impatient for blossoms.
Quick swifts and happy sparrows dipped, dove, and darted
after the falling seeds. My grandmother and I
danced about the backyard, arms outstretched, letting seeds
loose on the wind, joyfully dreaming of the wild
beauty that would fill the yard, and us, all summer.

— Amelia Campos

Make Connections

Describe how the speakers in the poems connect to their worlds. **ESSENTIAL QUESTION**

How do the connections described in the poems compare with your own experiences? **TEXT TO SELF**

Lyric and Narrative

Lyric poetry: • Expresses personal thoughts and feelings. • Has a musical quality and may include rhyme and rhythm. • Often contains imagery.

Narrative poetry: • Tells a story. • Has characters and dialogue. • May have meter. • Often contains imagery.

Find Text Evidence

I can tell that "To Travel!" is a lyric poem expressing the speaker's personal feelings. "Wild Blossoms" is a narrative poem that tells a story. Both poems contain imagery, or words that create a picture.

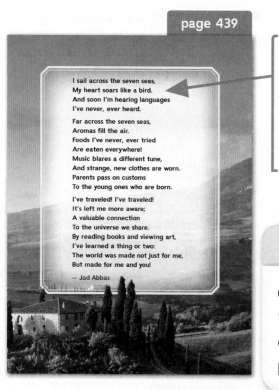

page 439

I sail across the seven seas,
My heart soars like a bird.
And soon I'm hearing languages
I've never, ever heard.

Far across the seven seas,
Aromas fill the air.
Foods I've never, ever tried
Are eaten everywhere!
Music blares a different tune,
And strange, new clothes are worn.
Parents pass on customs
To the young ones who are born.

I've traveled! I've traveled!
It's left me more aware;
A valuable connection
To the universe we share.
By reading books and viewing art,
I've learned a thing or two:
The world was made not just for me,
But made for me and you!

— Jad Abbas

"To Travel!" is a lyric poem. The line *My heart soars like a bird* expresses the speaker's feelings about traveling the world. The line *I sail across the seven seas* shows imagery of traveling.

Your Turn

Compare the way the speakers of "To Travel!" and "Wild Blossoms" express themselves. How are the poems similar and different?

Point of View

The **point of view** is the individual way the speaker of the poem thinks. Details such as word choice and the thoughts expressed are clues to the speaker's point of view.

 Find Text Evidence

"To Travel!" and "Wild Blossoms" are written in the first person, and they express individual points of view. I'll reread "To Travel!" to look for key details that help me figure out the speaker's point of view.

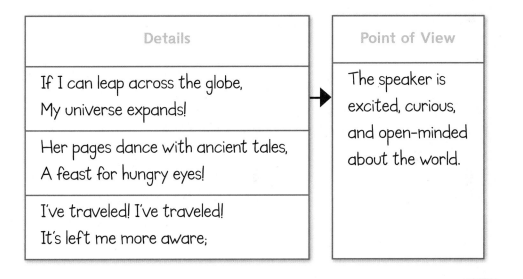

Details	Point of View
If I can leap across the globe, My universe expands!	The speaker is excited, curious, and open-minded about the world.
Her pages dance with ancient tales, A feast for hungry eyes!	
I've traveled! I've traveled! It's left me more aware;	

Your Turn

COLLABORATE

Reread the poem "Wild Blossoms." List key details in the graphic organizer. Use the details to figure out the speaker's point of view.

Go Digital! *Use the interactive graphic organizer*

Assonance and Consonance

Poets may repeat sounds in words for emphasis or effect.
Assonance is the repetition of the same vowel sound in two or
more words. **Consonance** is the repetition of a final or middle
consonant sound. The sounds contribute to a poem's feeling.

Find Text Evidence

Reread the poem "To Travel!" on pages 438 and 439. Look for
examples of assonance and consonance.

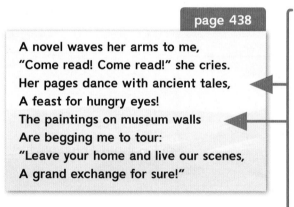

page 438

A novel waves her arms to me,
"Come read! Come read!" she cries.
Her pages dance with ancient tales,
A feast for hungry eyes!
The paintings on museum walls
Are begging me to tour:
"Leave your home and live our scenes,
A grand exchange for sure!"

The long a sound in pages,
ancient, *and* tales *is
repeated to emphasize the
contents of the novel. The
repetition of the /z/ sound
in the words* pages, tales,
eyes, paintings, museum,
walls, *and* scenes *creates a
feeling of how much there
is to see and do.*

Your Turn

Find examples of assonance and consonance in "Wild
Blossoms." Say the words in those lines aloud. What
feelings do the sounds contribute to the poem?

Personification

Personification is the use of human characteristics to describe non-human things, such as animals, objects, or ideas. Poets use personification to create vivid images and to help the reader picture a detail or understand an idea.

 Find Text Evidence

In "To Travel!" a novel is described as a person waving her arms and crying, "Come read!" The pages "dance" and eyes are described as "hungry." These human descriptions make books and their contents seem exciting and alive for the reader.

page 438

A novel waves her arms to me,
"Come read! Come read!" she cries.
Her pages dance with ancient tales,
A feast for hungry eyes!

 **Your Turn**

COLLABORATE

How is personification used to describe clouds in "Wild Blossoms"? What is the effect of this personification on the poem?

Pages 438–441

Write About the Text

Frank

I responded to the prompt: *Write a narrative poem about a thunderstorm.*

Student Model: *Narrative Text*

Under the Thunder

Thunder is nature's clatter

that vibrates in my ears.

Thunder is the rumble

that sparks some people's fears.

Me, I often listen

as thunder shakes the night.

Grammar

A **prepositional phrase** can act as an adverb that tells how, when, or where.

Grammar Handbook See page 472.

Strong Words

My poem includes sensory language to help readers experience the scene.

It echoes off the buildings

and growls with all its might.

Personification
I described the thunder with human characteristics.

The racket of thunder's grumble

slowly starts to fade.

Another roar breaks the silence—

a beating drum the skies have made.

Figurative Language
I used a metaphor to help readers think about thunder in a new way.

Your Turn

Write a narrative poem about the neighborhood you live in.

Go Digital!
Write your response online.
Use your editing checklist.

Jason Weingart Photography

Contents

Adjectives

Adverbs and Negatives

Interjections and Prepositions

Mechanics: Abbreviations

Mechanics: Capitalization

Mechanics: Punctuation

Sentences

Sentences and Sentence Fragments

A **sentence** is a group of words that expresses a complete thought. A sentence **fragment** is a group of words that does not express a complete thought.

My father builds a house. (complete sentence)
The plans for the house. (needs a predicate)
Changes his mind. (needs a subject)

Your Turn Write each group of words. Write *sentence* or *fragment* next to each item. Then rewrite each fragment to make a complete sentence.

1. My father looked at the house plans.
2. The front windows.
3. Added a staircase.
4. We decided to paint it blue.

Types of Sentences

There are four different types of sentences. Each begins with a **capital letter** and ends with an **end mark**.

A **declarative sentence** makes a statement. It ends with a **period**.	*We watched the meteor shower.*
An **interrogative sentence** asks a question. It ends with a **question mark**.	*How long will it last?*
A **imperative sentence** tells or asks someone to do something. It ends with a **period**.	*Look in the northern sky.*
An **exclamatory sentence** shows strong feeling. It ends with an **exclamation mark**.	*That was the brightest one yet!*

Complete Subjects and Complete Predicates

Every sentence has two important parts: the **subject** and the **predicate**.

The **subject** tells whom or what the sentence is about. The **complete subject** is all the words in the subject part.

The puppy next door barks all night.

The **predicate** tells what the subject does or is. The **complete predicate** is all the words in the predicate.

*The puppy next door **barks all night**.*

Your Turn Write each sentence. Underline the complete subject. Circle the complete predicate.

1. Our neighbor trains the new puppy.
2. The new dog is a golden retriever.
3. The poor little puppy trips on his dish.
4. He comes running at the sound of the whistle.
5. When can we play with the puppy?

Simple Subjects and Simple Predicates

The **simple subject** is the main word in the complete subject. It tells exactly *whom* or *what* the sentence is about.

*The amazing new **rocket** soared into the clouds.*

The **simple predicate** is the main verb in the complete predicate. It tells exactly what the subject *does* or *is*.

*The amazing new rocket **soared** into the clouds. It **was** great.*

Your Turn Write each sentence. Underline the simple subject. Circle the simple predicate.

1. The people pointed at the sky.
2. The smallest boy covered his ears.
3. We took pictures with our camera.
4. One of the people was a reporter.
5. Who brought binoculars to watch?

Compound Subjects and Compound Predicates

Use the **conjunctions** *and, but,* and *or* to combine sentences and create compound subjects or compound predicates.

A **compound subject** has two or more simple subjects that share the same predicate.

> ***Corey and Martha*** *walked along the shore.*

A *compound predicate* has two more simple predicates that share a subject.

> *Martha **jumped** in the water **and swam** for a while.*

Your Turn **Combine the sentence pairs to form one sentence. Then write whether the new sentence has a compound subject or a compound predicate.**

1. Corey tested the water. Corey decided it was too cold.
2. My sister waved to them. I waved to them.
3. What will Martha do next? What will I do next?

Compound Sentences

A **simple sentence** has only one complete thought. A *compound sentence* has two or more complete thoughts about different subjects. The **coordinating conjunctions** *and, but,* and *or* can be used to connect the complete thoughts in a compound sentence. The **correlative conjunctions** *either/or* and *neither/nor* can also be used in a compound sentence.

> *My mother exercises every day.* (simple sentence)
> *My mother runs every day, **but** my father rides his bike.*
> (compound sentence)
> ***Either*** *we stay here, **or** we head home.* (compound sentence)

Your Turn **Write each sentence. Then tell whether the sentence is *simple* or *compound*. If it is a compound sentence, circle the conjunction(s).**

1. My brother works out at the gym, and I tag along.
2. My sister teaches a class there, but I've never taken it.
3. Most days we do a variety of different exercises.

Combining Sentences

Use the **conjunction** *and, but,* or *or* to combine two simple sentences into a compound sentence. You can also use conjunctions to create compound subjects or compound predicates.

> *Nina kicked the ball. Nina scored. The crowd cheered.*
>
> *Nina kicked the ball **and** scored, **and** the crowd cheered.*

Your Turn Combine each pair of sentences by using a conjunction to form a compound subject, compound predicate, or compound sentence.

1. Our team won. The band played the school song.
2. The pep squad cheered. The pep squad danced.
3. My friends sang along. I sang along.
4. My sister went home. My father stayed with us.

Complex Sentences

An **independent clause** can stand alone as a sentence.

> *We built our fort.*

A **dependent clause** cannot stand alone as a sentence and begins with a **subordinating conjunction**. Some common subordinating conjunctions are *after, although, before, because, if, since, until, when, where,* and *while.*

> *where we could see the river*

A **complex sentence** contains an independent clause and one or more dependent clauses.

> *We built our fort where we could see the river.*

Use a **comma** after the dependent clause when it comes at the beginning of a sentence.

> *Because the rain lasted so long, we worried about flooding.*

Your Turn Write each sentence. Underline the independent clause. Circle the dependent clause.

1. We built a new fort because the old one fell down.
2. Although the work was hard, we finished in three days.
3. We couldn't use the new fort until my father inspected it.

Run-On Sentences

A **run-on sentence** contains two or more independent clauses without the proper conjunctions or punctuation.

The bell rang it startled me, I jumped out of my seat.

You can correct run-on sentences using one or more strategies to connect related clauses.

Break the independent clauses into separate sentences.	*The bell rang. It startled me. I jumped out of my seat.*
Create a compound subject or compound predicate.	*The bell rang and startled me. I jumped out of my seat.*
Create a compound sentence using coordinating conjunctions.	*The bell rang. It startled me, and I jumped out of my seat.*
Create a complex sentence using subordinating conjunctions.	*When the bell rang and startled me, I jumped out of my seat.*

Your Turn Correct each run-on sentence using one or more of the strategies described above.

1. I put my books in my bag I went home.
2. The dogs were excited, I took them for a walk.
3. One dog saw a squirrel he tried to chase it.
4. I got back inside I looked at my homework.
5. The problems were hard I called my friend, she helped me.

Nouns

Common and Proper Nouns

A **common noun** names a person, place, thing, or idea.

A **proper noun** names a particular person, place, thing, or idea and begins with a capital letter.

> The **teacher** opened the **atlas**. (common)
>
> **Mrs. Hunter** showed us **Australia**. (proper)

Your Turn Write each sentence. Underline each noun and write whether it is common or proper.

1. My mother has a collection of photographs.
2. The book contains pictures from India and China.
3. Mr. Turner taught the class about Asia.
4. My mother came to talk about her adventures.
5. The students listened as Mom told about a trip to Japan.

Concrete, Abstract, and Collective Nouns

A **concrete noun** names a person, place, or thing that physically exists and can be perceived with the senses. An **abstract noun** names a quality, concept, or idea that does not physically exist. Many abstract nouns have no plural form.

> **Ben** set the **painting** on the **easel**. (concrete)
>
> **Art** adds **beauty** to the **soul**. (abstract)

A **collective noun** names a group acting as a single unit. Collective nouns can also have plural forms.

> Our **band** performs tonight.

Your Turn Write each sentence. Underline each noun and write whether it is concrete or abstract. Circle any collective nouns.

1. Excitement filled the auditorium.
2. A trio of students appeared on the stage.
3. My heart filled with glee as the group sang.
4. All the singers in the choir sang with joy!

Singular and Plural Nouns

A **singular noun** names one person, place, thing, or idea. A **plural noun** names more than one person, place, thing, or idea. Most plural nouns are formed by adding *-s* or *-es*.

Singular nouns:	cat	box	beach	party
Plural nouns:	cats	boxes	beaches	parties

More and Irregular Plural Nouns

If a noun ends in a consonant + *y*, change *y* to *i* and add *-es*.	*ladies, berries, skies, libraries*
If a noun ends in a vowel + *y*, add *-s*.	*boys, monkeys, days, essays*
If a noun ends in *-f* or *-fe*, you may need to change *f* to *v* and add *-es*.	*chefs, roofs, leaves, hooves, knives*
If a noun ends in a vowel and *o*, add *-s*.	*studios, trios, duos, zoos*
If a noun ends in a consonant and *o*, add *-s* or *-es*.	*pianos, echoes, cellos, heroes*
Some nouns have the same singular and plural forms.	*deer, sheep, moose, fish, elk*
Some nouns have special plural forms.	*men, women, children, teeth, feet*

Your Turn **Write each sentence. Change the singular noun in parentheses ( ) into a plural noun.**

1. Many music (program) will be open to all (child).
2. The (girl) sent six (letter) and received only two (reply).
3. Both of the (piano) will repaired by (workman) today.
4. You hear strange (echo) at night in (zoo).
5. Our (park) protect the (life) of (deer) and other (creature).

Singular and Plural Possessive Nouns

A *possessive noun* is a noun that shows who or what owns or has something.

Add *'s* to a singular noun to make it possessive.

*The **boy's** friends knew the **game's** secrets.*

Add just an apostrophe (') to most plural nouns ending in *-s* to make them possessive. Other plural nouns add *'s*.

*The **employees'** lounge was next to **men's** clothing.*

Your Turn Write each sentence. Change the word in ( ) into a possessive noun.

1. My (brother) friends don't like video games.
2. They make movies on their (families) computers.
3. His friends wrote a series of (children) programs.
4. We saw his (friends) movies at school one day.
5. The (class) response was quite positive.

Nouns in Prepositional Phrases

A **preposition** is a word that relates a noun or pronoun to another word in a sentence. A **prepositional phrase** begins with a preposition (such as *in, on, over, at, under, near, to, for, by*, and *with*) and ends with a noun or pronoun. The noun or pronoun is called the **object** of the preposition.

*The boy **with the <u>hat</u>** rescued the cat **in the <u>tree</u>**. He placed the ladder **against the <u>trunk</u>** and climbed **up the <u>rungs</u>**.*

Your Turn Write each sentence. Underline the nouns that are objects of a preposition.

1. My friends and I walked to the fair.
2. We saw some horses near the entrance.
3. A man in a suit sold tickets to the rides.
4. At night, fireworks shot over the lake.
5. Sparkling trails of many colors filled the sky.

Verbs

Action Verbs and Direct Objects

An **action verb** is a word that tells of the action of the subject.

*Mom **turned** the key.*

A **direct object** is a noun or pronoun that tells whom or what is acted upon by the verb.

*She started the **engine**.*

Your Turn Write each sentence. Circle each action verb and underline any direct objects.

1. My brother opened the door.
2. Mom grabbed her phone.
3. Ben owns a repair shop in town.

Verb Tenses

A **present-tense verb** shows action that happens now.

*Today's weather forecast **calls** for sunshine.*

A **past-tense verb** shows action that has already happened.

*Yesterday's forecast **called** for rain.*

A **future-tense verb** shows action that may or will happen.

*Tomorrow's forecast **will call** for cloudy skies.*

A **progressive tense** shows action that continues over time. Use the verb *be* with the *-ing* form of another verb to create the **present progressive**, **past progressive**, or **future progressive** tense.

*I **am wearing** sunglasses. (present progressive)*

*I **was wearing** a raincoat. (past progressive)*

*I **will be wearing** a jacket. (future progressive)*

Your Turn Write each sentence. Underline the verb and tell what tense it is.

1. Next week we will visit my grandparents.
2. We received a letter from them last week.
3. What are we bringing in case of snow?

Avoiding Shifts in Verb Tense

In most cases, the verbs in a sentence or paragraph will be in the same tense. Be mindful of any shifts in the tense of the verbs.

You **scanned** the news and **smiled**.

My friend **listens** as his sister **sings**.

Your Turn Write each sentence. Use the correct form of the verb in parentheses.

1. I make toast while my sister (cook) eggs.
2. Mom asks if she (know) how to cook them.
3. My sister learned to cook when she (visit) our aunt.
4. She bought a cookbook and (learn) some recipes.
5. My family (enjoy) the meals she prepares.

Subject-Verb Agreement

A present-tense verb must agree with the subject of the sentence. Add *-s* to most verbs if the subject is singular. Add *-es* to verbs that end in *s, ch, sh, x,* or *z.* Do not add *-s* or *-es* if the subject is plural, or if the subject is *I* or *you.*

Caitlin **watches** the eagle. Her parents **look** for the camera.

Your Turn Write each sentence. Use the correct present-tense form of the verb(s) in parentheses.

1. The eagle (sit) in a tree out back.
2. The bird (stretch) its wings.
3. Caitlin (call) the neighbors on the phone.
4. They (look) out their windows.
5. Caitlin (take) a picture as the eagle (perch) on a branch.

Main Verbs and Helping Verbs

The **main verb** in a sentence tells what the subject does or is. A **helping verb** helps the main verb show an action or make a statement. The verb *be* is often used as a helping verb with a **present participle**, or a verb ending in *-ing*. The verb *have* is often used as a helping verb with a **past participle**, or a verb ending in *-ed*.

*Our family **is planting** a garden.*

Your Turn Write each sentence. Underline each main verb and circle each helping verb.

1. We have wanted a garden for many years.
2. My mother has studied some books on the topic.
3. My brother is tilling the ground.
4. We are growing corn, pumpkins, and squash.
5. I am already planning to make soups and pies.

Using *Can, May,* and *Must*

The verbs *can, may,* and *must* can be used as **helping verbs** with a main verb:

*I **may ask** if someone **can help** me.*

Your Turn Write each sentence. Underline each main verb and circle each helping verb.

1. We must raise money for our class trip.
2. How can we do it?
3. We may hold a bake sale.
4. We must all bring something tasty.
5. If we can sell enough, we may meet our goal.

Perfect Verb Tenses

The **present perfect tense** tells about an action that happened in the past. It also tells about an action that began in the past and continues in the present. Use the helping verb *have* or *has* followed by a **past participle**, which is usually the *-ed* form of the verb.

*I **have visited** five states in my lifetime.*

The **past perfect tense** tells about one past action that occurred before another past action. Use the helping verb *had* and a past participle to form the past-perfect tense.

*Before last summer, I **had visited** only three states.*

Your Turn Write each sentence. Use the present perfect or past perfect tense of the verb in parentheses.

1. I (travel) by plane only twice so far.
2. My father (purchase) tickets before the price went up.
3. My sister (worry) about flying every time.
4. This time, she (borrow) a book on airplanes from the library.
5. I (check) the book out before our last trip.

Linking Verbs

A **linking verb** links the subject with a word in the predicate. The word can be a **predicate noun**, which renames or identifies the subject, or a **predicate adjective**, which describes the subject. Some common linking verbs are *be, seem, feel, appear, become, smell,* and *taste*.

*Vonda **is** a chef. Her casseroles **taste** delicious.*

Your Turn Write each sentence. Underline the subject. Circle each linking verb. Then place a double underline beneath the predicate noun or predicate adjective that follows it.

1. "Something smells strange!" the chef shouted.
2. We are students in his cooking class.
3. "You seem nervous," he said.
4. I became anxious at the sight of smoke near the oven.
5. My cookies were a disaster!

Irregular Verbs

An **irregular verb** is a verb that does not end in *-ed* to form the past tense. Some also have special spellings when used with *have* in the perfect or progressive tenses. Below are some examples.

Present	Past	With *Have*
be (am/are/is)	was/were	been
begin	began	begun
bring	brought	brought
buy	bought	bought
catch	caught	caught
come	came	come
do	did	done
eat	ate	eaten
give	gave	given
go	went	gone
read (/rēd/)	read (/rĕd/)	read (/rĕd/)
ride	rode	ridden
run	ran	run
say	said	said
see	saw	seen
sing	sang	sung
take	took	taken
think	thought	thought
write	wrote	written

Your Turn **Write each sentence. Use the correct form of each verb in parentheses.**

1. Yesterday we (go) to the technology museum.
2. My father (bring) us to the computer exhibit.
3. I had (see) some of the machines before.
4. "Have you (think) about inventing something?" he asked.
5. "I have never (give) it a try," I (say).

Pronouns

Pronouns and Antecedents

A **pronoun** takes the place of one or more nouns. A **pronoun** must match the number and gender of its **antecedent**, which is the noun (or nouns) to which it refers.

*I gave the pen to my father. **He** used **it** to write a note.*

An **indefinite pronoun** refers to someone or something that is not known or specific, such as *anyone, anything, all, both, everybody, everything, everywhere, none, no one, somebody,* or *something*.

*I'll write **something** that **everyone** will enjoy.*

Subject and Object Pronouns

A **subject pronoun** is used as the subject of a verb. It tells who or what does the action. The pronouns *I, you, he, she, it, we,* and *they* can be used as subject pronouns.

An **object pronoun** is used as the object of either an action verb or a preposition. These include *me, you, him, her, it, us,* and *them* can be used as object pronouns.

*My sister and I bought a gift for our parents. **We** gave **it** to **them**.*

Reflexive and Relative Pronouns

A **reflexive pronoun** tells about an action that a subject does for or to itself. The ending *-self* is used with singular pronouns. The ending *-selves* is used with plural pronouns.

*My mother wrote **herself** directions. We drove **ourselves** to the city.*

A **relative pronoun** takes the place of its antecedent and introduces a dependent clause that tells more about the antecedent. Common relative pronouns are *that, which, who, when, whom,* and *whose*.

*We followed the signs **that** led to the city.*

Pronoun-Verb Agreement

A present-tense verb must **agree** with its subject, even if the subject is a pronoun.

*I **am** tired. She **is** sleepy. She and I **are** exhausted.*

Your Turn Write each sentence. Use the correct present-tense form of the verb in parentheses.

1. He (search) for the missing kitten.
2. She (think) about checking the basement.
3. While they do that, I (look) in the yard.
4. A few minutes later, they (call) me inside.
5. They point to the kitten as it (hide) under the bed.

Pronoun-Verb Contractions

Pronouns can be combined with all forms of the verbs *be, will,* and *have* to form **contractions**. An apostrophe takes the place of the missing letter or letters.

I have asked my father if he will know when you are ready.
***I've** asked my father if **he'll** know when **you're** ready.*

Your Turn Write each sentence. Replace each pronoun-verb pair in parentheses with a contraction.

1. My sister complains that (she is) always late.
2. My father is sure that (we will) be on time.
3. (I am) usually the last one out the door.
4. "(It is) the same thing every morning," Dad says.
5. "(You have) said that every time!" I reply.

Possessive Pronouns

A **possessive pronoun** shows who or what owns something. *My, your, her, his, its, our,* and *their* are possessive pronouns that come before nouns. *Mine, yours, hers, his, its, ours,* and *theirs* are possessive pronouns that can stand alone.

*I won't go into **your** room if you won't go into **mine**.*

Your Turn Write each sentence. Replace the words in parentheses with a possessive pronoun.

1. (My sister's) friends are visiting today.
2. They are older than (the friends I have).
3. I like to listen to (her friends') music.
4. You can't dance to (the music we own) very well.
5. What do you listen to in (belonging to you) house?

Pronouns and Homophones

Some possessive pronouns sound like pronoun-verb contractions but are spelled differently. A possessive pronoun does not contain an apostrophe because no letters are missing.

*__It's__ time for the family to have **its** dinner.* (**It's** = It + is; **its** is a possessive pronoun)

*__You're__ happy with **your** meal.* (**You're** = You + are; **your** is a possessive pronoun)

*__They're__ proud of **their** cooking.* (**They're** = They + are; **their** is a possessive pronoun)

*__There's__ no better pizza than **theirs**.* (**There's** = There + is; **theirs** is a possessive pronoun)

Your Turn Write each sentence. Choose the correct word in parentheses to complete the sentence.

1. "I need (you're, your) help," my father said.
2. "(Theirs, There's) a tree down across the driveway."
3. We tried pulling the tree by (it's, its) branches.
4. "(It's, Its) too heavy for just the two of us," I said.
5. "(You're, Your) right," Dad said. "Let's ask Mom to help."

Adjectives

Adjectives and Articles

Adjectives are words that describes nouns or pronouns. Adjectives tell **what kind** or **how many**.

*I saved my **two favorite** games for a **rainy** day.*

The words *the*, *a*, and *an* are special adjectives called *articles*. Use *a* and *an* to refer to any one item in a group. Use *the* to refer to a specific item or more than one item.

***The** girls will set aside **an** afternoon to watch **a** movie .*

Your Turn Write each sentence. Underline each adjective. Circle each article.

1. My three sisters wanted to watch a movie.
2. We picked a short movie with a scary title.
3. The film began with an eerie song.
4. The evil scientist prepared for an experiment.
5. A huge wolf jumped in through an open window.

Proper Adjectives

A **proper adjective** is formed from a proper noun and begins with a capital letter.

*The **Italian** car drove along the **Spanish** streets.*

Your Turn Write each sentence. Change the proper noun in parentheses into a proper adjective.

1. My father drove us to the (Mexico) restaurant.
2. We had been hoping for (China) food tonight.
3. We drove up near the (Canada) border.
4. Should we have taken our (America) passports?
5. The restaurant's design made it look like a (Mars) spaceship!

Adjectives That Compare

Add the word *more* or the ending *-er* to form a **comparative adjective** that compares two nouns. Add *most* or *-est* to form a **superlative adjective** that compares more than two nouns or pronouns.

If an adjective ends in a consonant and *y*, then change the *y* to *i* before adding *-er* or *-est*. If an adjective ends in *e*, then drop the *e* before adding *-er* or *-est*. If an adjective has a single vowel before a final consonant, then double the final consonant before adding *-er* or *-est*.

> This film is a **funnier** version of the book.
> The television series was the **most comical** version of all.

Your Turn Write each sentence. Use the correct form of the adjective in parentheses.

1. The school's computer has the (big) screen I've ever seen!
2. What is the title of the (popular) book in the library?
3. I think the magazines are (interesting) than the newspapers.

More and Most, Good and Bad

Use *more*, *better*, and *worse* to compare two people, places, or things. Use *most*, *best*, and *worst* to compare more than two people, places, or things.

> I have **many** pears. You have **more** pears than I do. He has the **most** pears of all.
> Joan is a **good** chef. Curt is a **better** chef than Joan. Hali is the **best** chef of all.
> She has a **bad** cold. He had a **worse** cold than she did. I had the **worst** cold of all.

Your Turn Write each sentence. Use the correct form of the adjective in parentheses.

1. We had the (bad) time ever at the beach last week!
2. There were (many) clouds than the week before.
3. The morning had (good) waves for surfing than the afternoon.

Irregular Comparative and Superlative Forms

In addition to *good, bad,* and *many,* the following adjectives also have irregular comparative and superlative forms: *little, much, far.* Use *less, more,* and *farther* to compare two nouns or pronouns. Use *least, most,* and *farthest* to compare more than two nouns or pronouns.

> Use the **least** amount of salt possible in the soup.

Like *more* and *most, less* and *least* can be used with other adjectives to compare nouns and pronouns.

> Breakfast was a **less tasty** meal than lunch.

Your Turn Write each sentence. Use the correct form of the adjective in parentheses.

1. I put (little) effort into today's practice than yesterday's.
2. Even so, I ran the (far) distance of anyone on the team.

Demonstrative Adjectives

This, that, these and *those* are **demonstrative adjectives** that tell which one or which ones. *This* and *these* refer to something nearby. *That* and *those* refer to something far away.

> Please put **these** hats with **those** gloves on **that** shelf.

Your Turn Write each sentence. Choose the correct word in parentheses to complete the sentence.

1. My sister tried on (that, these) jacket.
2. (This, These) pants are the same color.

Combining Sentences with Adjectives

Two sentences that tell about the same noun can be combined by moving an adjective into one of the sentences.

> We climbed the hill. The hill was **steep**. We climbed the **steep** hill.

Your Turn Combine each pair of sentences using the adjective.

1. The hikers looked at the view. The view was spectacular.
2. They could see the city. The city was distant.

Adverbs and Negatives

Adverbs

An **adverb** tells more about a verb. Adverbs often tell *how, when,* or *where* an action takes place. Many adverbs end in *-ly*.

The student **quickly** stepped **away**.

Your Turn Write each sentence. Circle each adverb and draw a line under the verb that each adverb describes.

1. The crowd slowly filled the theater.
2. The actors paced nervously.
3. My sister now worried about her scene.

Adverbs Before Adjectives and Other Adverbs

Adverbs can describe adjectives as well as verbs. Adverbs can also tell more about other adverbs.

The **amazingly** fast train **leaves** very soon.

Your Turn Write each sentence. Tell whether each underlined adverb describes a verb, an adjective, or another adverb.

1. I was waiting for an <u>extremely</u> late bus.
2. Time seemed to pass <u>incredibly</u> slowly.
3. I was <u>quite</u> certain a bus would arrive <u>soon</u>.

Good and *Well*

Good is an adjective that tells more about a noun. *Well* is an adverb that is tells more about a verb. As with *good*, the comparative and superlative forms of *well* are *better* and *best*.

The **good** doctor helped us feel **well**.

Your Turn Write each sentence. Choose the correct word to complete the sentence. Underline the word being described.

1. There is a (good, well) camp I want to attend this summer.
2. I must do (good, well) in school if I want to go.

Adverbs That Compare

Adverbs can be used to compare two or more actions. Use *more* before most adverbs to compare two actions. Use *most* before most adverbs to compare more than two actions. Add the ending *-er* or *-est* to shorter adverbs to compare actions.

> Shari sang **softly** and **more gently** than Kara.
>
> A. J. sang **softest** and **most gently** of all.

Your Turn Write each sentence. Choose the correct form of the adverb in parentheses.

1. Kara moved (gracefully) than Shari on stage.
2. A. J. danced (wildly) of all the band members.
3. The band finished (soon) than we were expecting.
4. Were you sitting (close) to the stage than me?
5. We clapped (energetically) after the third encore.

Negatives and Negative Contractions

A **negative** is a word that means *no*. Some negatives appear as the contraction *n't*, which is short for *not*. Do not use a **double negative** (two negatives) in one sentence.

> **Nobody** wants to go outside. I **can't** blame you for being afraid.

Your Turn Write each sentence. Change the word(s) in parentheses into a negative.

1. We could see (everything) in the darkness.
2. The howls in the distance (did) make us feel safe.
3. "That (is) an animal I'd like to meet," I said.
4. (Everyone) could sleep through the racket.
5. We (always) thought one night could last so long!

Interjections and Prepositions

Interjections

An **interjection** is a word or group of words that expresses strong feeling. Place a comma after a mild interjection. Use an exclamation mark after an interjection that expresses very strong feeling.

Hey! Did you see that? *Gee,* I wasn't looking.

Your Turn Rewrite each sentence using correct capitalization and punctuation.

1. Look here it comes again
2. Gosh it looked like a bat to me

Prepositions

A **preposition** comes before a noun or a pronoun. A preposition relates a noun or pronoun to another word in the sentence.

The tree **on** the corner swayed **in** the wind.

Common Prepositions					
about	above	across	after	against	along
among	around	at	before	behind	below
beside	between	by	down	during	for
from	in	inside	into	near	of
off	on	out	outside	over	through
to	under	until	up	with	without

Your Turn Write each sentence. Choose a preposition to complete the sentence.

1. We watched a report _____ the hurricane.
2. The storm was moving _____ the coast.
3. We bought emergency supplies _____ the store.
4. Bright streaks _____ lightning flashed in the sky.
5. The strongest winds blew _____ the night.

Prepositional Phrases

A **prepositional phrase** is a group of words that begins with a preposition and ends with a noun or pronoun. The **object of a preposition** is the noun or pronoun that follows the preposition.

Your Turn Write each sentence. Underline each prepositional phrase and circle each preposition. Then place an "O" above the object of the preposition.

1. My sister was elected president of the group.
2. She will meet with the principal tomorrow.
3. After the vote, the club served refreshments.
4. My sister told us the big news at dinner.
5. Mom gave her a book about leadership to read.

A prepositional phrase can be used as an **adjective** or an **adverb**. *The members **of the club** (adjective) voted **during the meeting** (adverb).*

In the sentence above, the phrase *of the club* is used as an adjective, modifying the plural noun *members*. The phrase *during the meeting* is used as an adverb, modifying the verb *voted*.

Your Turn Write each sentence. Underline each prepositional phrase. Then write whether the phrase is being used as an adjective or adverb.

1. The girl in the hall is joining a music group.
2. Her violin is in a brown case.
3. After lunch, she and the group will practice their music.
4. When rehearsal ends, the group of players will perform.
5. My friend from school is taking me to the concert.

Mechanics: Abbreviations

Titles and Names

An **abbreviation** is a shortened forms of a word. An **initial** is the first letter of a name. Titles and initials are capitalized and end with a period.

> *Mr. Plata brings Dr. T. J. Fenn's report to Ms. Ross.*

Your Turn **Write each sentence. Change the word(s) in parentheses into an abbreviation or initial.**

1. I want to volunteer at the (Paul Addison) West Animal Shelter.
2. I sent my application to (Mister) Corbin.
3. Bill Doran, (Senior), wrote me a recommendation.
4. (Doctor) Reese sometimes helps the dogs and cats.

Organizations

In both formal and informal writing, use abbreviations for certain organizations and government agencies. These abbreviations usually have all capital letters and no periods.

> *United Nations—UN   Federal Bureau of Investigation—FBI*

Internet Addresses

Use abbreviations for the end of Internet addresses.

> *commercial .com   educational .edu   government .gov*
> *organization .org   network .net   information .info*

Your Turn **Write each sentence. Change each word or group of words in parentheses into an abbreviation or initials.**

1. I found photographs of space at www.nasa.(government).
2. The (Environmental Protection Agency) was created in 1970.
3. I checked www.humanesociety.(organization) for articles about dogs and other animals.
4. My sister studied hard for the (Scholastic Achievement Test).

States

The **United States Postal Service abbreviations** for the names of states are two capital letters with no period at the end. Do not use a comma between the city and the state when using these abbreviations.

Alabama	AL	Kentucky	KY	North Dakota	ND
Alaska	AK	Louisiana	LA	Ohio	OH
Arizona	AZ	Maine	ME	Oklahoma	OK
Arkansas	AR	Maryland	MD	Oregon	OR
California	CA	Massachusetts	MA	Pennsylvania	PA
Colorado	CO	Michigan	MI	Rhode Island	RI
Connecticut	CT	Minnesota	MN	South Carolina	SC
Delaware	DE	Mississippi	MS	South Dakota	SD
District of Columbia	DC	Missouri	MO	Tennessee	TN
Florida	FL	Montana	MT	Texas	TX
Georgia	GA	Nebraska	NE	Utah	UT
Hawaii	HI	Nevada	NV	Vermont	VT
Idaho	ID	New Hampshire	NH	Virginia	VA
Illinois	IL	New Jersey	NJ	Washington	WA
Indiana	IN	New Mexico	NM	West Virginia	WV
Iowa	IA	New York	NY	Wisconsin	WI
Kansas	KS	North Carolina	NC	Wyoming	WY

Units of Measure

Use abbreviations for units of measure. Most abbreviations are the same for singular and plural units.

in.—inch(es)	*lb.—pound(s)*	*km.—kilometer(s)*	*L—liter(s)*
ft.—foot (feet)	*kg.—kilogram(s)*	*oz.—ounce(s)*	*hr.—hour(s)*

Mechanics: Capitalization

First Words

Capitalize the first word of a sentence. Capitalize the first word of a direct quotation. Do not capitalize the second part of an interrupted quotation. When the second part of a quotation is a new sentence, put a period after the interrupting expression and capitalize the first word of the new sentence.

> *"**Stop** playing that game," my sister said, "and go to bed."*
>
> *The game was over. "I'm ready," I replied. "That was fun!"*

Capitalize the first word and all the recipients in the greeting of a letter. Capitalize only the first word in the closing of a letter.

> *Dear **Sir** or **Madam**:   **Sincerely** yours,*

Your Turn Write each sentence. Use capital letters correctly.

1. to whom it may concern:
2. last week, my family visited your auto show.
3. my father said, "it will be fun to see the old cars."
4. "too bad, dad," i said, "because it looks like all new cars!"
5. all best wishes,

Titles of Works

Capitalize the first, last, and all important words in the title of a book, play, short story, poem, movie, article, newspaper, magazine, TV series, chapter of a book, or song.

> *Dad whistled "**Old MacDonald**" while I read "**Chicken Little**."*
>
> *I reviewed the book **Silent and Strong** for the **North School News**.*

Your Turn Write each sentence. Use capital letters correctly.

1. Our class sang "land of the free" at the talent show.
2. You could see a video clip on "news at nine."
3. The online article was called "a classy act takes the prize."
4. My sister's class performed "the queen and her court."
5. It was based on the book thrown from the throne.

Proper Nouns and Adjectives

Capitalize the names of cities, states, countries, and continents. Do not capitalize articles or prepositions that are part of the names. Capitalize the names of bodies of water and geographical features. Capitalize the names of sections of the country. Do not capitalize compass points when they just show direction.

Topeka, Kansas   *United States of America*   *northeast of Detroit*

Capitalize the names of streets and highways. Capitalize the names of buildings, bridges, and monuments.

Golden Gate Bridge   *Empire State Building*

Capitalize the names of stars and planets. Capitalize *Earth* when it refers to the planet. Do not capitalize *earth* when it is preceded by the article *the*. Do not capitalize *sun* or *moon*.

Venus is closer to the earth than Mars.

Capitalize the names of schools, clubs, teams, businesses, political parties, and products.

Science League at Northfield Elementary School

Capitalize the names of historic events, periods of time, and documents.

the Battle of Bunker Hill   *Declaration of Independence*

Capitalize the days of the week, months of the year, and holidays. Do not capitalize the names of the seasons.

Labor Day, a summer holiday, is the first Monday in September.

Capitalize the names of ethnic groups, nationalities, and languages. Capitalize proper adjectives that are formed from the names of ethnic groups and nationalities.

Swiss people may speak French, German, or Italian.

Your Turn **Rewrite each sentence. Capitalize appropriate words.**

1. The red hills book club is reading a russian novel.
2. They meet at the old farm diner on miller street.
3. The main character moves from rome to moscow.
4. Mom read the book from memorial day through june.

Mechanics: Punctuation

End Punctuation

A **declarative sentence** makes a statement. It ends with a **period (.)**.

An **interrogative sentence** asks a question. It ends with a **question mark (?)**.

An **imperative sentence** makes a command or a request. It ends with a **period (.)** or an **exclamation mark (!)**.

An **exclamatory sentence** expresses strong emotion. It ends with an **exclamation mark (!)**.

Do you like fishing? Watch that crazy bird fly! I'm learning to swim.

Your Turn Write each sentence. Use the correct end punctuation.

1. How many fish did you catch so far
2. That's the first nibble I've had all day
3. I'm having way too much trouble reeling it in
4. What will you do if the line breaks
5. You wouldn't believe how much work this is

Periods

Use a **period** at the end of an abbreviation. Use a period after initials in a name. Use a period in abbreviations for time. Use a period after numbers and letters in an outline.

Dr. M. Fitz will speak to our group at 9:45 A.M. on Jan. 12.

Your Turn Write each sentence. Insert periods where needed.

1. I need to get across town by 11:30 AM.
2. I have an interview with Ms Flynn at her office.
3. She is the owner of G B Rascal's Hobby Shop.
4. Does the Island Ave bus stop at Riley Rd downtown?
5. My outline for the interview begins, "1 Main St Shops."

Colons

Use a **colon** to separate the hour and minute when you write the time of day. Use a colon after the greeting of a business letter.

Dear Mr. Davis:

I will be late to the 11:30 rehearsal today.

Hyphens

Use a **hyphen** or **hyphens** in certain compound words. Use a hyphen to show the division of a word at the end of a line. Always divide the word between syllables. Use a hyphen in compound numbers.

*Her **real-life** movies are based on the **in-credible** stories of **twenty-six** teenagers.*

Apostrophes

Use an **apostrophe (')** and an *s* to form the possessive of a singular noun. Use an apostrophe and an *s* to form the possessive of a plural noun that does not end in *s*. Use an apostrophe alone to form the possessive of a plural noun that ends in *s*. Do not use an apostrophe in a possessive pronoun.

Use an apostrophe in a **contraction** to show where a letter or letters are missing.

***They're** putting the **teachers'** lists on their **school's** computer.*

Your Turn Write each line of the printed letter below. Insert the correct punctuation where needed.

1. Dear Dr Metcalf
2. Thank you for loaning your full size model
3. of a skeleton to our school. Our biology stu
4. dents in the 915 class will enjoy it. Theyll try
5. to identify thirty one of the models bones.

478

Commas

Use a **comma (,)** between the name of a **city** and the complete name of a **state**. Use a comma after the name of a state or a country when it is used with the name of a city in a sentence. Do not use a comma between the name of a city and the postal service abbreviation for a state.

We flew from Dayton, Ohio, to Paris, France, in one day.

Use a comma between the day and the year in a **date**. Use a comma before and after the year when it is used with both the month and the day in a sentence. Do not use a comma if only the month and the year are given.

We met on June 9, 2003, but lost touch in April 2008.

Use a comma after the **greeting** in a friendly letter and after the **closing** in all letters.

Dear Uncle Phil,   Very truly yours,

Use a comma before *and, but,* or *or* when it joins simple sentences to form a **compound sentence**. Use a comma after an introductory **prepositional phrase** or **dependent clause**.

After the alarm buzzed, Mom woke up, but Dad stayed asleep.

Use a comma to set off a **direct quotation**. Use a comma to set off a noun of **direct address** or an **appositive** within a sentence.

"Jill, when I called," she asked, "did you know it was I, your sister?"

Use commas to separate three or more items in a **series**. Use a comma to separate three or more subjects in a **compound subject** or three or more predicates in a **compound predicate**.

She painted the waves, gulls, and boats at the shore.

Use a comma after the words *yes* or *no* or other **introductory words** at the beginning of a sentence. Use a comma before a **tag question** that comes at the end of a sentence.

Hey, Ethan, you fed the dog, didn't you? Yes, I did.

Your Turn Write each sentence. Add commas where needed.

1. The town of Gladville Maine is a great place to live.
2. Mountains lakes and rivers provide many places to visit.
3. I asked "Linda how long have you lived here?"

Quotation Marks

Use **quotation marks** before and after the exact words that a speaker says or writes. Use a **comma** or **commas** to separate a clause, such as *he said*, from the quotation itself. Place the comma outside the opening quotation marks but inside the closing quotation marks. Place a **period** inside closing quotation marks. Place a **question mark** or **exclamation mark** inside the quotation marks when it is part of the quotation.

> *"What are you working on?" my father asked.*
>
> *"I'm writing a story," I replied, "and it's due tomorrow."*

Use **quotation marks** around the title of a short story, song, short poem, print or online article, or chapter of a book.

> *I finished my story, "The Path to the Summit."*

Your Turn Write each sentence. Add punctuation where needed.

1. My brother wrote a poem called Up on the Mountain.
2. I asked Where did you get the idea for that?
3. I wrote it after reading your story he replied.
4. How dare you copy my idea I exclaimed.
5. I wrote an essay called Can You Believe My Brother?

Italics (Underlining)

Use italics or underlining for the title of a book, movie, television series, play, magazine, or newspaper.

> *My family went to see the movie **Adventure!** last spring.*

Your Turn Write each sentence. Underline titles where needed.

1. The author of the book The Fun Years visited my class.
2. She also wrote the screenplay for Laugh It Off.
3. She contributes articles to Modern Comedy magazine.
4. Have you seen her new television series, Make Me Smile?
5. I read her column on jokes in The Weekly Chuckle.

California Common Core State Standards

At the bottom of some pages in this book, you will see letters and numbers. What do these numbers and letters mean? In **RL.5.1**, **RL** stands for **R**eading Standards for **L**iterature. The number **5** stands for Grade 5. The number **1** is the standard number.

Subject Area	Grade Level	Standard number
RL	5	1

This California standard is about explaining answers based on information in the text to show what you have learned.

> 1. Quote accurately from a text when explaining what the text says explicitly and when drawing inferences from the text.

This means that you will learn to use exact details from the text to support what you have learned. You will learn to understand what the author says directly in the text. You will also learn to find deeper meaning in the text by using details and clues. The author put these clues into the story. It is the reader's job to figure them out!

The Grade 5 California Standards for Reading and Language Arts have six subject areas.

RL = Reading Standards for Literature

RI = Reading Standards for Informational Text

RF = Reading Standards for Foundational Skills

W = Writing Standards

SL = Speaking and Listening Standards

L = Language Standards

Your standards in all of these subject areas follow. **Take a look!**

English Language Arts & Literacy in History/ Social Studies, Science, and Technical Subjects

Grade 5

Reading Standards for Literature	
Key Ideas and Details	
RL.5.1	Quote accurately from a text when explaining what the text says explicitly and when drawing inferences from the text.
RL.5.2	Determine a theme of a story, drama, or poem from details in the text, including how characters in a story or drama respond to challenges or how the speaker in a poem reflects upon a topic; summarize the text.
RL.5.3	Compare and contrast two or more characters, settings, or events in a story or drama, drawing on specific details in the text (e.g., how characters interact).
Craft and Structure	
RL.5.4	Determine the meaning of words and phrases as they are used in a text, including figurative language such as metaphors and similes. (See grade 5 Language standards 4–6 for additional expectations.)
RL.5.5	Explain how a series of chapters, scenes, or stanzas fits together to provide the overall structure of a particular story, drama, or poem.
RL.5.6	Describe how a narrator's or speaker's point of view influences how events are described.
Integration of Knowledge and Ideas	
RL.5.7	Analyze how visual and multimedia elements contribute to the meaning, tone, or beauty of a text (e.g., graphic novel, multimedia presentation of fiction, folktale, myth, poem).
RL.5.8	(Not applicable to literature)
RL.5.9	Compare and contrast stories in the same genre (e.g., mysteries and adventure stories) on their approaches to similar themes and topics.
Range of Reading and Level of Text Complexity	
RL.5.10	By the end of the year, read and comprehend literature, including stories, dramas, and poetry, at the high end of the grades 4–5 text complexity band independently and proficiently.

Reading Standards for Informational Text

Key Ideas and Details

RI.5.1 Quote accurately from a text when explaining what the text says explicitly and when drawing inferences from the text.

RI.5.2 Determine two or more main ideas of a text and explain how they are supported by key details; summarize the text.

RI.5.3 Explain the relationships or interactions between two or more individuals, events, ideas, or concepts in a historical, scientific, or technical text based on specific information in the text.

Craft and Structure

RI.5.4 Determine the meaning of general academic and domain-specific words and phrases in a text relevant to a *grade 5 topic or subject area*. (See grade 5 Language standards 4–6 for additional expectations.)

RI.5.5 Compare and contrast the overall structure (e.g., chronology, comparison, cause/effect, problem/solution) of events, ideas, concepts, or information in two or more texts.

RI.5.6 Analyze multiple accounts of the same event or topic, noting important similarities and differences in the point of view they represent.

Integration of Knowledge and Ideas

RI.5.7 Draw on information from multiple print or digital sources, demonstrating the ability to locate an answer to a question quickly or to solve a problem efficiently.

RI.5.8 Explain how an author uses reasons and evidence to support particular points in a text, identifying which reasons and evidence support which point(s).

RI.5.9 Integrate information from several texts on the same topic in order to write or speak about the subject knowledgeably.

Range of Reading and Level of Text Complexity

RI.5.10 By the end of the year, read and comprehend informational texts, including history/social studies, science, and technical texts, at the high end of the grades 4–5 text complexity band independently and proficiently.

Grade 5

Reading Standards for Foundational Skills

Phonics and Word Recognition

RF.5.3	Know and apply grade-level phonics and word analysis skills in decoding words.
RF.5.3a	Use combined knowledge of all letter-sound correspondences, syllabication patterns, and morphology (e.g., roots and affixes) to read accurately unfamiliar multisyllabic words in context and out of context.

Fluency

RF.5.4	Read with sufficient accuracy and fluency to support comprehension.
RF.5.4a	Read on-level text with purpose and understanding.
RF.5.4b	Read on-level prose and poetry orally with accuracy, appropriate rate, and expression on successive readings.
RF.5.4c	Use context to confirm or self-correct word recognition and understanding, rereading as necessary.

Writing Standards

Text Types and Purposes

W.5.1	Write opinion pieces on topics or texts, supporting a point of view with reasons and information.
W.5.1a	Introduce a topic or text clearly, state an opinion, and create an organizational structure in which ideas are logically grouped to support the writer's purpose.
W.5.1b	Provide logically ordered reasons that are supported by facts and details.
W.5.1c	Link opinion and reasons using words, phrases, and clauses (e.g., *consequently, specifically*).
W.5.1d	Provide a concluding statement or section related to the opinion presented.
W.5.2	Write informative/explanatory texts to examine a topic and convey ideas and information clearly.
W.5.2a	Introduce a topic clearly, provide a general observation and focus, and group related information logically; include formatting (e.g., headings), illustrations, and multimedia when useful to aiding comprehension.
W.5.2b	Develop the topic with facts, definitions, concrete details, quotations, or other information and examples related to the topic.
W.5.2c	Link ideas within and across categories of information using words, phrases, and clauses (e.g., *in contrast, especially*).

W.5.2d	Use precise language and domain-specific vocabulary to inform about or explain the topic.
W.5.2e	Provide a concluding statement or section related to the information or explanation presented.
W.5.3	Write narratives to develop real or imagined experiences or events using effective technique, descriptive details, and clear event sequences.
W.5.3a	Orient the reader by establishing a situation and introducing a narrator and/or characters; organize an event sequence that unfolds naturally.
W.5.3b	Use narrative techniques, such as dialogue, description, and pacing, to develop experiences and events or show the responses of characters to situations.
W.5.3c	Use a variety of transitional words, phrases, and clauses to manage the sequence of events.
W.5.3d	Use concrete words and phrases and sensory details to convey experiences and events precisely.
W.5.3e	Provide a conclusion that follows from the narrated experiences or events.

Production and Distribution of Writing

W.5.4	Produce clear and coherent writing (including multiple-paragraph texts) in which the development and organization are appropriate to task, purpose, and audience. (Grade-specific expectations for writing types are defined in standards 1–3 above.)
W.5.5	With guidance and support from peers and adults, develop and strengthen writing as needed by planning, revising, editing, rewriting, or trying a new approach. (Editing for conventions should demonstrate command of Language standards 1–3 up to and including grade 5.)
W.5.6	With some guidance and support from adults, use technology, including the Internet, to produce and publish writing as well as to interact and collaborate with others; demonstrate sufficient command of keyboarding skills to type a minimum of two pages in a single sitting.

Research to Build and Present Knowledge

W.5.7	Conduct short research projects that use several sources to build knowledge through investigation of different aspects of a topic.
W.5.8	Recall relevant information from experiences or gather relevant information from print and digital sources; summarize or paraphrase information in notes and finished work, and provide a list of sources.
W.5.9	Draw evidence from literary or informational texts to support analysis, reflection, and research.

W.5.9a	Apply *grade 5 Reading standards* to literature (e.g., "Compare and contrast two or more characters, settings, or events in a story or a drama, drawing on specific details in the text [e.g., how characters interact]").
W.5.9b	Apply *grade 5 Reading standards* to informational texts (e.g., "Explain how an author uses reasons and evidence to support particular points in a text, identifying which reasons and evidence support which point[s]").

Range of Writing

W.5.10	Write routinely over extended time frames (time for research, reflection, and revision) and shorter time frames (a single sitting or a day or two) for a range of discipline-specific tasks, purposes, and audiences.

Speaking and Listening Standards

Comprehension and Collaboration

SL.5.1	Engage effectively in a range of collaborative discussions (one-on-one, in groups, and teacher-led) with diverse partners on *grade 5 topics and texts*, building on others' ideas and expressing their own clearly.
SL.5.1a	Come to discussions prepared, having read or studied required material; explicitly draw on that preparation and other information known about the topic to explore ideas under discussion.
SL.5.1b	Follow agreed-upon rules for discussions and carry out assigned roles.
SL.5.1c	Pose and respond to specific questions by making comments that contribute to the discussion and elaborate on the remarks of others.
SL.5.1d	Review the key ideas expressed and draw conclusions in light of information and knowledge gained from the discussions.
SL.5.2	Summarize a written text read aloud or information presented in diverse media and formats, including visually, quantitatively, and orally.
SL.5.3	Summarize the points a speaker or media source makes and explain how each claim is supported by reasons and evidence, and identify and analyze any logical fallacies.

Presentation of Knowledge and Ideas

SL.5.4	Report on a topic or text or present an opinion, sequencing ideas logically and using appropriate facts and relevant, descriptive details to support main ideas or themes; speak clearly at an understandable pace.
SL.5.4a	Plan and deliver an opinion speech that: states an opinion, logically sequences evidence to support the speaker's position, uses transition words to effectively link opinions and evidence (e.g., *consequently* and *therefore*), and provides a concluding statement related to the speaker's position.

SL.5.4b	Memorize and recite a poem or section of a speech or historical document using rate, expression, and gestures appropriate to the selection.
SL.5.5	Include multimedia components (e.g., graphics, sound) and visual displays in presentations when appropriate to enhance the development of main ideas or themes.
SL.5.6	Adapt speech to a variety of contexts and tasks, using formal English when appropriate to task and situation. (See grade 5 Language standards 1 and 3 for specific expectations.)

Language Standards

Conventions of Standard English

L.5.1	Demonstrate command of the conventions of standard English grammar and usage when writing or speaking.
L.5.1a	Explain the function of conjunctions, prepositions, and interjections in general and their function in particular sentences.
L.5.1b	Form and use the perfect (e.g., *I had walked; I have walked; I will have walked*) verb tenses.
L.5.1c	Use verb tense to convey various times, sequences, states, and conditions.
L.5.1d	Recognize and correct inappropriate shifts in verb tense.
L.5.1e	Use correlative conjunctions (e.g., *either/or, neither/nor*).
L.5.2	Demonstrate command of the conventions of standard English capitalization, punctuation, and spelling when writing.
L.5.2a	Use punctuation to separate items in a series.
L.5.2b	Use a comma to separate an introductory element from the rest of the sentence.
L.5.2c	Use a comma to set off the words *yes* and *no* (e.g., *Yes, thank you*), to set off a tag question from the rest of the sentence (e.g., *It's true, isn't it?*), and to indicate direct address (e.g., *Is that you, Steve?*).
L.5.2d	Use underlining, quotation marks, or italics to indicate titles of works.
L.5.2e	Spell grade-appropriate words correctly, consulting references as needed.

Grade 5 · Language Standards (continued)

Knowledge of Language	
L.5.3	Use knowledge of language and its conventions when writing, speaking, reading, or listening.
L.5.3a	Expand, combine, and reduce sentences for meaning, reader/listener interest, and style.
L.5.3b	Compare and contrast the varieties of English (e.g., dialects, registers) used in stories, dramas, or poems.
Vocabulary Acquisition and Use	
L.5.4	Determine or clarify the meaning of unknown and multiple-meaning words and phrases based on *grade 5 reading and content*, choosing flexibly from a range of strategies.
L.5.4a	Use context (e.g., cause/effect relationships and comparisons in text) as a clue to the meaning of a word or phrase.
L.5.4b	Use common, grade-appropriate Greek and Latin affixes and roots as clues to the meaning of a word (e.g., *photograph, photosynthesis*).
L.5.4c	Consult reference materials (e.g., dictionaries, glossaries, thesauruses), both print and digital, to find the pronunciation and determine or clarify the precise meaning of key words and phrases and to identify alternate word choices in all content areas.
L.5.5	Demonstrate understanding of figurative language, word relationships, and nuances in word meanings.
L.5.5a	Interpret figurative language, including similes and metaphors, in context.
L.5.5b	Recognize and explain the meaning of common idioms, adages, and proverbs.
L.5.5c	Use the relationship between particular words (e.g., synonyms, antonyms, homographs) to better understand each of the words.
L.5.6	Acquire and use accurately grade-appropriate general academic and domain-specific words and phrases, including those that signal contrast, addition, and other logical relationships (e.g., *however, although, nevertheless, similarly, moreover, in addition*).